The
MOFFATT
NEW TESTAMENT COMMENTARY
Based on *The New Translation* by the
REV. PROFESSOR JAMES MOFFATT, D.D.
and under his Editorship

THE EPISTLE OF PAUL
TO THE GALATIANS

THE EPISTLE OF PAUL
TO THE GALATIANS

BY

GEORGE S. DUNCAN, D.D.

*Professor of Biblical Criticism
in the
University of St. Andrews*

HARPER AND BROTHERS PUBLISHERS
NEW YORK AND LONDON

EDITOR'S PREFACE

MOFFATT'S NEW TESTAMENT COMMENTARY

THE aim of this commentary is to bring out the religious meaning and message of the New Testament writings. To do this, it is needful to explain what they originally meant for the communities to which they were addressed in the first century, and this involves literary and historical criticism ; otherwise, our reading becomes unintelligent. But the New Testament was the literature of the early Church, written out of faith and for faith, and no study of it is intelligent unless this aim is kept in mind. It is literature written for a religious purpose. 'These are written that ye might believe that Jesus is the Christ, the Son of God.' This is the real object of the New Testament, that Christians might believe it better, in the light of contemporary life with its intellectual and moral problems. So with any commentary upon it. Everything ought to be subordinated to the aim of elucidating the religious content, of showing how the faith was held in such and such a way by the first Christians, and of making clear what that faith was and is.

The idea of the commentary arose from a repeated demand to have my New Testament translation explained ; which accounts for the fact that this translation has been adopted as a convenient basis for the commentary. But the contributors have been left free to take their own way. If they interpret the text differently, they have been at liberty to say so. Only, as a translation is in itself a partial commentary, it has often saved space to print the commentary and start from it.

As everyman has not Greek, the commentary has been written, as far as possible, for the Greekless. But it is based upon a first-hand study of the Greek original, and readers may rest assured that it represents a close reproduction of the original writers' meaning, or at any rate of what we consider that to have been. Our common aim has been to enable everyman to-day to sit where these first Christians sat, to feel the impetus and inspiration of the Christian faith as it dawned upon the minds of the communities in the first century, and thereby to realize more vividly how new and lasting is the message which prompted these New Testament writings to take shape as they did. Sometimes people inside as well as outside the Church make mistakes about the New Testament. They think it means this or that, whereas its words frequently mean something very different from what traditional associations suggest. The saving thing is to let the New Testament speak for itself. This is our desire and plan in the present commentary, to place each writing or group of writings in its original setting, and allow their words to come home thus to the imagination and conscience of everyman to-day.

The general form of the commentary is to provide a running comment on the text, instead of one broken up into separate verses. But within these limits, each contributor has been left free. Thus, to comment on a gospel requires a method which is not precisely the same as that necessitated by commenting on an epistle. Still, the variety of treatment ought not to interfere with the uniformity of aim and form. Our principle has been that nothing mattered, so long as the reader could understand what he was reading in the text of the New Testament.

JAMES MOFFATT.

PREFACE

THE commentator on Galatians is fortunate in his predecessors, and I gratefully acknowledge how much I owe to those who have laboured in this field before me. A certain novelty of treatment however has been demanded by the conditions of the present series. And in regard to the many difficulties in the exegesis of the Epistle my aim has been less to provide my readers with a solution than to take them with me in the effort to find one.

In one respect I may claim a certain measure of originality. The problem of the destination of Galatians, over which so much controversy has raged in the past and still rages, must now be widened to include the problem of the date of the Epistle and the general circumstances of its origin. The present volume is the first recent commentary of its size and scope[1] to be based on the hypothesis that Galatians was written before the Apostolic Council of Acts xv., in which case it would be the earliest of all the extant Epistles of St. Paul. A work like the present is obviously not the place for an exhaustive examination and justification of this hypothesis, or for a rebuttal of the various critical theories (e.g. those involving a reconstruction of the narrative in Acts) which are put forward in opposition to it. It is in the exegesis of the Epistle that the surest test of the hypothesis will ultimately be found.

The hypothesis of an early date for Galatians, though it has many friends in Britain and America, has not so far commended itself to Continental scholars. Among the latter, indeed, there is even a tendency to question the South Galatian theory regarding the destination of the Epistle, and only if we are 'South-Galatians' regarding the destination can we go on to postulate an early date. Even at a time like the present, when a quickened interest in Biblical Theology is unfortunately accompanied by a measure of indifference to questions of 'mere Introduction,' it must be evident that the problem of

---

[1] I should like to mention with appreciation the shorter commentaries of Emmet (*Readers' Commentary*), Knox (*Gore's Commentary*), Dow (*Abingdon Commentary*), and Blunt (*Clarendon Bible*), all of which are based on the hypothesis of an early date.

the date of Galatians raises grave issues for the student of Christian Origins and of New Testament Doctrine. There is need for a revision of some of our ' established ' critical theories regarding the various stages of St. Paul's missionary activity, and more especially regarding the development of his doctrinal ideas. To take one example, Paul like other Christians rejoiced from the first in the gift of the Holy Spirit and looked forward eagerly to the Coming of Christ. And if the apocalyptic hope receives more emphatic and detailed treatment in the Thessalonian Epistles than in Galatians, this is in itself no proof that the former belong to an earlier period than the latter—the converse may indeed be the case, as I have ventured to suggest on p. xlvi. Galatians itself is not to be understood apart from the eschatology which is implied in it.

My thanks are due to various friends, notably Professor J. Y. Campbell, formerly of Yale University, and Professor John Dow, of Toronto, who have given me helpful criticisms and suggestions ; and to my wife and my brother, the Rev. D. A. Duncan, Doune, for assistance in preparing the book for the press.

G. S. DUNCAN.

August 1934.

CONTENTS

INTRODUCTION

COMMENTARY

CONTENTS

CONTENTS

xi

INTRODUCTION

INTRODUCTION

I. The Character and Purpose of the Epistle

For an understanding of the character and outlook of the Apostle Paul there is no better introduction than his Epistle to the Galatians.

(i.) It is in large measure a personal letter. Fully one third of it is occupied with a statement of personal history. In the rest, where he is dealing with the foundations of the Christian faith, it is his own personal faith he is expounding. The Christ of whom he tells us is One of whom he says : ' He loved *me* and gave Himself up for *me*.'

(ii.) It is a controversial letter. We see the apostle measuring himself against opponents. Two things have been challenged which are dearer to him than life itself—the truth of his gospel, and his right to preach it. In such circumstances he reveals all the vigour of his mind, all the passion of his soul—and, we may add, all his humanity and tenderness.

(iii.) Once we have learned to view it aright, the issue in Galatians is simple and clear. In Paul's other Epistles it is not always possible for us to disentangle with confidence the various strands that enter into the complicated situations with which he is confronted. In Galatians there are two vital questions with which he deals in turn, the first a personal one, concerning the validity of his apostleship, the second dealing with a theme of vital importance for religious faith, viz. the terms on which sinful man can win acceptance with God.

(iv.) If the view maintained in this commentary is correct, then Galatians has the added interest of being the earliest of all the Pauline letters.[1] We see Paul, still a young man and untried, engaged in his first big conflict for the gospel's sake.

[1] It may even be regarded as the earliest of all the New Testament writings.

His other letters for the most part reveal him as the seasoned campaigner ; here he is David facing his Goliath.

Apart from the light it sheds on the career and thought of the apostle, we cannot forget the importance which this Epistle has for the formulation of Christian Doctrine, and the significance which has attached to it in some of the great controversies of the Church.   In particular it stirred the soul of Luther into new life, and contributed more than any other writing to his epoch-making onslaught on the errors of Rome. He himself said of it : ' The Epistle to the Galatians is my epistle ; I have betrothed myself to it : it is my wife.'

The situation which called forth this great Epistle would appear to have been as follows :

When Paul had preached to the Galatians his universalistic gospel of redemption through the death of Christ, he had been welcomed with extraordinary enthusiasm (iv. 14 f.), and many Gentiles had embraced the faith.   Apparently a second visit followed (iv. 13).   But shortly before this letter was written, the churches which Paul had founded had been visited by members of a Judaizing[1] party in the Church, who, while they were Christians, accepting Christianity as the fulfilment of the Jewish hope, nevertheless believed that it must operate within the sphere of Judaism.   God's holy People, they said, could not be separate from Israel.   Hence, if the Galatians wished to be members of God's People, it was not enough, as Paul claimed, that they should have been baptized in Christ's name, and have received the gift of the Spirit ; they must be initiated into Israel by undergoing the rite of circumcision, and like all true Israelites they must accept the obligations of the Jewish Law.   These arguments were reinforced by others directed against Paul's claim to apostolic authority.   Who was this Paul ?   He was not one of the original Twelve, or accredited by the Jewish ' authorities.'   In admitting Gentiles to the Church without demanding circumcision, he had no

[1] The term ' Judaizers ' is applied to Jewish-Christians who were zealous to maintain Jewish customs and traditions.

support from the real leaders of the Church—though (man-pleaser as he was) he submitted to their authority when he was personally present in Jerusalem.

News reaches the apostle that his Galatian converts are lending a ready ear to the specious arguments of the Judaizers, and at once he despatches to them this letter of remonstrance, argument and appeal. The first part is devoted to a historical sketch in which he controverts certain misrepresentations which his enemies have circulated against him—in particular, he asserts that the gospel which he preaches had been given him by revelation from God, and so, too, had his commission to preach it ; the other apostles had recognized the validity of his call and the adequacy of his gospel ; and at Antioch he had even dared to vindicate his position against Peter's compromising conduct. The Epistle runs on like a mountain torrent. He starts sentences and breaks them off ; in the part dealing with Peter he begins by quoting what he said to his brother apostle, then suddenly he soars aloft into a soliloquy as he contemplates what Christ has done for his own soul ; he turns abruptly and addresses his readers as if he were speaking to them face to face ; at the beginning of the letter he dashes into his theme without a word of thanksgiving, an omission to which there is no parallel in any other of his letters ; and near the end, after calling attention to the character of his handwriting, he appends a closing message of guidance and appeal.

Without doubt it is a great Epistle—the Magna Charta of Evangelical Christianity. It shows how Paul saved Christianity from sinking to be a mere sect of Judaism, or, as he himself felt, degenerating into a form of paganism. It is no wonder that it stimulated Luther in his fight against the errors and the bondage of Rome. And it will continue to stimulate men always when they are called to resist a challenge to the liberty and the truth of the Gospel.

II. CRITICAL PROBLEMS

Galatians is happily free from some of the critical difficulties which confront us in certain other N.T. writings.

(*a*) Its *authenticity* is unquestioned. In every line it betrays its origin as a genuine letter of Paul. It was unchallenged in the second century by the heretic Marcion, as it was in the nineteenth by the negative criticism of the Tübingen School.

(*b*) Neither is there any doubt regarding its *unity*. It came 'red-hot' from the apostle in the form in which we to-day have it.

But in other respects it is the most tantalizingly difficult of all Paul's letters. Three problems in particular arouse great diversity of opinion among scholars.

1. The destination of the Epistle. Who were the Galatians?
2. The date and occasion of writing.
3. The source of the trouble in Galatia, and the character of Paul's opponents.

These three problems necessarily hang together, and our solution of any one will to some extent determine, and be determined by, our solution of the others. No attempt can be made here to touch on all their varied aspects. In the present commentary special attention is given to the second problem, and if the solution proposed for it be accepted, viz. that the Epistle was written before the Apostolic Council of Acts xv., all doubt is removed regarding its destination, and considerable light is shed on the precise nature of the controversy that occasioned it.

1. The Destination of the Epistle

In the heart of the peninsula which to-day we call Asia Minor there dwelt a Celtic people who, coming originally from Gaul, had preserved the name Galatians. When Rome spread her conquests eastwards, this wild people retained the status of a dependent kingdom (189 B.C.); a century and a half later the country passed into various hands, and ultimately in

25 B.C. came to be governed under the Roman provincial system. At the time of Paul the province which went under the name of Galatia included the old kingdom of Galatia to the north, and also parts of Lycaonia, Pisidia and Phrygia which adjoined it to the south.

The problem therefore emerges : when Paul refers to Galatia, is he thinking in a restricted sense of *the old kingdom* of Galatia —which, for convenience' sake, we may call North Galatia ? Or does Galatia mean for him *the Roman province* of that name ? If the former, we have no detailed information from Acts of any missionary work carried on in that region, the only possible references (and it may even be questioned whether they refer to North Galatia at all) being the mention of the place-name in Acts xvi. 6 and xviii. 23, in the accounts of the second and third missionary journeys. On the other hand, if Paul is thinking of the Roman province, it becomes possible for us to hold that the Galatian churches are in the southern part of the province, viz. the churches of Pisidian Antioch, Iconium, Lystra and Derbe, which were founded by Barnabas and Paul on their first missionary journey.

Thus we have the two hypotheses—the North Galatian and the South Galatian. And inasmuch as the Galatian churches would appear from the references in the Epistle (iii. 1-3 ; iv. 13 ff.) to have been all founded at one and the same time, these two hypotheses are mutually exclusive. The churches to which Paul writes were *either* those in South Galatia, founded on the first missionary journey, *or* they were in North Galatia, founded apparently on the second journey. To this we may add that while we have a fair amount of information from Acts regarding the South Galatian churches, we are almost completely in the dark regarding the alleged visits to the northern area. Did Paul penetrate, we may ask, as far into the interior as Ancyra or even Tavium, or did he (as seems a more reasonable hypothesis) go no further than Pessinus and neighbourhood ? No towns are mentioned by name, and nothing is said about the founding of churches.

Among the ancients it was accepted without question that the Galatians of our Epistle were the inhabitants of North

Galatia, and until comparatively recent years this was still the predominant view. But during the nineteenth century it began to be seriously challenged. Advocated seventy years ago by Perrot and Renan, the South Galatian theory must now for ever be associated with the name of Sir William Ramsay, who, bringing to its support his wide and intimate knowledge of the geographical and political conditions of Asia Minor in the Græco-Roman period, has by his numerous contributions to the subject presented the case in so masterly and cogent a fashion that (in the words of so cautious a scholar even as the late Professor C. H. Turner[1]) he has ' swept the opposing theory from the field.'

Nevertheless there are still many eminent scholars, e.g. Moffatt, Lietzmann, Lagrange, who either accept the North Galatian theory whole-heartedly or indicate a preference for it. If the destination of the Epistle could be discussed as an isolated problem, perhaps the fairest verdict would be *non liquet*. The present writer inclines strongly to the South Galatian hypothesis, but he does so largely because on that hypothesis we can reach, as he believes, a far more satisfactory exegesis of the Epistle, and, in particular, because the early date to which he feels compelled to assign the Epistle rules out the North Galatian theory as impossible.

One or two minor questions of interest may be referred to before we leave this part of our enquiry.

(i.) It is by no means so certain as Ramsay sought to make out that the references in Acts xvi. and xviii. exclude a visit to some part of North Galatia. But even if that be conceded, it does not follow that it was to converts made on those two occasions that Paul writes in the Epistle. Thus Burton, the editor of the *International Critical Commentary* on Galatians, is willing to believe that ' on his second missionary journey Paul passed through the western edge of old Galatia, there finding or making a few disciples but founding no churches,' but he holds nevertheless that it was to the churches in South Galatia that Paul addressed his Epistle.

(ii.) The references to Barnabas in the Epistle (ii. 1, 9, 13)

[1] Inaugural Lecture at Oxford, 1920.

suggest that he was in some way known to the recipients, and they would have added significance if he was known to them personally (cf. especially the pregnant reference ' even Barnabas ' in verse 9). But it was only in South Galatia, i.e. on the first missionary journey, that Barnabas was associated with Paul ; by the time of the visits to North Galatia, Barnabas and he had parted company. With regard to the fact that Barnabas' name is not joined with Paul's in the opening words of the Epistle, see commentary on i. 2.

(iii.) Is it likely, we may ask, that there would have been a special outburst of Judaistic propaganda in North Galatia ? If, as is generally accepted, the Judaizers came from outside (from Jerusalem, probably), had they passed by South Galatia, where there were organized churches, to go on to North Galatia, where probably there were at most only small bands of believers ? Lagrange deduces from the Epistle that the people to whom it was addressed had until now been outside the range of Judaistic controversies ; but the true explanation of this is not that they dwelt in a remote part of Asia, untouched by the great trade-routes, but that the Epistle was written at an early date when Judaistic propaganda was only beginning.

(iv.) In iii. 1, Paul addresses his readers directly : ' O senseless Galatians ' ; and it is sometimes urged that it would have been foolish and unnatural for him to use this mode of address to people who, though they were Galatians for purposes of administration, were certainly not Galatians by birth. The objection is by no means convincing. There was no other comprehensive designation for the wide varieties of nationality to be found in the southern area of the province ; and it may even have been a designation which would have evoked a sense of pride.

2. The Date and Occasion of Writing

We proceed now to consider the date of Galatians. Here is a line of approach along which, more than any other, we may hope to reach a solution of our critical difficulties. The question of the date is moreover of first-rate importance for the exegesis of the Epistle, for our answer to it will determine our view of the circumstances in which the apostle was placed when he wrote this great letter, of the stage he had reached in his thinking and missionary activity, and of the development of that opposition which pursued him throughout all his ministry.

Various possible dates

If, as seems the natural interpretation of iv. 13, the apostle had paid *two* visits to the Galatian churches, then on the N. Galatian theory the epistle was not written till some time after the visit of Acts xviii. 23—i.e. it cannot have been written before his ministry in Ephesus (Acts xix.).

On the S. Galatian theory, on the other hand, the second visit may either be that referred to in Acts xvi. 6, or (to go further back) it may be equated with the return visit on the first missionary journey (Acts xiv. 21). A more precise dating requires that we determine whether the Epistle was written very soon after the completion of the first missionary journey, or at some time during (or subsequent to) the second missionary journey. Put otherwise, the question is: was it written before or after the Apostolic Council at Jerusalem of Acts xv. ?

Is the visit to Jerusalem in Galatians ii. 1–10 to be identified with that in Acts xv. or with that in Acts xi. 30 ?

The Epistle must clearly be later than the latest event recorded in it ; and as criticism for long maintained, with scarcely a dissentient voice, that Paul's second visit to Jerusalem recorded in Gal. ii. was obviously the same as the one paid at the time of the Council of Acts xv., it was regarded as established beyond cavil that Galatians was later than the Council. Another view, however, which has of late found increasing support in Britain and America (it has been adopted by Ramsay, Streeter, Burkitt,[1] and is the view maintained in this Commentary) is that the visit of Gal. ii. corresponds to

[1] Professor Kirsopp Lake also supported it strongly in his *Earlier Epistles of St. Paul*; but in Vol. V. of the *Beginnings of Christianity* he has gone over to the view that Acts xi. 30 and Acts xv. give two presentations of one and the same visit (see p. xxiv.).

the visit narrated in Acts xi. 30, when Barnabas and Paul
went up with a contribution from the Christians in Antioch
to relieve distress among the Jewish-Christians of Jerusalem.
If this second view is established, it becomes possible on the
S. Galatian theory (it may even be said that it becomes essential) to date Galatians before the Apostolic Council,[1] when the
apostle paid a third visit to Jerusalem.   On this view Galatians
is earlier than the Thessalonian Epistles, which were not
written till the second missionary journey.   It becomes, in
fact, the earliest of all the Pauline Epistles.

Those who identify Gal. ii. with Acts xv. find their initial
(and in the end their main) justification in the alleged simil-
arity in the circumstances of the two visits.   In each case we
have Barnabas and Paul consulting with the Jerusalem leaders
on the question of the admission of Gentiles to the Christian
Fellowship, and in each case they win their way in the face
of vehement opposition.   But the resemblances can be over-
stressed ; there are differences which are even more striking
than the resemblances ; and with regard to the visit of Acts
xi. 30 it may be claimed that there too we have Barnabas and
Paul going up to Jerusalem, and that what we know about
that visit makes it certainly not impossible (but rather, as
we shall see, makes it probable) that it provides the true setting
for the events of Gal. ii. 1–10.

Objections to identifying Gal. ii. with Acts xv.

(1) At the outset there is this fact to which due weight must
be given.   If there is one passage more than another in his
Epistles where Paul is stating unchallengeable facts, it
is in Gal. i. and ii.   Faced with bitter misrepresentations
regarding his relations with the Jerusalem ' authorities ' he
sets himself to state his case with a fearless regard for accuracy
and truth.   ' I am writing you the sheer truth, I swear it
before God ! ' he says in i. 20.   He begins by telling how,
some three years after his conversion, he went up to Jerusalem
from Damascus—an account which agrees in general with
that given in Acts ix.   Then ' after fourteen years,' he says,

---

[1] It is interesting to note that this dating was accepted by Calvin.

' I went up again to Jerusalem along with Barnabas.' Thus what is the *second* visit to Jerusalem in the narrative of Galatians, where every sentence is carefully weighed, is to be identified (say the critics) with a visit which in Acts is the *third* visit. The discrepancy is so serious that one would have thought that the obvious solution was to discard the premise which gives rise to it, in other words to abandon the identification of Gal. ii. with Acts xv. If, however, that identification is to be maintained, how is the discrepancy to be accounted for ? The explanations put forward have assumed three main forms, no one of which can be regarded as satisfactory.

(*a*) We pass over the drastic solution, rarely now put forward, that the visit described in Acts xi. 30 is unhistorical.

(*b*) A second explanation is that Paul omits all reference to the visit of Acts xi. 30 because on that occasion he saw only the presbyters, not the apostles. This is a mere evasion of the difficulty. Even if it be conceded that Paul's concern in Galatians is to tell, not of his *visits to Jerusalem*, but of his *relations with the apostles*, is it conceivable that he would in such a narrative have omitted altogether to mention the intervening visit, when in a few words he could have safeguarded himself by saying that on that occasion the apostles were not present in the city ? Further we may doubt whether the fact that only the presbyters are mentioned in the Acts narrative means that the apostles were certainly absent (see p. 38).

(*c*) A third explanation, maintained by Schwartz and McGiffert and now adopted by Kirsopp Lake, is that in Acts xi. 30 and Acts xv. we have the same visit narrated from two different points of view, owing to the author's dependence on different sources. Thus Acts is made to conform to Galatians in having only two visits ; the Apostolic Council, which took place on the second of these, is dated at the same time as the famine-relief visit (possibly as early as the year 46) ; and just as there are two versions of the one visit to Jerusalem, so also there are two versions of the one mission to Galatia, (i.) in Acts xiii. and xiv. and (ii.) in Acts xvi. 6 ff. Whatever attractiveness such a hypothesis may have as a critical *tour de force*, we can have no confidence that it is *true* ; and is it not at once more reasonable and more satisfactory to accept the general outline of Acts as we have it?[1]

(2) A further objection to seeing in Gal. ii. 1–10 Paul's version of the narrative of Acts xv. is that the two accounts do not harmonize.

(*a*) In Acts there is a formal conference ; in Galatians Paul has a private interview with the Jerusalem leaders.

(*b*) At the Council in Acts decrees are passed which are embodied in a letter to be sent down to the churches concerned. Paul in Galatians makes no reference to decrees, and indeed makes it plain that no decrees were passed. ' The authorities,' he says, ' made no addition to my gospel, they fully acknowledged my apostleship, and merely asked me to remember the poor ' (ii. 6–10). This is not the place to examine the various problems raised by the narrative in Acts xv.—how far e.g. is that account reliable, what were the exact terms of the decision, and did it represent a compromise or a complete endorsement of Paul's Gentile-policy ? But unless we are to dismiss it as completely unreliable, then in any attempt to identify the two accounts we are faced with the baffling question: 'Why, if a formal ruling on the situation was arrived at, is there no reference to it in the Epistle?' Surely the Judaizers would readily have appealed to it if it had represented a compromise ; or if it represented a triumph for Paul, the apostle had only to refer to it to silence all controversy. No satisfactory explanation of this difficulty has yet been forthcoming.

(3) A third objection to the identification of Gal. ii. and Acts xv. is provided by the narrative in Gal. ii. 11 ff., regarding the question of Jewish and Gentile Christians eating together at Antioch. One naturally assumes that the episode related in those verses took place *after* the events related in verses 1–10. But how could a difficulty such as is there described have developed if verses 1–10 represent a formal conference at which this very difficulty had already been discussed and settled ?

[1] The view that Acts xv. combines the accounts of *two* Councils (see essays by W. F. Howard in the *Study Bible* volume on Acts and by H. Lietzmann in *Amicitiæ Corolla*) is likewise exposed to grave objections.

It may be urged that this is scarcely a fair statement of the case. The Apostolic Council, it may be said, dealt solely with the terms on which Gentiles could have a place in the Christian Fellowship, not with the question of Jewish and Gentile Christians associating with one another. But is it conceivable that at the date of the Council, when (according to the evidence of Acts) the work at Antioch had been going on for perhaps three years and there had been a Gentile-embracing mission through South Galatia, the question of the admission of Gentiles *into* the Fellowship could be discussed as an isolated question apart from the other question of the corporate relations of Jews and Gentiles *within* the Fellowship ? This practical issue must certainly have presented itself to the Council. Accordingly, if Gal. ii. 1–10 is a narrative of the Council, critics are driven to suggest that the incident of Peter at Antioch in verses 11 ff. took place *before* the events described in verses 1–10. In other words, Paul relates first of all his two visits to Jerusalem, and then goes back to recount an incident at Antioch which took place before the second of these. Such a reversal of chronological order, of which there is not a hint in Paul's narrative, is so highly improbable that only as a last expedient ought it to be accepted as an explanation.

A historical reconstruction of the development of events

At Antioch work among Gentiles had, under the supervision of Barnabas and Paul, been going on for approximately a year (Acts xi. 26) before the visit to Jerusalem related in Acts xi. 30 (=Gal. ii. 1). The visit had as one of its objects the taking of a relief-fund to Jerusalem ; but the narrative in Galatians reveals that it was undertaken on Paul's part as a result of divine guidance, and that he was concerned to inform the apostles in Jerusalem of the new and wonderful developments which were taking place in regard to the acceptance of the Gospel by Gentiles. At this stage, therefore, the question at issue was the fundamental one of the terms on which Gentiles should be accepted into the Christian Fellowship. It concerned, to use Paul's phrase, the truth of his gospel.

When Paul went up to Jerusalem at this time, knowing well that this question must be raised, his position was by no means secure. He was still a young man, unknown to most members of the Church, remembered by others with lingering prejudice, and viewed with suspicion and hatred by the non-Christian Jews, with whom the Christians of Jerusalem desired to live as amicably as possible. His own claim was that he had been called by God to be an apostle, and had received a special commission to go to the Gentiles ; but would the Jerusalem authorities, however much they might be impressed by his sincerity and missionary zeal, be completely satisfied as to his apostolic claims and give him *carte blanche* to work among Gentiles without demanding from them circumcision and the keeping of the Law ? Conversations took place on the subject—there is no indication in Gal. ii. of a formal Conference, and indeed the time was not ripe for that ; and it speaks volumes, both for the cogency with which Paul presented his case and for the extent to which the leaders of the Jerusalem church were ruled by the Spirit of Christ, that these latter acknowledged the genuineness of his apostleship and fully endorsed his interpretation of the gospel. Gal. ii. 1–10, therefore, represents quite an early stage in the development of events.

But the settlement of one question means the raising of others. The practical question next emerged of the relation of Jews and Gentiles within the Fellowship. Even at the Jerusalem meeting above referred to, that problem had created a difficult situation : the demand was raised that Titus, a Gentile who accompanied Paul, must be circumcised if he was to have full and free fellowship with his brother-Christians in Jerusalem, and Paul, who could *reculer pour mieux sauter*, consented (as I believe) to his circumcision. But already it was plain to his clear vision that, if Gentiles were to be admitted to the Fellowship, then within the Fellowship Jews and Gentiles must be *one*. On his return to Antioch, therefore, Paul himself joined in table-fellowship with Gentile members of the Church (he had no doubt done so even *before* his visit to Jerusalem). So too did Barnabas ; other Jewish-Christians were probably encouraged to do likewise ; and when Peter visited Antioch,[1] he too fell in with a practice which, though it was altogether novel to him, appealed to his honest and sympathetic nature. Then there arrived emissaries from James in Jerusalem who took exception to this table-fellowship. They did not deny that the Gentiles might become Christians without first becoming Jews ; but they insisted that, as Jews were forbidden by the Law to eat with Gentiles, Jewish-Christians and Gentile-Christians must keep separate.

Here then was an issue which cut Paul to the quick. Was the Fellowship of Christ to be split into two sections, a Jewish and a Gentile ? By prompt and decisive action he saved the situation at Antioch, and unity was, for a time, restored. But clearly trouble was brewing. Soon it would become so threatening that a formal Conference on the subject would be necessary. Meanwhile two other developments took place which served to bring matters to a head. One was the initiation by Barnabas and Paul of a great missionary-crusade—they went out into the highways and the byways of the world, constraining the Gentiles to come in ; and ' a door of faith ' was opened in the towns of S. Galatia (Acts xiv. 27). The other was that Jewish opposition marshalled itself for attack. Among extreme Jewish-Christians (and in this they would have the sympathy and support of non-Christian Jews) it became apparent that Pauline Christianity meant a denial of some of the fundamental principles of Judaism. Hence they demanded that, if unity was to be maintained in the Church, Gentile-Christians must come under the same God-given ordinances as Jewish-Christians. The claim put forward by Paul, and endorsed by the Jerusalem apostles, that Gentile-Christians should be free from the Law must be abandoned. To press home their case, and to save the situation before Paul (regarded as a false apostle and a traitor to his nation's faith) had irretrievably ruined it, judaizing propagandists appeared in Antioch,[2] and even

---

[1] This was probably before the missionary journey of Barnabas and Paul to Galatia.

[2] Acts xv. 1. No time-indication is given in this verse ; and it is probable that these emissaries from Judæa had arrived in Antioch some considerable time previous to the events described in chap. xv.

pursued Barnabas and Paul in their missionary tour through Galatia ; and as we see from the Epistle, they achieved no little success in persuading Gentile converts to accept the Jewish Law.

This was the situation that called forth from Paul his Epistle to the Galatians. Can we define the situation still more precisely ? Where was Paul when word reached him of the havoc the Judaizers were making among his Galatian converts ? Was he (as seems most probable) in Antioch, where Acts says that he spent a considerable time on his return ? Was he on his way up from Antioch to Jerusalem to attend the Council ?[1] May it even be that he had not yet had time to reach Antioch on his way back from Galatia ? The interval need not have been a long one—experience of ' revivals ' shows that enthusiastic converts lend a ready ear to fresh demands by which, as they think, they can testify to the genuineness of their faith and make their calling and election sure. At the very opening of the letter Paul expresses his astonishment that the Galatians should have deserted Christ *so soon* (see note on i. 6). The Judaizers may have followed him relentlessly from town to town, keeping close on his heels all the way : the language of i. 9 reveals that, even during the time he spent with the Galatians, Paul was conscious of the dangers of a rival gospel being preached among them ('I have said it before'; see note on that passage and on 'again' in v. 3). Sufficient time, however, has elapsed for the trouble to have reached alarming proportions and for Paul to have passed right away from Galatia. He is now in a place where he cannot easily reach those to whom he writes (iv. 20). It seems best to picture him as being in Antioch.

We may continue our historical retrospect one stage further. The question which had been raised involved vital religious interests ; and from the first there must have been many in the Church who found it difficult to know how they ought to react to it. The extreme Judaizers had a point of view which

---

[1] This has been conjectured because of the vague phrase (without any place-reference) in i. 2 : ' the brothers who are beside me.' On that phrase see commentary *ad loc.*

deserves to be studied with sympathy and patience. Even the Jerusalem apostles who (at the time of the earlier conversations) had given their blessing to Paul and his work must have viewed with concern certain possible results of his policy. There is a significant phrase in ii. 14 which helps us to appreciate their difficulty. It speaks of men who were true-born Jews coming to forget their traditions and learning to ' live like the Gentiles.' How far, it might be asked, were Jewish-Christians to be made to go for the sake of fellowship with their Gentile brethren? Brotherhood in Christ might lead a Jewish-Christian to welcome a Gentile-Christian to his table, but was he in turn to accept an invitation to the table of the Gentile, where he might be asked to eat food such as no Jew ought to eat? There were other difficulties, too, apart from those which concerned food. Was a Jewish-Christian, e.g., to become lax in his observance of the Sabbath because his Gentile brother did not observe it?

On all such matters Paul had one clear principle to guide him. ' The Law was temporary and provisional; the will of Christ is final; and therefore the Christian must go as far as the Spirit of Christ requires that he should go.' Hence we have his insistence (as in chaps. v. and vi.) on the life of the Spirit and on the law of Christian Love. But the matter was less clear for others who did not wish to turn their back on their past or show themselves disloyal to the religion of their fathers.

It would be interesting if we knew more definitely how Barnabas viewed the issue. What we know of him inclines us to believe that he would go as far as possible with his young colleague. When the matter was referred to the Jerusalem Council, he certainly supported Paul on the general question; but so also (as is shown by the decision of the Council)[1] did Peter and James and the other leaders of Jewish-Christian opinion. But did Barnabas go with Paul all the way?[2] At

[1] The decree avoided explicit mention of table-fellowship, i.e. it did not recommend that fellowship such as Paul encouraged was either *essential* or *right*; it merely proposed a *modus vivendi* which would make fellowship *possible*. Gentile-Christians were asked to abstain from fornication and to avoid foods which were especially repugnant to Jews.

[2] No safe argument may be deduced from the fact that Barnabas is not associated with Paul in the writing of Galatians (i. 1) (see p. 10).

one time certainly he wavered (ii. 13). And he did not accompany Paul on the second missionary journey. Though we do not have sufficient evidence for a decision, are there indications that the liberal policy of Paul scarcely carried the *full* approval of the older apostle ?

Doctrinal features of the Epistle, and their bearing on the question of date

Even if we accept Galatians as the earliest of all his letters, we must not forget that at this date Paul had already been a Christian for perhaps seventeen years, and in its essential features his gospel was already formed. But as at least *pointers* in the direction of an early date we may cite the character of his references to the Church (see pp. xliv. f.) and the fact that, though he comes so near to it in thought, he never uses the expression ' the body of Christ.' Similarly, he does not use the term ' the mystery ' with regard to the Gospel, even though all that is implied by that phrase in Col. i. 25 ff. is already present to his mind. The simple expression found in iii. 29, v. 24, ' those who belong to Christ ' (lit. ' who are of Christ '; see p. xliv.) has a parallel in the name ' Christ's men ' (*Christianoi*) which about this time came to be applied to the believers at Antioch (Acts xi. 26).

The thought which Paul develops in his later Epistles, that believers share in the Lord's risen life, is not expressed in that way in Galatians, where the benefits of salvation are connected with Christ's redemptive death and the gift of the Holy Spirit.

Paul's apocalyptic teaching in the Thessalonian Epistles (written during the second missionary journey) is certainly not to be explained as representing a cruder and a more primitive stage in his religious thinking (see p. xlvi.). And as regards the affinities of our Epistle with Romans, which dates from the third missionary journey, it is entirely fallacious to imagine that these necessarily imply that Romans (at least in its present form) and Galatians were written at approximately the same time.

Chronology

On the obscure subject of chronology a word must suffice. Paul's second visit to Jerusalem (Acts xi. 30 ; Gal. ii. 1) may be connected, as Acts indicates, with a famine in Judæa. On the evidence of Josephus there was a famine in Judæa about the year 46—after the death of Herod in 44. A probable date for the Apostolic Council (Acts xv.) is 48, which may therefore be taken also as the date of our Epistle. Paul's first visit to Jerusalem, approximately fourteen years before the second visit, may be placed about 33, and his conversion two years earlier (see i. 18 and ii. 1).

3. The Source of the Trouble in Galatia

If the reconstruction given on pp. xxvi. ff. be accepted as a reasonable interpretation of the development of events, there is no need to doubt the traditional explanation of the trouble in Galatia, viz. that it was caused by Jewish-Christian emissaries who came in from outside, probably from Jerusalem. That view, however, has in recent years been challenged from two sides.

(1) It has been pointed out that in the Epistle there is no clear indication that the people who caused the trouble had come from Jerusalem. May it not therefore be that the trouble arose in Galatia itself ? And as there is no reason to believe that the Church in Galatia was to any large extent Jewish-Christian, may it not be that the opposition came in the main from local Jews ? To quote Kirsopp Lake's statement of this position : ' So far as Romans and Galatians deal with the Law it is not because there was a Jewish-Christian mission in rivalry to Paul, but because Paul wished to protect his converts from the efforts of Jewish teachers to persuade them to come over to the true Mother Church—the Synagogue —and accept whole-heartedly all the teaching of the Old Testament on which Paul himself relied for the proof of so much of his teaching ' (*Beginnings of Christianity*, Vol. V., p. 215).

If we had merely Galatians to go on, this might be accepted as a *possible* explanation of the facts before us. It may be doubted, however, whether it is a *true*, or at least a *complete*, explanation.

In Jerusalem and Judæa, where Jewish Christianity was a living force, there certainly was a party *within the Church* which insisted on setting Christianity within the framework of Judaism. Acts xv. 5 definitely refers to Christian Pharisees who demanded that Gentiles must be circumcised and told to keep the Mosaic Law; and the false brothers whom Paul denounces in ii. 4 were, of course, Christians. But they were, as we may say, Jews first and Christians afterwards; and they would fight to the uttermost any interpretation of Christianity which, when carried to its inevitable conclusion, was to separate them from the commonwealth of Israel, and link them up in a new unity with ' Gentile sinners.' In this they were sure of support from their non-Christian Jewish brethren, whose attitude to Pauline Christianity was one of deep resentment and finally of active opposition.

Thus the opposition to Paul in Galatia may have had the backing of non-Christian Jews; but the driving force came from Jewish-Christians. And the probability is that they were Jewish-Christians from Judæa. Emissaries from Judæa found their way to Antioch, according to Acts xv. 1; and if their real aim was to do all in their power to wreck Paul's work, then the probability is that they pursued him into Galatia.

(2) In the second place it is urged[1] that, in addition to Jewish (or Judaizing) opposition, Paul had to face trouble of an exactly opposite kind, viz. from a Gentile party of ' spiritual perfectionists ' who, priding themselves on their possession of the Spirit, claimed to be superior to the authority of the Jewish Law, or even to the recognized principles of morality. This party, it is said, is referred to in vi. 1 (' you who are spiritual '); and it was with them in mind that Paul issued his stern warning that Christian freedom is not to be made

[1] For this view see J. H. Ropes' *The Singular Problem of the Epistle to the Galatians.*

'an opening for the flesh' (v. 13). As a further argument in support of this hypothesis, we are asked to believe that when Paul develops, as he does in chaps. iii. and iv., his contention that those who are Christ's are the true offspring of Abraham, he is combating the pretensions of those Gentile 'spirituals' who wished to sever altogether the connection between Judaism and a truly spiritual Christianity. On this view it is Paul who is the Judaizer, seeking to link up his converts with a Jewish past with which they themselves wish to have nothing to do !

Paul's correspondence does indeed reveal that, in some of his churches at a later date, he had trouble from people of this type ; but the existence of such a party at this date in Galatia is a gratuitous assumption. The errors which Paul combats in his doctrine of Christian freedom are the errors, not of Gentile perfectionists, but of Jewish legalists. Faced with the Judaizing contention that the only alternative to adherence to the Jewish Law is a lapse into heathen licence, Paul reminds his Gentile readers that they know the ethical and spiritual standards of the Gospel, and that those who have received the Spirit must learn to walk by it. And when he emphasizes how Christians are linked up with Abraham (' if you are Christ's, then you are Abraham's offspring'—iii. 29), he is not asserting this connection in the face of those who deny it, but expounding its meaning to those who misunderstand it. The true sons of Abraham, he declares as against the assertions of the Judaizers, are not those who are linked together by the covenant-rite of circumcision and the keeping of the Law, but those who through Christ, the true 'Offspring' of Abraham, have learned to trust God in faith as Abraham did.

III. THE THEOLOGICAL BACKGROUND OF THE EPISTLE

The Epistle to the Galatians is not a theological treatise ; it is a religious appeal. Yet behind that appeal there lies a definite outlook on life and destiny, an ordered system of thought on the purposes and activities of God as these have been revealed in Christ. Paul could not have pled as he does in Galatians if he had not had a clear theology.

In one of the opening verses the apostle gives expression to a thought which is of cardinal importance for the interpretation of all that follows. He says that ' Christ gave Himself for our sins, to rescue us from the present evil world ' (i. 4). At the heart of Paul's appeal there lies a doctrine of *redemption*. With this verse as a guide we may examine Paul's thought under three heads :

1. The Prelude to Redemption.
2. The Redemption accomplished by Christ.
3. The Consequences of Redemption.

1. The Prelude to Redemption

Man's Separation from God

It was a widely accepted view that the world as a whole lay under the domination of the powers of evil. His very belief in a Holy God forced the Jew to recognize that mankind was enslaved to sin, doomed therefore to death which was the penalty for sin, and cut off from perfect knowledge of God or participation in His life-giving Spirit. Along with the powers of evil other powers were recognized which were not so much hostile to God's purpose as indifferent to it. Paul knew how the pagan world looked with awe on the mysterious forces which ruled the natural order, notably the powers of the heavenly spheres to which he alludes by the name of Elemental Spirits (Gal. iv. 3, 9), and he himself had inherited from his Jewish upbringing a belief in various ' principalities and powers.' All these powers held sway over the present evil world and came between man and God. In view of this separation God aimed at ultimate reconciliation of man to Himself ; as a means to that end He sought to redeem man from the powers that enslaved him ; and the devout looked forward in faith to the age to come, when sin should give place to righteousness and death to life eternal, and when God Himself should dwell with His people.

God's Covenants with Abraham and Israel

The pious Jew was ready to acknowledge that in the working out of this gracious purpose God looked out on humanity as a whole : He was the God of all the earth. Yet He must establish contact where contact could be found. He began by calling one man Abraham through whom He could work—promising that in him and in his seed all nations would be blessed. The acceptance of any one man must always mean the passing-over of others, even though the passing-over may be temporary and leave open the possibility of ultimate acceptance. Thus of Abraham's seed Isaac was chosen but not Ishmael : Jacob but not Esau. After their deliverance from Egypt, which typified a greater deliverance to come, the earlier covenant with Abraham and his seed was renewed on Sinai with the children of Israel *as a people*, representing that branch of the family of Abraham through which the promises were to be fulfilled ; and in virtue of it they were now not merely *sons of Abraham* and *children of Israel* but *the people of God*.

All good Jews held firmly by these two covenants ; but different interpretations came to be held with regard to their character and content. To the more evangelically minded they were essentially expressions of the self-manifestation and redeeming activity of God, whose primary and indeed sole demand was for trust. In this respect the covenant with Abraham was *par excellence* a covenant of Promise, to which Abraham responded in faith. There were other Jews, however, who, partly on grounds of narrow nationalism, partly on grounds of stern righteousness, interpreted the covenants as if they were two-sided agreements, according to which the human recipients came under certain obligations, in the one case to circumcise their children, in the other to keep the Law given on Sinai. On this view God's blessing was only for those who ' kept the covenant.'

In Galatians the foundation of the religion of Jehovah is placed by Paul in the covenant of Promise which God made with Abraham. It is God from whom all saving activity comes ; and such a God ' accepts ' (' justifies ') man never in terms of what man has accomplished but solely in terms of his faith and receptivity. So thoroughly is this covenant of Promise the foundation for Paul that he insists that the later covenant of the Law was essentially secondary—the Law was imposed for a special purpose, and held merely for a temporary period. And when Christ came, says Paul, He came in fulfilment of the covenant of Promise ; and with His coming the covenant of Law has come to an end.

The Law of God

At this point we may ask ourselves (i.) what precisely was meant by the Law which under the covenant Israel had pledged itself to obey ; and (ii.) what was the attitude to the Law of those who ranged themselves against Paul.

(i.) The word translated into Greek as *nomos* and into English as *Law* was in Hebrew *Torah*, and it signified not Law in a legalist sense but the revealed Will of God. Thus the Will of God and the Law of God were at basis synonymous terms. As regards the covenant with Israel made on Sinai, the Torah which God communicated there might be interpreted of the ten commandments (Exod. xxxiv. 28), or even of the foundational demand that Israel was to have no other God save Jehovah ; but the term came to be applied to the five sacred books in which, as every good Jew believed, Moses incorporated what had been revealed by God as His demands for the people. Even the prophetic teaching was in a sense Torah : Isaiah can speak as if what he has to declare is God's law no less than God's word (Isa. i. 10) ; but a distinction came to be drawn between the Law and the Prophets, even though it was recognized that, as in each case the Voice was the Voice of God, what the prophets declared was in reality an interpretation of what was written in the books of Moses. Lastly, as the Law constantly required reinterpretation and formulation to make it applicable to the changing conditions of life, the term Torah was made to cover the dedicated work of the scribes who, now that prophecy had ceased, were accepted as continuing the work of the prophets in the task of interpreting the Law ; and alongside the written law a place was found for the unwritten law of tradition. Hence it was that though, to the pious Jew, the fundamental demand of God was still that men should hearken to His word and obey His will, and though from this point of view much that Paul says of the Law must appear unsympathetic and even unjust, nevertheless the Law of God came to be interpreted too much in a legalistic and too little in a spiritual sense, and even those who did not feel it (as Paul did) an intolerable burden must have been conscious that it did not give them freedom and joy and power in their religious life. It was possible to give heed to the Law and not hear the authoritative and life-giving Voice of God, or be in touch with His Spirit.

(ii.) Nevertheless the good Jew regarded the Law with unqualified honour and devotion. The springs of devotion came first of all from personal piety. God could never be for him, as for so many in our modern world, merely the end of the great human quest ; God was the beginning, who spoke to men and called them to hearken and obey. The facts of history served in certain quarters to deepen their devotion. Shut in on every side by a paganism which threatened to engulf it, Judaism had come to believe that only by a scrupulous regard for Jehovah's revealed will in the Law could the nation preserve its identity and witness for Him to other nations that knew Him not. Going a stage further, Jewish thinkers declared that the Law received by Israel on Sinai had, from the very nature of things, existed with God from the beginning, and must, therefore, exist to all eternity—a copy, as it were, of the Law eternally existent in heaven. Lastly, while many pious Jews were ready to recognize that in the eyes of a holy God the Jew was as truly a sinner, and as worthy of condemnation, as the Gentile was, nevertheless they clung to the belief (*a*) that it was in the Law that God had defined, fully and finally, what He expected of His people, and (*b*) that the real significance of the Promise lay in this, that God would continue to show a special measure of favour to the seed of Abraham, a favour in which the Gentiles could only share if they accepted the covenant-rite of circumcision and pledged themselves to keep the covenant-obligation defined in the Law.

On all these grounds it was natural that even among those Jews who became Christians there should be many who refused to believe that the Law could be set aside or superseded. Jesus Himself, they recalled, had come not to destroy the Law but to fulfil it. Further, in proclaiming God's righteousness among the Gentiles, they held that they must go with a complete message, embracing the Law of God as well as the Gospel. Had not Israel received the Law that she might pass it on to the nations ? And how, if they were not made to accept the Law, would it be possible for Gentiles to leave behind their old lawlessness and rise to the heights of the righteousness of God ?

It is against such contentions that Paul has to fight in Galatians. The orthodox Jewish view of the Law he attacks unmercifully (chaps. iii.–v.). No doubt the strength of his attack came from the witness of religious experience—he recognized, as others had done before him, that man is sinful and cannot of himself keep the Law of God. But this conviction is reinforced by a denial of the whole theological system on which the traditional view of the Law was based. A fundamental fact for him was that the whole of mankind, being enslaved to sin and under the domination of the powers of this world, was separated from direct communion with the living God. God's redemptive purpose had, it is true, been advanced a stage when contact was established with the seed of Abraham and when later the covenant was renewed with the children of Israel. But sin was not yet cast out ; the powers of this world were not yet dethroned. Until the time came for God to effect *deliverance*, Israel under the Law was in no better case than the other nations outside the Law. The Law, no matter how exalted or how literal a view was taken of it, could not of itself bring men to God or mediate to them the divine Spirit ; all it could do was to make them realize their failure and bring home to them their need of salvation. Indeed, it put men meantime under its condemnation and curse, and that very condemnation was in itself something from which those who were under it must be delivered before they could attain to God's blessing. Lastly, it is in the

Promise rather than in the Law that the true character and purpose of God are revealed. The Promise will stand when the Law is abrogated. And now in Christ the Promise is being fulfilled ; and the true inheritors of it are not those who are ' of Israel ' in the sense that they are Abraham's seed after the flesh, but those who are ' of Christ,' who alone is the true seed of Abraham.

Flesh and Spirit

Bound up with Paul's view of the world is his doctrine of man, and his teaching on flesh and Spirit. In revealed religion *man* is not to be explained except by reference to *God* who created him in His own image and has marked him out for a heavenly destiny. Man is therefore not mere *flesh*, because he is constantly exposed to the influence of the divine *Spirit*. But apart from this influence from the divine Spirit there is strictly no such thing as the human spirit ; and man truly lives only in so far as he is in living contact with the Spirit of God. Man however has fallen from his high estate ; he has become a prey to the powers of evil ; and until he is delivered from them the Spirit of God cannot fully operate in his life. It was in the *flesh* that these evil powers carried out their attacks on him and established their sway over him—for the flesh, though not in itself evil, is weak and easily corrupted when it is not dominated by the Spirit ; and if man was ever to attain his destiny as a spiritual being it was in the flesh that evil must be fought and overcome. Meanwhile man awaits a Deliverer. If he needs deliverance from the condemnation of God's Law, a still more radical need is to be delivered from the power of evil that resides in his flesh, so that he may come under the sway of God's Spirit.

2. The Redemption Accomplished by Christ

The looked-for Deliverer, says Paul, came in Jesus Christ. ' When the time had fully expired, God sent forth His Son, born of a woman, born under the Law, to ransom those who were under the Law, that we might get our sonship ' (iv. 4).

(i.) Jesus came from God. He did not arise among men to be their Leader and Champion ; He was the Son of God, who had come from God to be their Redeemer. That He was truly the Son of God was proved for Paul by the fact that God raised Him from the dead (Gal. i. 1 ; Rom. i. 4) ; and His resurrection and exaltation revealed Him too as ' The Lord,' to whom all the powers of the present world were made subject.

(ii.) As a pre-condition of effective deliverance, Jesus in His coming among men identified Himself thoroughly with those whom He sought to deliver. (*a*) Born of a woman, He took flesh, and became truly man ; in this way He experienced all the onslaughts that the powers of this world make against man, and finally He was able to offer Himself as a representative on behalf of His brother-men. (*b*) Further, as it was through His covenanted people that God was seeking to advance His redemptive purposes for humanity as a whole, Jesus was born a son of Abraham, and came under the Law, even sharing in that curse which the Law imposed on those who were under its jurisdiction ; and so He was able to offer Himself as a representative on behalf of His brother-Israelites. (*c*) In this representative capacity He accepted crucifixion, the innocent for the guilty ; and by taking on Himself the condemnation and punishment which belonged to the brethren, He became in a double sense their Deliverer—those who were under the Law might now be ransomed from its curse, and men everywhere might rise above the conditions of sin and servitude which seemed an inevitable accompaniment of life in the present age, and attain to the freedom of sons of God.

From first to last Galatians connects this redemptive work of Christ with His *death*. ' He died for our sins ' (i. 4) ; ' He gave Himself up for us ' (ii. 20) ; ' then indeed Christ's death was useless ' (ii. 21) ; ' Jesus Christ the crucified ' (iii. 1) ; ' He became accursed for us ' (iii. 13) ; ' the cross of Christ ' (vi. 12; 14). There is only one direct reference to the resurrection of Christ, viz. in i. 1. In some of his later Epistles Paul represents believers as sharing in the resurrection-life of their Lord (e.g. Col. iii. 1). This is not so in Galatians. Here

Christians are not those who share Christ's resurrection, but those who accept in faith the benefits purchased by His death.

For a fuller study of Paul's teaching on Christ's death we may refer the reader to the commentary on the passages quoted above.

3. The Consequences of Redemption

To understand Paul's teaching on the consequences of Redemption we must look at the far horizon and consider his eschatology. Eschatology does not come prominently to expression in Galatians ; but it is pre-supposed, as it is in all the New Testament writings ; and no interpretation of Galatians can afford to neglect it.

There is no reason to think Paul's eschatological teaching at this stage differed in essentials from that of Jesus.[1] Jesus seems to have taught men to expect the Kingdom of God to be inaugurated by the triumphal appearance of the Messiah (Son of Man) before whom the dead of all ages would appear, some to pass to life eternal, the others to pass to punishment or death. Paul likewise has his doctrine of the two ages (i. 4) ; and in I Thessalonians, written shortly after this, he has given us a picture of the appearance of Christ and the gathering together of His saints (iv. 15–17).

Justification and the Gift of the Spirit

In his teaching in Galatians Paul does not deal with the coming judgment or the life to come, but with the true approach to God which will ultimately lead to life eternal. He believes that in the day of judgment a man cannot base his claims on anything that he himself has accomplished, for anything that is really worth while is the result of what God Himself has done for him. The first fact we must recognize, here and now, is that Christ died to ransom us ; and we are called to accept His redeeming work and in simple faith to yield ourselves to God. When we thus turn to God in Christ, God on His part accepts us—and that acceptance is what

[1] A different view is maintained by Schweitzer, in his great book *The Mysticism of Paul the Apostle*.

is called Justification. The acceptance follows on our faith —hence the expression 'justification by faith'; and God signifies that His acceptance of us is real by giving us His Holy Spirit. This gift of the Holy Spirit has a cosmical significance, for it shows that men are not entirely under the sway of the powers of this world but may be brought into living contact with God Himself; but it has a significance also for the individual believer, who now knows that, though he is still in the flesh, the flesh need no longer dominate him, —here and now he may have growing in his life the fruit of the Spirit. Life in the Spirit is thus characterized less by scrupulous endeavour than by quiet growth. If the Spirit has full sway in a man's life, that man may in the end attain to spiritual completeness. If on the other hand he allows the flesh to reassert itself, he is in no better case than if he had not received the Spirit, and his initial justification will be rendered futile.

When Paul speaks of a man being justified he means, not that he has been made righteous, but that he has been accepted as righteous. And in two important respects his doctrine of justification differs from that of the Judaizers with whom he is in opposition. In the first place he insists that man can never win acceptance by the due performance of the divine requirements—the transcendent holiness of God and the depravity and servitude of man combine to make that way of acceptance impossible. Man cannot be justified by his own works but simply by faith in *God*. In the second place acceptance need not be postponed till that final day when we stand before Christ for judgment: man may be justified here and now, so soon as he turns to God in faith and flings himself on God's mercy. It is this which adds point to the apostle's expostulation with the Galatians in iii. 1-6. 'You have already received the Spirit,' he implies, 'without your having first pledged yourselves to keep the Law, and your reception of the Spirit shows that God has accepted you. Why then should you now imagine that in the end you may not be accepted by Him unless you do keep the Law?' As conceived by the Judaizers, however, justification came not at the beginning, but at the end of the process ; it came not before the gift of the Spirit, but at the day of judgment ; and the special significance of the gift of the Spirit was that it enabled the recipients so to live that they might in the end be justified. It was a noble ideal ; but in Paul's eyes it was not Christian, for the simple reason that it reverted to the legalist conception of a man being judged and justified by works. It ignored the distinctly Christian truth that Christ had died to redeem men ; and if man can win acceptance by what he does, then there was no need that Christ should die for him (Gal. ii. 21).

Those who belong to Christ—the Church of God

By accepting the benefits which Christ has purchased for him the believer comes to ' belong to Christ '—a simple and significant phrase which Paul uses in iii. 29 ; v. 24. At baptism the Christian crucifies the flesh (v. 24) and ' puts on ' Christ (iii. 27) ; he ceases to live his own life, for Christ now lives in him (ii. 20). Justification is thus only the initial, though all-important, step towards the complete self-identification of the believer with Christ. It is this self-identification which modern theology has in mind when it speaks of ' Christ-mysticism.' ' In Paul there is no God-mysticism ; only a Christ-mysticism by means of which man comes into relation to God. The fundamental thought of Pauline mysticism runs thus : " I am in Christ ; in Him I know myself as a being who is raised above this sensuous, sinful and transient world and already belongs to the transcendent ; in Him I am assured of resurrection ; in Him I am a child of God " ' (Schweitzer, *The Mysticism of Paul the Apostle*, p. 3).

But the believer's relation to Christ is never merely an individual one. Old Testament and New Testament alike teach that God's aim is the winning for Himself of *a people* ; and the individual who is justified by Christ and receives the Holy Spirit is thereby incorporated into the Holy People which is already in existence and waiting to receive him. While Paul holds that Christ is, in a unique sense, the Son of God (iv. 4), and the only true ' offspring of Abraham ' (iii. 16), he goes on to show how those who are Christ's constitute God's redeemed family (iv. 5), and collectively are Abraham's offspring and inheritors of the Promise (iii. 29). For Paul's use of the phrase ' in Christ ' to denote this corporate relationship to Christ see note on p. 103.

In pre-Christian thought it was accepted that the people of God was Israel (or a righteous remnant), including, of course, any who should be incorporated into Israel ; and a name frequently applied to it was the *ecclesia* or *church* of God. This conception is taken over into the New Testament, and the *ecclesia* of God now includes those who belong to Christ. Thus in Galatians Paul applies to the Christian Fellowship the designation of ' the church of God ' (i. 13). But his use of the phrase in i. 13 suggests that it is a transferred designation, purposely used to cover a body of people whom Paul now sees to be members of God's *ecclesia*, though at the time referred to he had included them rather among God's enemies. In his later Epistles Paul's use of the term becomes at once more bold and more frequent. As a definite breach developed between ' the Christian Church ' and ' the Jewish Church ' Paul dared to claim the name, *the ecclesia of God*, as the natural and exclusive prerogative of the Fellowship that is ' in Christ.' As an indication that the apostle has not yet definitely adopted that exclusive position, we may refer to his significant reference in i. 20 to ' the *Christian* churches[1] of Judæa,' where the addition of the word ' Christian ' seems to imply that the name of *Church* might be claimed by other assemblies which were not Christian. If this is so, it is (as Professor Anderson Scott notes)[2] ' an echo, perhaps the latest, of this consciousness of sharing a common status with the Jewish Church ; it would also be a point in favour of an early date for the Galatian Epistle.' Significance in this connection may also attach to the designations *the household of the faith* (vi. 10) and *the Israel of God* (vi. 16, where see note).

[1] The plural ' churches ' in this passage and in i. 2 signifies local congregations of the one *ecclesia* or Church.
[2] Essay on ' What happened at Pentecost ? ' in the volume entitled *The Spirit* (edited by B. H. Streeter), p. 135.

The Ingathering of the Gentiles

When Gentiles began to accept the Gospel, the question was naturally raised in the Church whether it was sufficient that they should ' belong to Christ,' or must they also put themselves alongside their Jewish-Christian brethren by adhering to the commonwealth of Israel. It was not Paul who first raised the question ; but he recognized more clearly than any other how vital the issue was, and once battle was joined on it he fought the fight to a finish.

Paul saw the problem in its eschatological setting. The determining factor was not the sacred inheritance of the past but the wonder of the dawning age in which all things were made new. If in Christ Gentiles were redeemed from the present evil world and made heirs of life eternal, what call was there that they should submit themselves to ordinances which, however sacred in their origin, had reference to the present age from which they had been delivered ? For, as Paul saw clearly, the Law was at best a God-given ordinance for the regulation of life within the present world ; it was in no sense a means of deliverance from it.

In another way Paul's work among Gentiles and his conceptions of the End reacted on one another. While it was only to be expected that among the elect should be many out of Israel, it was also in line with the teaching of the prophets that there should be many Gentiles in the number ; and to that special task of gathering in the Gentiles Paul knew that he had been called by God. Now when he wrote his Epistle to the Galatians Paul was conscious that that work had as yet scarcely begun. Hence at this time he did not nurse the expectation of an immediate Coming of Christ, as some of the early disciples did who lacked his range of vision or his conception of the gospel. Later, as the work among the Gentiles advanced, his thoughts dwelt more on the approach of the End (e.g. in the Thessalonian Epistles). But no such anticipation is expressed in Galatians. In urging his converts to lead the Christian life he bases his appeal not on the nearness of the End but on the fact that they have been redeemed.

IV. The Dominant Religious Ideas in the Epistle

The dominant religious issue in Galatians concerns Justification—is a man justified in God's sight by doing the works of the Law or by faith in Jesus Christ ? So stated, the issue may appear to be of interest primarily for theologians. How Paul would have been amazed, and grieved, could he have imagined that any one would so misunderstand his meaning ! It was not as a theologian that he sat down to write this Epistle, but as ' an apostle ' (i. 1). The people to whom he writes are not pupils to whom he addresses a theological exposition, but converts whom he has himself won for the faith and whom he is concerned to re-establish in it—' dear children,' as he himself writes, ' with whom I am in travail once again till Christ be formed within you ' (iv. 19). Indeed, we may go further. Paul writes as he does to the Galatians because there has been granted to him in his own soul a revelation of the Son of God (i. 15). He dares to appeal to them to rest their justification on Christ alone because he knows that in his own life there is nothing now that he can call his own— ' it is no longer I who live; Christ lives in me ' (ii. 20). Hence if we would understand Galatians aright, we must think of it, not primarily as a theological treatise, but as the passionate outpouring of the apostle's soul in vindication of the gospel which he has been commissioned to preach, and of the faith which has made all things new for himself.

Righteousness

It may help to bring home to us the vitally religious significance of the issue if we recall that the terms ' justification ' and ' righteousness ' are represented in the Greek by one and the same word (*dikaiosynē*). But what precisely is meant by righteousness, and what are the standards by which it is to be judged ? In ordinary thinking we tend to connect it with right dealing as between man and man, and we test it by certain recognized human standards, e.g. established law and custom. In daily life a man may pass as righteous if he pays his debts and his general conduct is that of a gentleman.

From this point of view there can be no doubt that righteousness comes by *works*. In revealed religion, however, righteousness is a relationship, not between man and man, but between man and *God*. Indeed, it is to God that righteousness primarily, and in a strict sense solely, belongs. The fundamental fact is that *God is righteous* ; and if we are to attain to righteousness in our dealings with Him, it can only be in response to His righteous dealings with us. When that is recognized, the assertion that righteousness comes by works may require re-examination.

The Righteousness of God

A common tendency in our references to the righteousness of God is to assume (*a*) that it is primarily an *attribute*, a distinguishing mark of His character ; (*b*) that it is one attribute among many, to be set alongside His grace, His wisdom, His power ; (*c*) that it is the attribute specially associated with His character as Judge, and therefore to be contrasted, e.g., with His grace. No true understanding of God's righteousness is to be reached along those lines. When the Hebrew thought of the righteousness of God, he thought of God *in action*, God working out a righteous purpose, a purpose which must certainly include a final judgment, but in which judgment is going on all the time. God's righteousness is nothing less than the divine ordering of human history and the divine ordering of human lives. Everything that He does is the expression of His righteousness—He manifests it equally when He visits the meek and when He dethrones the presumptuous ; and all is directed towards the ultimate triumph of righteousness and the establishment of His Kingdom, a goal which those who acknowledge Him are summoned also to seek (Matt. vi. 33).

When, therefore, we think of the righteousness of God, one conception of Him which must be dismissed is the primarily forensic one of the Judge who merely sits on the judgment seat to test how far we have risen to or fallen short of His standards. Nearer to the truth is the conception of Him as the Legislator or Governor who is concerned to see that His universe is governed according to righteous principles. Yet in the last resort it is no great gain to substitute one legalistic conception for another. For it is not by laws merely that God rules the universe. There is assuredly a place for law in His providential scheme : but that place can never be more than provisional and secondary (cf. iii. 19–iv. 6). God accomplishes His righteous purpose by being Himself in the fray, overcoming all that sets itself up against Him, and imparting His Spirit to all who are concerned to be on His side. And He can never seek to accomplish His ends in any way that is inconsistent with His own righteous character. His methods are not those of *law* but of *grace* ; in other words, He must give Himself. Therefore righteousness and grace are not two collateral and, at times, opposing attributes. All that God does is a manifestation at once of His righteousness and of His grace.

Redemption

The transcendent sublimity of the righteousness of God becomes apparent when we see how it deals with human suffering and misery, and above all with that dread fact from which so much suffering and misery arise, viz. human sin. The scriptural teaching about man is that, though God made him in His own image, he has fallen from his high estate ; he is a sinner, and as such is subject to death and liable to eternal condemnation. The modern mind rarely takes sin as seriously as the scriptures do. In ordinary thinking sin is an occasional lapse on the part of the individual from recognized ethical standards. In the scriptures, on the other hand, it proceeds from the acknowledgment by man of some other Power than the Lord God ; and it implies an active, even if unwilling, opposition to God's holy will, a thwarting of His righteous purposes, an undermining of the very foundations on which He seeks to build His Kingdom. And humanity as a whole is inextricably involved in it.

Hebrew thought pondered deeply on the dread power and universality of human sin and sorrow, and in the two centuries preceding the Christian era it came to associate these evils with certain ' powers of this world ' which held humanity in their grasp. The great vision of the ultimate triumph of God's righteousness was never lost, but it was seen that as a preliminary to this triumph God must do something to overthrow those powers of evil and accomplish man's deliverance. The conception of a Messiah, who was to be at once a World Conqueror and a Deliverer of his people, may have assumed some unspiritual forms, but it witnessed to the belief that a new age will not be ushered in by the mere development of human ideals and the exercise of human endeavours. Humanity, as God sees it, is enslaved and requires deliverance. Before progress can come there must be redemption.

Justification and Reconciliation

The Christian Gospel tells how Christ died to accomplish our redemption, and we are summoned to have faith in One who thus gave Himself for us. On the basis of that faith God accepts us (' justifies ' us), forgiving our sins and imparting to us His holy Spirit. This is the truth which Paul set himself to vindicate in Galatians.

It is sometimes said that the doctrine of Justification by Faith is of the very essence of the gospel. But such a statement lends itself to misrepresentation. In the first place it is not by our faith that we are justified, but by *faith in God* through Jesus Christ. In other words the terms on which salvation is possible for us are dictated by what God in Christ has done to make salvation possible. It is not on our faith that we rely for salvation, but on Christ. In the second place justification is only the initial step on the way to salvation. God's aim is not merely to justify us, but to reconcile us to Himself. The justified man must learn to *live in the Spirit*, otherwise his justification lacks reality and will lead to nothing.

Nevertheless it is of fundamental importance for the truth of the gospel that it should be recognized that it is by faith in Christ alone that man can be justified, and not by conformity to legal regulations. We now turn to enquire into that issue more closely.

1

INTRODUCTION

The Truth and the Freedom of the Gospel

What then was the real religious issue in Galatians ? And wherein did Paul, as a Christian, differ from non-Christian Jews, and, more particularly, where did he differ from those Jewish-Christians who sought to impose their views on his Galatian converts ?

(*a*) The Jew believed, no less than the Christian, that God was working out a purpose of righteousness, and that in the Torah He had given men a revelation which might be as a lamp unto their feet and a light unto their path. And even if there was a tendency to interpret the Torah in the terms of the scribe rather than of the prophet, he could claim with reason that it is only in a community disciplined and dominated by a recognition of the sovereign Law of God that the voice of God is likely to be listened to. A lawless world is not, apart from its sheer need, a good seed-plot for the word of God.

(*b*) Paul would have agreed with this. But firstly he insisted that a revelation by God of His sovereign demands does not, when it is unaccompanied by some redemptive power, reconcile man to God, but rather serves to increase the gulf that lies between them. Preoccupation with Law may indeed shut out the vision of God. Even ordinary human idealism readily turns to disillusionment and despair : but for the idealist who acknowledges the righteousness of *God*, moral failure demands that God must either *condemn* or *save* ; He must allow sin to work *death*, or He must Himself intervene to bring *life*. And, in the words of the Fourth Gospel, God sent not His Son into the world to condemn the world, but that the world through Him might be saved.

Secondly, on the more positive side, Paul turned from God's revelation in the *Law* to that other revelation in His *Son*. What arrested the soul of Paul was that the Law could do nothing but enunciate God's demands ; whereas such was the *grace* of the Lord Jesus Christ that He came nearer and ever nearer to us, leading us to see both our achievements and our failures in the light of the Father who had marked us out for sonship, and finally giving His life for us that He might

li

reconcile us to God. Over against the failure of *Law* Paul
sets the efficacy of *Grace*.

(c) But Paul's controversy in Galatians was not with the
non-believing Jew, but with the Jew who had become Christian
and still remained a Jew at heart. The point of view of the
Judaizers deserves to be studied with all care and sympathy.
It may be that in the end we shall agree with Paul that they
were distorting the gospel and imposing a policy of enslavement ; but they themselves would not have accepted that
interpretation of the position. Nothing is so certain to obscure
for us the true issue in Galatians as the unwarranted assumption that Paul's opponents were blind and unspiritual bigots.

Like Paul the Judaizers had accepted Jesus as Lord and
Christ, and they rejoiced that through Him the Holy Spirit of
God was operative among men, enabling them to rise to the
heights of God's righteousness. Where they differed from
Paul was in interpreting the righteousness of God in terms
of the old revelation given in the Torah : God, they said, had
given men His Spirit to enable them to live in accordance
with His Law. To Paul such an interpretation emptied the
new revelation of its meaning ; that men should order life in
accordance with regulations when God has given His own
Spirit for the ordering of it was to him as retrograde a step as
for children to continue to crawl when they have learned to
walk. Indeed it was worse : it was as if slaves who had been
set free should welcome a reimposition of bondage.

But was not Paul, it may be asked, in danger of confusing
the ideal and the actual ? Even if a man is ' justified,' i.e.
accepted as righteous, so soon as he turns in his need to God,
nevertheless God's aim is ultimately to *make* him righteous ;
He cannot rest content with an ' imputed ' righteousness which
is not really there. Exposed as he is to all the temptations
of the flesh and of the world, does man not require to be
trained in righteousness and to be subjected to the discipline
of the divine commandments ? Or, to turn from the individual
to the Fellowship, Paul might regard the Church as the Fellowship of the Spirit, sharing even here on earth in the life of
the world to come ; but in actual fact was it not rather a

Fellowship of earnest endeavourers, who were safeguarded from the evil of the world and prepared for ultimate salvation? So conceived the problem is one which constantly arises in ecclesiastical history, and is very much with us to-day.

Paul saw the issue clearly—in theory at least, though his solution had still to be tested by prolonged experience. Both for the individual and for the fellowship, he insisted, the Christian life needs no other discipline or training save that provided by the Spirit, for under the influence of the Spirit righteousness grows like the harvest. Above all he based his teaching always on the fact that Christ had *died* to make this new life possible for men. Before Christ came men were at best *safeguarded* from the evil of the world ; now they are *redeemed* from it ; and as redeemed men they can, in the power of their Redeemer, overcome temptation without again becoming entangled in rules and regulations. A religion of grace has, of course, its obligations and its laws, no less stern than those of a religion of law ; for where much is given, much also is required. Christ did not abolish law and leave men lawless, but placed them under a new law, the law of love (cf. v. 14, vi. 2, 1 Cor. ix. 21).

Both in the personal life and in the life of the Church the weakness of human nature works against the Pauline doctrine ; and so legalism creeps in as an ally to the gospel, until under its influence even the gospel becomes—what the Law had become—not a means of deliverance from the world but at best a help towards regulation within it. Then in the providence of God there arises an Augustine, a Luther, or a Barth, to sound again the trumpet-notes of *sola gratia* and *sola fide*. And though the fight goes on *within* the Church, and the outside world seems to care little for the issue, nevertheless to the protagonists on one side it always seems (as it seemed to Paul in his day) that the very truth and liberty of the gospel are being challenged by influences which are really pagan. If righteousness comes by way of obedience to law or the pursuit of ideals, then indeed Christ's death was useless (ii. 21).

Paul delivered the Christian Church from bondage to the

Jewish Law. That does not mean that the Church, as an organized society existing in the world, can forgo the right or escape the necessity of ordaining laws of its own. Paul himself came to realize this, as we can see from repeated references in his later Epistles when he has occasion to deal, not as here with the purely religious question of man's relation to God, but with specific practical problems of the relation of the Church to the world and of Christians to one another and to their fellows. On the Church's right and duty to enact such laws and regulations its whole system of organization, discipline, and worship is based. On the other hand history abundantly illustrates the dangers inherent in ecclesiasticism. The law of the Christian Church may become as great a burden and a tyranny as the law of the Jewish Church, and even the churches of the Reformation must constantly ask themselves whether much that they ordain in the sacred name of religion does not reflect a state of servitude rather than of sonship.

On this matter the Epistle to the Galatians has still its message for us. While resolutely combating anything that savoured of anarchy and disorder in the Church of the living God, Paul has once and for all vindicated the position that, whatever enactments the Church may ordain, it must be prepared continually to test these by relation to the living Spirit. For the Spirit is the Church's life, and the ordinances of the Church are mere regulations : and it is not by slavish obedience to ordinances, but by the power and leading of the Holy Spirit, that the Church lives and fights and advances.

COMMENTARY

COMMENTARY

I. INTRODUCTION TO THE EPISTLE

(i. 1–10)

i. 1–5 : *Paul addresses his readers, reminding them that he has a right to do so as an apostle, and that the Christ in whose name he writes is One by whom we are redeemed out of the present evil world*

i.

Paul an apostle—not appointed by men nor commissioned by 1 any man but by Jesus Christ and God the Father who raised him from the dead—with all the brothers who are 2 beside me, to the churches of Galatia ; grace and peace 3 to you from God our Father and the Lord Jesus Christ 4 who gave himself for our sins to rescue us from the present evil world—by the will of our God and Father, to whom 5 be glory for ever and ever : Amen.

The opening sentences of a Pauline Epistle generally repay careful and detailed study. They often reveal the thoughts that dominate the apostle as he begins to write, and so provide a key-note for the rest of the letter. This is notably the case in Galatians.

Paul's letters open with a salutation after the style of the 1 ordinary correspondence of the time : *A to B, greeting*—the nearest approach to this simple formula being seen in 1 Thessalonians. But generally the salutation is expanded in a way which strikes at the outset a note of solemnity and dignity. Thus in most of his letters **Paul** not merely gives his name ; he adds the designation **an apostle.** Commonly the designation given is : ' an apostle of Jesus Christ,' with the addition of the words ' by the will of God.' When Paul so describes himself, it is as if he is presenting his credentials : he is an ambassador from the court of Jesus Christ. In no letter, however, does he describe his commission with such fullness or emphasis as here, where he defines it not merely affirmatively, but also by means of a double negative. His enemies had denied his apostleship ; all the more uncompromisingly will he assert it.

It is a curious fact that the Greek word *apostolos*, in the sense of ' a man sent forth with a commission,' should be so seldom found till we meet it in the New Testament ; and the frequency and prominence of its use there may be taken as a measure of the new emphasis which the early Christians had learned to place on this conception of a man being ' sent forth ' from God. How is this new emphasis to be explained ?

The question takes us back to the words of Jesus Himself. According to Luke iv. 16 ff. He began His ministry at Nazareth by applying to Himself the words of Isaiah's prophecy : ' *He has sent me* ' (verse 18). This claim that God had sent Him He frequently repeated (e.g. Mark ix. 37, Matt. xv. 24) ; and when in turn He chose Twelve men and sent them forth in His name, He seems to have called them by an Aramaic name for which the Greek *apostolos* provided the nearest equivalent : they were ' *men who were sent forth.*'

There is evidence, however, in the New Testament that the term came to be applied to others besides the Twelve. Paul claimed to be an apostle; and his claim was recognized by some if not by all (ii. 7 ff.). Barnabas is described as an apostle in Acts ; and there are other cases where the evidence is more doubtful—e.g. the references to James (i. 19), ' the brothers of the Lord' (1 Cor. ix. 5), and Andronicus and Junias (Rom. xvi. 7). It would be natural that the name should be confined at first to the Twelve whom Christ Himself had chosen, and the fact that the first official act of the Eleven after the death of Judas was to choose a man to fill the vacancy points to an idea on their part that their number was somehow fixed at twelve. But apart from this one piece of evidence there is no clear proof that the number did remain at twelve ; and in a society like the Christian Church, facing an ever-expanding task and rejoicing in the life of the Spirit, it is unlikely that any such restriction could for long be accepted as binding.

An essential condition in the case of Judas' successor was that he should have been associated with the others during the whole of the Lord's earthly ministry, and should have been a witness of the resurrection, for as an accredited envoy of Jesus he was expected to be able, out of his own experience, to testify to the risen Christ, and to do so with a full knowledge of the things which Jesus had said and done from the beginning. If the attempt was made to lay down like conditions in each successive vacancy, the task before the remaining members would become increasingly difficult : death would reduce the ranks of those who had the requisite qualifications, and there would always be the danger of unworthy candidates, ' false apostles,' men who, whatever other qualifications they might have, were without the true apostolic gifts and apostolic call. On the other hand it was in accordance with the fundamental principles of Christian belief that He who in the days of His flesh had called some men to be apostles was still free, as the risen Lord, to call others. We ought probably, therefore, to allow for two different attitudes in the early Church on this question of apostleship. There was the conservative attitude which limited apostleship to the Twelve and to those whom, from time to time, the original members selected for association with themselves ; and there was the other attitude which was in line with the prophetic tradition, according to which the Lord chooses those whom He wills, bidding them go to those to whom He shall send them (cf. Jer. i. 7). On either view the apostle still remained primarily one who was *sent*. The true apostle could never owe his appointment merely to men.

Paul was perfectly clear in his own mind and soul that he was *an apostle of Jesus Christ* : God Himself had revealed His Son to him, and had duly commissioned him to go forth throughout the world as an accredited preacher of the gospel. But it is not surprising that there were some who refused to recognize his apostleship : perhaps even the Twelve for a time had been chary about it, and when he went up to Jerusalem on the fateful visit related in ii. 1-10 it was by no means certain that his claims would be accepted. For apart from the fact that there were doubts about the form in which he preached the gospel, he had not associated with Jesus and the original apostles during the days of the earthly ministry ; even with regard to the resurrection he had not seen the risen Lord when the other witnesses had seen Him (previous to the event described as the Ascension)—being in this respect, as his detractors said (and he accepts the description), ' a child born out of season ' (1 Cor. xv. 8). In answer, Paul insisted on going back to the fundamental facts regarding apostleship. Whether he had or had not known Jesus in the flesh was to him a matter of quite secondary importance ; the vital matter was that he had seen the risen Lord (cf. 1. Cor. ix. 1), or rather that the risen Lord had appeared to him, and that he had received from God Himself his apostolic commission. Of the validity of that commission he himself had no doubt, but if proof were wanted, there was the obvious fact that the blessing of God rested on his work (cf. what he says about ' apostolic signs ' in 2 Cor. xii. 12) ; and when it was seen that the same Lord who equipped Peter for work among Jews had equipped Paul to work among Gentiles (ii. 7, 8) the other apostles accorded full recognition to his apostleship.

Paul is therefore ready to make positive assertion of his apostleship, as given him direct from heaven. But first of all he defines his apostleship negatively (there is no parallel to this in the salutation of any other epistle), and the negative he employs here is two-fold. He was **not appointed by men nor commissioned by any man.** The two phrases, taken literally, are *neither from men* (plural) *nor through man* (singular), as if the former referred to the ultimate source of the authority, the latter to the medium through which the authority (or the power accruing from it) had been transmitted. It is doubtful if the distinction should be drawn too finely, for the ' from ' (Greek *apo*) in the former is doubtless determined to some extent by the prefix in the word *apostolos*, while the ' through ' (Greek *dia*) in the latter may be paralleled by the common Pauline phrase ' an apostle by (*dia*) the will of God ' ; cf. here ' by (*dia*) Jesus Christ and God the Father.' But accepting the phrases as we have them, we may say that in the former Paul implies that it is from a divine and not from a human source that his appointment originally derives : ' if I am an apostle, as I am, it is not because I appeared as a candidate before a body of men and was elected by them, but because God Himself elected me ' (cf. i. 15). When in his second negative he declares that his apostleship is *not through man*, it is possible to take this with reference to his investiture, or, as we should say, his ordination, as if he meant to say, ' I am an apostle no matter whether others have recognized and approved of my commission or not ' ; but it is more likely that he is thinking, not of his setting apart, but rather of the training he had received to equip him for the work of an apostle. It is as if at the outset he was concerned to assert, what he does so much more fully in the body of the epistle, that his apostolic *gospel* is not derived and secondary, something which has been transmitted to him *through man*, but has come to him, as he says later in i. 12, *by (dia) revelation of Jesus Christ*.

In both of these negative phrases Paul's language is perfectly general—he is merely working out the contrast between God and man as the ultimate source of authority and power (cf. Acts v. 29). But clearly he has in mind, as had also his opponents, the question of his relation to the Jerusalem authorities. Let us not, however, imagine that this emphatic and detailed assertion of independence on Paul's part implies any radical cleavage between him and the earlier apostles. His apostleship was not ' *from men* ' : he did not, that is, appear, as Joseph and Matthias did (Acts i. 23), before the other apostles as a candidate for apostleship, as if the ultimate question was whether they would accept or reject him. No, in his own soul he believed he was an apostle whether they recognized him or not ; but at the same time he welcomed such recognition, and would have been distressed if any differences had arisen which would have caused that recognition to be withheld. Similarly, with regard to his claim that his apostleship was not ' *through man*,' the gospel which he as an apostle proclaimed was not one which he had derived by sitting at the feet of another, nor was its authority dependent on the question of its agreement with the teaching of the other apostles ; he had received from God a revelation of His Son, and the implications of that revelation were worked out in what he called ' my gospel.' But while concerned to make this claim, Paul was also convinced, and indeed regarded it as a matter about which there need be no dispute, that as regards the great essentials of the faith he was quite in line with the teaching of the Twelve, passing on what he himself had received ; and in regard to possible differences, he was eager to submit his gospel to them for their consideration, in case (as he says in ii. 2) his work should be found to be leading nowhere.

Turning now from negatives to positives, Paul asserts that his apostleship came to him (here again his phrase is a double one) **by Jesus Christ and God the Father.** The first part of this expression, where the preposition is the same as in the preceding phrase ' not by man,' refers primarily to the channel through which the apostolic power has been conveyed to him ; but the latter part, by its very reference to God, must certainly include the idea of the ultimate source from which the authority and power originate. And the very fact that Paul can combine these two ideas in one composite prepositional phrase shows that for him the action of God as Originator and that of Jesus Christ as Transmitter are not separate and distinct, but together constitute a direct divine intervention which leaves no place for dependence on human agencies. When the names of Jesus and God are thus combined, God is regularly described as **the Father** (cf. the formula in salutations, as in verse 3). It was as Father that Jesus Himself addressed God, knowing His own relation to God to be primarily that of Son, and it was as Father that the Christian believers thought of Him, knowing that through Jesus they had been made sons (cf. iv. 5). The designation **Christ,** though never losing its original significance as the Anointed, the Messiah, God's chosen agent for the establishment of His Kingdom, came quite early to be applied to Jesus as practically part of His name.

What is especially significant here is that the names Jesus and God are linked together by the words ' **who raised him**

8

from the dead.' Why are these words added ? The explanation which most naturally suggests itself is that it was from the *risen* Christ that Paul claimed to have received his commission as an apostle. It ought, however, not to be forgotten that what Paul is concerned to vindicate in this Epistle is not his apostleship merely, but the very gospel with which he claimed to have been commissioned (cf. his emphatic statement in verses 11 and 12) ; and the content of that gospel, no less than his call to preach it, was given him by the revelation of Christ, risen and ascended. It is true that less is said in this Epistle on the resurrection than on the death of Christ, for it is apparently in his interpretation of Christ's *redemptive* work that Paul sees the fundamental difference between himself and the Judaizers ; still neither he nor they would have had a gospel of any kind to preach had not Jesus been raised by God from the dead and been thereby made Lord and Christ.

In his opening salutations Paul normally associates with 2 himself his fellow-missionaries or special companions. Here the apostle associates with himself, without naming them, **all the brothers who are beside me.** Is the reference to all the members of the Christian community in the place (whatever it is) from which he writes ? This is not likely ; for in that case he would probably rather have written ' all the brethren who are in A.' The reference is almost certainly to a limited number of companions. On the view which is adopted in this Commentary that the Epistle was written before the Council of Jerusalem (Acts xv.), the phrase might conceivably be taken either of Paul's fellow-workers at Antioch, or of those who at the time of writing accompanied him on a journey, e.g. the journey from Antioch to Jerusalem for the Council (Acts xv. 1–3). But Paul's mention of these brethren here apparently means more than that they join with him in the salutation ; quietly but boldly he insinuates that in the position which he is to take up in the letter he has their support. This is probably more than he could justifiably claim if the reference were to all the members of some congregation, even Antioch, though it would be applicable to the case of those who were travelling with him to Jerusalem to support him in the plea he was to make there. But perhaps the true explanation of the phrase (which in the Greek is literally ' those with me ') is that it denotes ' those who share my position.' The Greek preposition used here is *syn*, not *meta*, and there seem to be cases where, as contrasted with the latter, the former denotes some closer association than that of bodily presence.[1]

If this interpretation is accepted, has it any bearing, we may ask, on the omission of the name of Barnabas from the super-scription of the letter ? Did Paul refrain from joining Barnabas' name with his own because he could not commit Barnabas to all the positions maintained in the Epistle ?[2] This is doubtful deduction. Paul writes in his own name because it is he and he alone whom the Judaizers have attacked; it is his own personal position (his apostleship and his gospel) that must be vindicated.

The letter is addressed **to the churches of Galatia.** The view taken in this Commentary is that Galatia is to be interpreted not of the old kingdom of Galatia but of the Roman province which went by that name (see Introduction, p. xix.), and that the churches of Galatia are the churches of Derbe, Lystra, Iconium and (Pisidian) Antioch, situated in the southern part of the province. On the word ' churches ' see p. xlv.

3 The greeting is **grace and peace.** ' Peace ' is, of course, the familiar Jewish salutation (*shalôm*) ; and ' grace ' may have seemed to Gentile readers merely a Christian variation of the Greek word (*chairein*) regularly used in greetings, though the origin of its use in this connection, especially in association with ' peace,' can scarcely be dissociated from the thought of Jehovah's ' graciousness ' in the Aaronic bene-diction of Num. vi. 24-26. Behind the term ' grace ' as

[1] We may note its use in Acts xiv. 4 and in Phil. iv. 21 : in the latter case it is perhaps implied that the apostle did have *beside* him some Christian brothers who were not truly *with* him. That some Christian preachers did at the time dissociate themselves from him is a fact of which he has himself told in an earlier part of that Epistle, Phil. i. 14 ff.

[2] On this see Introduction, p. xxx. The absence of Barnabas' name constitutes, of course, no problem if the Epistle was written at a later period when Barnabas was no longer with Paul.

applied to God or Christ there is always the thought that in Christ God has, on His own initiative, given expression to the goodness and mercy which are of the very essence of His nature, and which those who experience them know that they have done nothing to deserve. Thus, instead of the conventional greeting of every-day life, Paul uses a word which, more than any other, sums up all the new-found sense of God's gracious goodness which has come to the Christian through Jesus Christ. By the words of salutation, therefore, as well as by the assertion of his apostleship, Paul at once makes clear the religious bond which holds writer and readers together. It is a mere confusion of form with substance to assert, as Deissmann does, that Paul's letters differ from those of the every-day correspondent 'not as letters, but only as the letters of Paul' (*Bible Studies*, p. 44). Paul writes, not as a private individual, or with the mere desire to assist in temporary and local difficulties, but as one whom God has commissioned to be an apostle for the building up of the fellowship of His Church. And it is not surprising that the Christian Church should soon have made collections of his Epistles, and have been led to treat them as sacred scriptures.

' Grace and peace ' come to the Christian from **God our Father and the Lord Jesus Christ,** who again (as in verse 1) are viewed in an indissolvable unity. It is because all who are Christians participate in His grace that God is now described as ' *our* Father.' And Jesus, whom God raised from the dead, is here accorded the name of *Lord.* This name, which in the Old Testament is associated with God, is in the New Testament applied to the risen and ascended Christ, denoting evidently that He is ruler over all the powers of this present world (cf. Phil. ii. 6–11). That Lordship is His in virtue of His exaltation ; but before attaining to it **he gave** 4 **himself for our sins.** The introduction of these words here is doubtless meant to emphasize an aspect of the gospel which Paul desires to vindicate in face of ignorance and opposition. Not that Paul's Judaizing opponents would have denied that ' Christ gave himself for our sins '—that indeed was a fundamental belief of the Christian Church which would be accepted by all, and which, stated thus simply, may have been part of an early Christian confession (cf. 1 Cor. xv. 3). But not all recognized as vividly as Paul did the significance of Christ's death as the central act in the great divine scheme of redemption ; not all recognized that Christ died **to rescue us from the present evil world.**

By asserting thus early in the Epistle that Christ died to deliver men from the present evil world (or age), Paul gives expression to a thought which is of first-rate significance for the understanding of the Epistle as a whole (see Introduction, pp. xxxv. ff.).

The word translated ' world ' is more strictly ' æon ' or ' age '—world-history being regarded as a succession of ages each with its own distinctive type of life. A special development of this conception emerged in Jewish religious thinking in the century before Christ, when a decisive distinction was drawn between *two* ages, viz. the age that now is, and that other age (the age to come) which will supervene after the Messiah has come to set up His Kingdom. The difference between the two ages was of course not merely one of time. The present age was characterized by sin and death, and was under the sway of ' principalities ' and ' powers ' which intervened between man and God ; whereas in the age to come sin and death would be no more, and God would be present in the midst of His redeemed people.

In heathen thought too there were ideas analagous to these. The present world was regarded as ruled by dread, inhuman forces—among them those ' elemental spirits ' of the firmament to which, as we are to read later in the Epistle (iv. 3, 9) the Galatians paid a slavish devotion before they were won to a nobler faith in Christ ; and apart from Christianity there were various cults which offered men a way of escape from the iron necessities of life, and pointed to a higher and a better world. Thus among Gentiles as among Jews the way was being prepared for a message of redemption and victory.

The early Christians took over the conception of the two ages ; and, interpreting it in the light of what they had learned from Jesus, not merely by His life and teaching, but above all by His death and resurrection and the gift of the Spirit, they proclaimed with ardour and assurance that Jesus was the looked-for Messiah, that He might be expected to come soon to inaugurate His Kingdom, and that only those who were ' His ' could share in the new life. In support of their conviction they appealed primarily to the resurrection of Jesus, which broke the authority of the powers of the present world, and to the gift of the Holy Spirit, which showed that the powers of the world to come were already operative among men. But they knew that their Lord's resurrection was not to be separated from the redemptive work which He had carried out during His life on earth, and which found its fullest expression in that death which He had spoken of as a ransom-price (Mark x. 45). They knew, too, with a strong sense of spiritual reality, that a necessary precondition for entry into the perfect life of the future was redemption from the sin and death of the present age. And when Christ, the sinless Son of God, voluntarily submitted Himself to the powers of this world, so far as these could exercise authority over Him, and allowed them to bring Him even to death itself, they recognized that this supreme sacrifice of His was on their behalf and in their stead ; He died that their sins might be forgiven, and that as forgiven men they might enter that new life over which neither sin nor death could prevail.

When Paul had preached to the Galatians, he had found them predisposed to listen to his message of the age that was to be, and of the victory accomplished by the risen Christ over the powers of the age that now is ; and, placarding before their eyes the crucified Christ (cf. iii. 1), he had forced them also to recognize (1) that they themselves were sinful men who could have no hope of entering on that new life unless their sins were forgiven, and (2) that by the death of Christ they could at the great judgment day come before God as men whose sins were covered, and who could thus by God's grace enter on life eternal. And, as we saw in the Introduction (pp. xxxix. xliii. f.), there was reason why Paul should lay special emphasis on this teaching at the very outset of the Epistle.

For the Judaizers seemed to him, in their form of the gospel, to be robbing the redemptive work of Christ of its real value. Christ did not die, says Paul, merely to lead men to live better lives in this age : He died to accomplish men's deliverance, and so enable them to attain to life eternal.

That Christ's death was that of a *Redeemer*, and not merely of a *Martyr*, is brought out by the addition of the words **by the will of our God and Father.** It is not enough for Paul to think of Christ as dying at the hands of wicked men (cf. Peter's sermon, Acts ii. 23). The cross of Christ had once been for Paul a stumbling-block, and he who was crucified on it could not be other than accursed (1 Cor. xii. 3). But now that the Crucified One had been revealed to him as the Lord, an interpretation had to be found for the meaning of the Cross. It was not merely something which God had *permitted*, it was something which God the Father had *willed* ; and His purpose behind it was the redemption of His children from the present evil world.

5   Why does Paul at this point break forth into a doxology ? It is because his whole soul expands at the thought of the wonderful deliverance achieved through the redeeming love of Christ (cf. Rom. xi. 35). ' *He gave Himself for our sins— to rescue us from the present evil world* ' : this is not for Paul a mere theological statement, it is a spontaneous outburst of faith proceeding from a deep well of spiritual experience. When Paul so describes his Lord, it is in a spirit less of polemic against those who underestimate the significance of the Saviour's work than of personal gratitude towards the Saviour. It is well to remember that Paul is conscious that he himself is one of those whom Christ died to rescue : he writes as a redeemed man, one who has known what it is to be entangled in a body of death and to be rescued from it (Rom. vii. 24 f.) ; and in this very letter his loyal and grateful soul overflows as he tells of Him ' who loved me and gave Himself up for me ' (ii. 20). If we would understand Paul's letters aright, we must be prepared to dig down till we reach the deep pure springs of his personal religion.

i. 6–9 : *Why Paul is constrained to write*

**I am astonished you are hastily shifting like this, deserting 6
Him who called you by Christ's grace, and going over to
another gospel. It simply means that certain individuals 7
are unsettling you ; they want to distort the gospel of
Christ. Now even though it were myself or some angel 8
from heaven, whoever preaches a gospel that contradicts
the gospel I preached to you, God's curse be on him ! I 9
have said it before and now I repeat it : whoever preaches
a gospel to you that contradicts the gospel you have already
received, God's curse be on him !**

In Paul's letters (as indeed in ordinary contemporary
correspondence) the opening salutation is often followed by
a word of thanksgiving : he likes to give thanks for the
progress his readers are making in Christian faith and life,
and his thanksgiving is often accompanied by a prayer that
their progress will go on from more to more. In Galatians
there is no such thanksgiving or prayer. In some epistles,
e.g. 2 Corinthians, Ephesians, and 1 Peter the thanksgiving
appears in the form of an ascription of praise, in which God is
blessed for His saving grace in Christ and incidentally for the
effects which that saving grace is producing in the lives of the
believers ; and in much the same way the doxology here
(verse 5) may be claimed as taking the place of a general
thanksgiving. Paul can and does give glory to God for His
grace revealed in Christ (cf. verse 5 and the thought behind
verse 6) ; the tragedy is that on the side of the Galatians that
grace is being spurned.

Hence, instead of a word of praise, the Epistle opens with 6
an abrupt and passionate outburst, not softened in the Greek
even by an introductory particle : **I am astonished.** Not for
a moment can the apostle keep back what presses so heavily
on his soul. In some other epistles he clearly realizes, as he
begins to write, that ere he closes he will have to utter strong
words of warning and rebuke, but generously and tactfully
he restrains himself until first of all he has paid tribute to the

15

progress which his correspondents have made in the Christian life. Thus among the Thessalonians there are faintheartedness and disorderliness and impurity, but in the opening words of his First Epistle to them there is nothing but praise for their magnificent response to the Gospel-message. More significantly we may take the case of 1 Corinthians, where though the apostle proceeds almost at once to deal with the factions which are dividing the congregation he first acknowledges in glowing terms the spiritual gifts with which it is so richly endowed. Some such acknowledgment is expressed later in Galatians—they had begun well, he says (v. 7; cf. iii. 2 ff.); but at this point the thought that is uppermost is regret for their back-sliding.

Even so, however, it is significant that in such a situation Paul's opening word should be an expression, not of anger or vituperation, but of surprise. And this initial note of astonishment is maintained throughout the whole Epistle, even in passages where passion might so easily have degenerated into mere denunciation. Paul's attitude throughout is that of the man who, in Christian love, is 'always eager to believe the best, always hopeful, always patient' (1 Cor. xiii. 7). It is because of his own deep sense of the magnitude of Christ's grace that he is at a loss to understand how any who have once experienced it should lightly turn away from it.

Yet if there is Christian charity in Paul's language, there is sternness too. He accuses the Galatians of shifting and deserting—this double idea is brought out by one compound verb in the Greek, which implies a wilful change of allegiance, a going-over from one side to another. True, the apostle uses the present tense : the defection is not yet complete ; it may be possible still to arrest it. Yet defection it is, and defection of the worst type, for what you are really doing, he says, is turning your back on Him who called you by Christ's grace.

Part of the surprise is occasioned by the fact that all this has happened so *quickly*. Advocates of a late date for the Epistle are disposed to interpret this of the rapidity with which the defection developed after it had once begun : hence the

translation ' **hastily.**' But the simpler explanation is surely
also the right one, viz. that Paul is thinking of the lamentably
short time during which the Galatians have remained loyal
to Him who called them.   Hence the two words translated
' hastily like this ' are perhaps best taken in close conjunction,
' so quickly.'   But just as Hamlet expostulates with regard to
his mother's remarriage :

> ' That it should come to this !
> But two months dead !—nay, not so much, not two :
> So excellent a king ; that was, to this,
> Hyperion to a satyr,'
>
> (Act I., Sc. ii.)

so here Paul, amazed though he is that the defection should
have followed so soon, is even more amazed at the miserable
exchange it has involved. *Deserting Him who called you by
Christ's grace !*   There is a minor difficulty as regards the
syntactical construction of this phrase.   Keeping the same
Greek words, some would adopt the rendering : *deserting Christ
who called you in grace,* or *by His grace ;* others, following
Marcion and some of the Latin Fathers, omit the name of
Christ altogether and translate : *deserting Him who called you
in grace.*   The syntactical differences are not without a certain
theological significance.   Passages such as Matt. ix. 13 and
xxii. 3 remind us that God's call to men may be thought of
as mediated through Christ or conveyed through the messen-
gers whom God sends in His name.   But to Paul, with his
grasp of fundamental issues, the call never ceases to be a
call from God, who speaks to men not through the commands
of the Law, but through the grace of the Lord Jesus Christ.
So vividly is this contrast present to his mind that he dares
to tell the Galatians that, in seeking to come under the Law,
they are actually *deserting God* (cf. his language in ii. 20, 21).
And that he fully means all that these words imply is made
abundantly clear by the words which follow, where, after
saying that the Galatians have gone over to another gospel,
he corrects himself and says that ' gospel ' is not a word to be
used in such a connection ; that other is indeed no gospel
at all.

7 Here again the syntax causes difficulty. A more or less literal translation (see Authorized Version and Revised Version) is : ' to another gospel, which is not another ; only there are some who trouble you,' where it is to be noted that the word ' another ' is in the two cases represented in the Greek by different words, the distinction between which, however, is not to be pressed. Dr. Moffatt, like the American Revisers in their marginal reading, connects the second ' another ' with the words which follow, as if the sense were : ' which is nothing else than a case of people troubling you.' Whatever the syntax, the sense is scarcely in dispute. It is as if, having inadvertently slipped into the phrase ' another gospel,' Paul pulls himself up with the reflection : ' Why no ! that other teaching has indeed no gospel in it. There is only the one gospel of Christ, and what these disturbers would substitute, if they had their way, is a mere perversion of it.' By ' the gospel of Christ ' Paul means something far more than the ' news ' (of the Kingdom) which Jesus had heralded : it is the gospel of which Christ is the very essence and substance (cf. the phrase ' preach Him ' in verse 16)—how that, through the life, crucifixion, and resurrection of His Son-Messiah, God had established a new relationship with His people, redeeming them out of an evil world and calling them to life eternal.

Verse after verse at this point reiterates this note of ' the gospel ' (cf. 1 Cor. ix. 12 ff.)—a measure at once of Paul's pride in it and of his revulsion at anything that would rob it 8-9 of its splendour and its truth. Tag on to this glorious gospel of grace, he seems to say, the demands of a legalistic relationship, and what you get is not another and legitimate form of the gospel, but a distortion of it so essentially evil that those who advocate it deserve to be cut off from the Messiah and His people and from all participation in the benefits He brings (cf. Rom. ix. 3 ; Eph. ii. 12). Conjuring up firstly in purely general terms a situation so hypothetical as to be outside the bounds of possibility, then descending in the next verse from this imaginative flight to face the all too tragic reality of the present situation among his converts (' **whoever preaches to you** '), he deliberately repeats an imprecation such as we cannot

18

imagine him using had it been merely his personal prestige, or the success of his missionary labours—anything, in fact, but the gospel of Christ—which was at stake. With this furious outburst we may contrast Paul's mellower outlook in Phil. i. 15–18 ; but there what he has in view is the motives of the preachers, not the truth of their message. Truer parallels in tone to the present passage may be found in 1 Cor. v. 2–5 ; 2 Cor. xi. 4 ff., 13–15; Phil. iii. 2, and in some denunciations of the Pharisees in the Gospels. Its terrible significance is not to be toned down. We are rather to see reflected in it the apostle's passionate devotion to the true gospel of which he had been put in trust, and for the sake of whose furtherance among his own nation he says he would willingly himself (cf. ' myself ' verse 8) become ' accursed and banished from Christ ' (Rom. ix. 3).

An interesting question is raised by the phrase : **I (better we) have said it before.** As the Greek shows, Paul does not mean by this merely that he is repeating for emphasis' sake what he has just said in verse 8 ; he is thinking of a previous warning, delivered (as is most natural to suppose) when the missionaries were personally present (hence the contrast between ' we said before ' and ' I say now,') the occasion perhaps being the second visit (Acts xiv. 21 ff.). Now if the missionaries on that earlier occasion had found it expedient to issue such a warning, they must already have realized the possible danger of subversive propaganda. This conclusion has been used by some critics to lend support to the view that the occasion referred to is later than the Jerusalem Council, and that the date of the Epistle, therefore, is not earlier than the period of the third missionary journey. But a preferable interpretation is that even by the time of the first missionary journey Paul recognized that his interpretation of the Christian gospel was disowned by many of his Jewish brethren who would not scruple to propagate their destructive views among his Galatian converts. It is therefore no surprise to Paul to learn, as he does now, that Judaistic propaganda is going on in Galatia : what does surprise him, as he says in verse 6, is that it is achieving so immediate and so signal a success.

i. 10 : *A Parenthetical Expostulation*

10 Now is that ' appealing to the interests of men ' or of God ?
Trying to ' satisfy men ' ? Why, if I still tried to give
satisfaction to human masters, I would be no servant of
Christ.

10   This verse ought to be taken closely with what goes before,
rather than, according to the paragraph arrangement commonly adopted, with what follows. Paul is arrested by the
uncompromising boldness of the language he has just used.
And by contrast he recalls some of the denunciations with
which, he has heard, his traducers are seeking to undermine
his authority.

More frequently than is often recognized, Paul in his
Epistles reproduces controversial words and phrases which
have already played a part in discussions or correspondence.
Sometimes these are derived from a letter which has reached
him from his converts—there are traces of this in the Corin-
thian Epistles. In the present case it is probable that in the
report which he has received regarding the trouble in Galatia
he has been told in some detail of the arguments by which the
Judaizers were seeking to establish their case. One of the
minor exegetical problems in Galatians is to determine what
phrases in the Epistle are ' echoes ' in this sense. An attempt
is made in the translation to express these by means of inverted
commas.

Verse 10 contains two of these ' catch-phrases.' Paul's
opponents had said (i.) that he was ' appealing to the interests
of men ' ; (ii.) that he was trying to ' please ' or to ' satisfy
men.' In the first of these taunts the word used (wrongly translated ' persuade ' in the Authorized Version) denotes the process
of presenting a case so as to win approval. Paul, it was said,
was like a sophist or demagogue, whose sole object was to get
men to agree with him. Concerned to win adherents, he made
the gospel easy, but cared little either for the truth of what he
preached or for the ultimate salvation of those who accepted it.
The second taunt is more general : Paul was a ' man-pleaser '

—which may mean either that he was concerned to win popular applause, or (better) that it was man and not God who dictated for him his standards of conduct.

Both these accusations Paul indignantly repudiates. There is indeed a sense in which he might have accepted the first and gloried in it. The very nature of the gospel necessitates that whoever preaches it should seek to ' win ' men ; and so thoroughly was this Paul's ambition that, as he himself proudly claims, he became ' all things to all men ' (see especially I Cor. ix. 19–23). But in all this he saw no cause for reproach : it was all done ' for the sake of the gospel.' Hence, with the words he has just dictated (verses 8, 9) still resounding in his ear, he stops short and indignantly asks whether, when a man can express himself as he has just done (this is the force of now in the Greek) it is men he is appealing to, or God ? This contrast between ' men ' and ' God ' is more a matter of deep religious feeling than of logic ; for, while in the one case what is sought is *man's adherence* (i.e. to the gospel as thus presented), in the other it is *God's approval*. There is no lack of logic, however, in the final summing-up. ' No man can serve two masters,' or seek at the same time to please both men and God (for this frequent contrast in the New Testament cf. I Thess. ii. 4 ; Eph. vi. 6 ; Col. iii. 22). So, of course, the Judaizers had contended on their side, and had condemned Paul as one who tried to give satisfaction to human masters. Paul, in turn, accepted the issue as thus presented ; and, convinced beyond argument that he *was* a servant of Christ, claimed that on this very ground he stood acquitted of the charge of man-pleasing. ' Servant ' is an inadequate translation—what Paul calls himself here, as in the opening words of Philippians and Romans, is a ' slave (bond-servant) of Christ ' (Greek *doulos*). It is unfortunate that, except in such a phrase as ' bond and (or) free,' our English translations should so consistently fail to give this word its true meaning, thereby encouraging the false conception of Christian ' service ' (as something essentially voluntary and part-time) so characteristic of modern religious idealism. The ' bond-servant of Christ ' is not free to offer or withhold his ' service ' ; his life is not his own, but belongs entirely to his Lord. Hence the scorn with which Paul repudiates the suggestion that there can be any place in his life for ' man-pleasing.'

If I still tried to please men ! Why ' *still* '? This does not mean : ' after all I have experienced,' still less ' as I used to do in earlier days.' The sense is the strictly logical one, viz. ' if I, who am and claim to be a bond-servant of Christ were, despite this, to seek to satisfy men, then my alleged devotion to Christ as Lord would be a delusion and a sham.' And that there is no delusion about it, but that both his life and his gospel are based on a rock foundation, Paul now proceeds to maintain in a lengthy *apologia*.

II. A HISTORICAL APOLOGIA (i. 11–ii. 21)

Paul tells how it was that the gospel came to him, not through human agency but by divine revelation ; how he reacted at the outset to this new experience ; and how it had dictated for him all his subsequent career and conduct. Since God Himself had thus revealed the gospel to him, he had felt no need to consult the Jerusalem ' authorities ' regarding its interpretation. Such relations as existed between him and them were marked by cordiality and mutual recognition : but in no sense was he ever in subjection to Jerusalem.

i. 11, 12 : *Paul tells how the gospel came to him by special revelation*

11 **No, brothers, I tell you the gospel that I preach is not a human**
12 **affair ; no man put it into my hands, no man taught me what it meant, I had it by a revelation of Jesus Christ.**

11 The confidential character of what follows is marked by the introduction of the word ' brothers.' What was true of Paul's apostleship (verse 1), viz. that it came to him not from man but from God, was even more fundamentally true of the gospel which he was commissioned to preach. He begins with the

quite general statement that the gospel is **not a human affair**—
as we might say to-day, it is not to be regarded as a product
of human evolution or explained solely by reference to so-
called historical origins. This he proceeds to illustrate by an 12
appeal to what happened *in his own case* : there is at this point
in the Greek an emphatic first personal pronoun which ought
not to be ignored. *With regard to myself,* he says (i.) **no man
put** the gospel **into my hands** and (ii.) **no man taught me what
it meant.** In these two clauses he probably has already in
mind the two stages in his religious life (before and after his
conversion) of which he is to tell in verses 13 ff. Under (i.),
which is literally ' I did not receive it from man,' i.e. by a
process of handing on a tradition, he means more than that
he did not inherit the Christian tradition from those who were
Christians before him ; he indicates *inter alia* that his apprehension of the gospel is not to be explained by reference to his
early environment and religious education (cf. verses 13, 14).
By (ii.) he wishes to make clear that his understanding of the
gospel did not come to him through sitting at the feet of
teachers who explained to him its essential truths. **I had it,**
he adds, **by a revelation of Jesus Christ.** It is hard to say
whether by this he means that Jesus Christ was the agent who
revealed the gospel to him (*a revelation from Jesus Christ*), or
that Jesus Christ himself was revealed to him in such a way
that as a result he now had a gospel to preach. Probably the
latter is to be preferred ; cf. the phrase in verse 16, ' He chose
to reveal His Son to me.' All that Paul subsequently preached
was determined by his experience on the Damascus road,
when Jesus Christ was revealed to him in His true significance.
Jesus was to be thought of no longer merely as one who had
been crucified and was therefore accursed ; He was the Christ,
the Son of God, who had died to win men's salvation, and who
was now exalted as Lord.

i. 13, 14 : *He recalls how little his early life predisposed him
towards the gospel*

You know the story of my past career in Judaism ; you know 13
how furiously I persecuted the church of God and harried

14   it, and how I outstripped many of my own age and race
       in my special ardour for the ancestral traditions of my
       house.

13   In proof of what he has asserted regarding the God-given
     character of his gospel in verses 11, 12, Paul recalls in one
     short but vivid sentence the main features of his life before
     the gospel was revealed to him. **The story** he has to tell
     is one which the Galatians already know—the Greek may
     even imply that he had himself told it to them, reinforcing
     his preaching by personal testimony. It deals, be it noted,
     with his **past career in Judaism**—a career which, as we
     gather from this passage and from Phil. iii. 4–6, was one
     of surpassing promise according to the standards by which it
     was regulated and inspired. Unlike Augustine, Paul never
     associated his pre-Christian days with moral turpitude and
     degradation—it was not in that sense that he could call him-
     self 'the foremost of sinners' (1 Tim. i. 15). The thought from
     which he could never get away was rather that that career
     of his, into the prosecution of which he had flung himself with
     so much earnestness and zeal, had been running, until it was
     arrested, along lines directly contrary to the purposes of God.
     ' That fellowship of the followers of Jesus Christ, which now
     I know to be none other than **the church of God,** God's chosen
     holy people, **I persecuted furiously** (lit. beyond measure,
     ' putting more than ordinary zest into my persecution') **and
     harried it** (seeking, that is, to destroy it). This last verb
     seems to have been commonly used to describe Paul's activity
     against the Church ; cf. verse 23, and Acts ix. 21. Paul never
     ceased to be staggered by the thought that it was to him, a
     persecutor and a blasphemer, that Christ had appeared (cf.
     1 Cor. xv. 8, 9 ; 1 Tim. 12–14) ; and in that fact, which from
     one point of view was a supreme revelation of the ' grace of
     God ' (cf. verse 15), he saw also, as here, an irrefutable proof
     of the truth of his gospel as coming from God and not from
     man.

14   Apart from this persecuting zeal, Paul claims that his whole
     mentality predisposed him to be an opponent of such a gospel

as now he preached. He recalls how ' in Judaism ' (this prepositional phrase has been omitted in the translation) he outstripped many of his Jewish contemporaries, *being* (to adopt
here a more literal translation) *more exceedingly zealous*, i.e.
than those others were, *for the traditions of my fathers* (meaning
by this probably the traditions of his race rather than of his
own family or house).   Here we have, from his own pen, an
invaluable sketch of Paul, the brilliant and eager young
student of the law, dedicating his outstanding gifts of mind
and spirit to the service of his ancestral religion.   As evidence
of the change which Christ has made in his whole outlook we
may note how he, a Jew by nationality, is able here and in
the preceding verse to talk objectively of ' Judaism,' as if it
were something from which he was now completely dissociated,
and how, *per contra*, he, an Israelite after the flesh, can refer
to the ' church of God ' as if the right to that title was now
passing from the old Israel to the new.[1]   ' Outstripping in
Judaism ' includes much in its reference.   Judaism was a
doctrinal system ;   and already Paul would have begun to
show that amazing grasp of the Law and the Prophets which
later was to reveal itself in his Christian Epistles.   It was also
a way of life, separated as by a gulf from the ways of heathendom ;   and Paul probably means us to understand that he
was no Hellenist, ready to look with sympathy on non-Jewish
ways of life and thought, but a staunch Hebrew (cf. Phil. iii. 5),
concerned to maintain ancestral traditions.   Above all, it was
a religion, the worship of One than whom there was no other
God ;   and it may thus be that part of that ardour to which
Paul alludes was a religious enthusiasm for the God of his
fathers, a passionate desire to see Jehovah's name known and
His righteousness established among all the nations. If, even
in his pre-Christian days, Paul was not merely the brilliant
student and the scrupulous traditionalist but was already
nursing in his soul something of the vision and the fire of the
prophet, one can better understand how it was that when, on
the Damascus road, he received a vision of the Son of God,

[1] See Introduction, p. xlv.

he soon realised that his mission was to preach his gospel to the Gentiles.

In thus emphasizing the purity and the ardour of his early attachment to Judaism Paul's concern was to justify his contention that the gospel, when it came to him, had not a human origin (verse 12). But those who read his words must also have been prompted to ask themselves the question : if for so ardent a Jew as Paul the gospel involved a radical breach with his religious traditions, how can it be that for us who are Gentiles by birth the gospel is incomplete unless we add to it the tenets of Judaism ?

i. 15–17 : *After the revelation that came to him he did not seek to learn the meaning of the gospel from human sources*

15 But the God who had set me apart *from my very birth* called
16   me by his grace, and when he chose to reveal his Son to me, that I might preach him to the Gentiles, instead of
17   consulting with any human being, instead of going up to Jerusalem to see those who had been apostles before me, I went off at once to Arabia, and on my return I came back to Damascus.

15   Paul's narrative in these verses is to be understood as a continuation of, and not a contrast to, what he has related in verses 13, 14 ; hence the introductory particle ought to be ' and ' rather than ' but.' The logical emphasis is to be found in what he has now to say regarding his conduct *after* his conversion (verse 17), and despite the clumsiness of the sentence it would have been better if the translation could have followed the Greek (cf. Authorized Version) in confining the description of the conversion itself to a subordinate clause of time, designed to give the setting for the statement which follows. Paul's argument is that, as *before* his conversion, so also *after* it the circumstances and environment of his life were such that in no sense could the gospel as he understood and preached it have been ' evolved ' out of them. His gospel was given him directly because God Himself had broken in upon his life and given him a special revelation.

Nevertheless Paul's reference to the conversion is not entirely incidental. He describes it with some fullness, and with a sense alike of rapture and of awe, recognizing as he does that his claim to be independent of merely human authority is ultimately based on the fact that at his conversion it was *God* who had done everything for him. Every word in the description tells of the divine purpose and initiative : Paul himself was a mere recipient. Tracing the hand of God in his life from the beginning, and recalling, apparently, how Jeremiah (i. 5) had described his own call, how Isaiah (xlix. 1) had described the call of Israel, he dares to say of himself, '**God set me apart,**' as he set them, '**from my very birth** ' (MS. authority on the whole favours the omission of the name ' God ' in this phrase : ' He who had set me apart '). In fulfilment of an eternal purpose God likewise **called him,** as according to the Isaiah passage He had called Israel—' called ' him who persecuted the Church of God to have himself a place in the fellowship, ' called ' him who was a blasphemer to become an apostle ; no wonder that at the very thought of it Paul is moved to add that here God acted **by his grace.** Lightfoot associates the ' call ' with the conversion ; but the language of Isa. xlix. 1 (cf. Rom. viii. 30) indicates rather that the call of God may be addressed to man long before man himself is able to hear the call or is prepared to answer it. The time came when, in the fulfilment of His purpose, **God 16 chose to reveal his Son to me** (lit. *in me*). Here again the initiative is entirely with God : He acts of His own good pleasure, and Paul claims no credit for religious insight. Following his identification of the call with the conversion, Lightfoot refers this phrase to Paul's entry on his missionary career, as if the Greek meant ' to reveal his Son *through me* (i.e. to others).' But the context of the passage, together with Paul's use of the word ' reveal,' puts it beyond doubt that the apostle is here concerned to tell of a revelation which God made to his own soul. By using the phrase ' his Son ' in this connection Paul implies that God had opened his eyes to see Jesus in His true character—He was not a mere teacher ; neither, despite His crucifixion, was He an accursed blasphemer ; rather He was one whom God acknowledged as His Son (cf. Rom. i. 4). In his own descriptions of his conversion (e.g. here and in 1 Cor. ix. 1 ; xv. 8 ; 2 Cor. iv. 6 ; 1 Tim. i. 12 ff.) Paul always emphasizes the reality of the *inward* experience—in contrast to the account in Acts ix. 1 ff. (and to a lesser extent the other accounts in Acts xxii. 6 ff. and xxvi. 12 ff.) where stress is laid on the *external* phenomena accompanying it.

A revelation so wonderful and so unexpected clearly had a divine purpose behind it, and for the benefit of his readers Paul mentions in passing what the purpose was : it was **that I might preach him** (i.e. the Son of God) **to the Gentiles.** As they are introduced here, he asserts nothing more by these words than that the work on which he is now engaged as a missionary to the Gentiles (including the Galatians) is in accordance with the plan and purpose of *God*, who gave him the initial revelation. Whether this interpretation of his mission was present to *his own* mind from the moment of his conversion is not stated. All the accounts in Acts (ix. 15 ; xxii. 15 ; xxvi. 16 ff.) indicate that he was led almost at once to interpret his work universally, as being for Gentiles as well as for Jews ; and according to Acts xxii. 17–21 it was during the first of his subsequent visits to Jerusalem that he received the revelation to ' leave Jerusalem ' and go ' afar to the Gentiles.'

Paul tells what his *immediate* reaction was to this divine revelation and call—in the Greek the word for ' at once ' is placed for emphasis at the very opening of the statement. Intent still on asserting his independence of human authority, Paul defines his reaction (*a*) negatively, (*b*) positively.

(*a*) The direct and overwhelming character of the experience convinced Paul from the outset that here he had to deal with God and not with man ; and it was from God Himself that he must now learn what his next step was to be. Any question therefore of **consulting with any human being** was immediately ruled out, even though at Damascus as elsewhere there were Christians and even honourable Jews whose counsel and sym-
17 pathy at such a time might have been helpful. In particular

he did not take what might have seemed the obvious step of going up at once to Jerusalem to see the recognized leaders of the Christian movement. By this emphatic double negative (cf. i. 1) Paul seems to be meeting the taunts of his opponents, who may have alleged that his knowledge of the gospel was dependent on what he had learned from Ananias in Damascus (Acts ix. 10 ff. ; xxii. 12 ff.) and later from the Jerusalem authorities. His triumphant sense of independence is conveyed even by the words ' those who had been apostles before me.' We know how, at the time of writing, Paul was proudly yet humbly conscious that he was called to be an apostle quite as fully as those others were ; but here he perhaps indicates that that conviction went back to the time of the conversion experience itself. The call which he then received (verse 15) was a call to *apostleship*—a claim which is in accordance with the statement put into his mouth in Acts xxvi. 16 f. It was accordingly not from fellow-men, or even from fellow-apostles, that he must seek guidance at such an hour, but from God Himself, who had called him to the work.

(*b*) Next comes the positive assertion of what he *did* do. I went off at once to Arabia, and on my return I came back to Damascus. It is only from Galatians that we know of this visit to Arabia. The Nabatæan Arabs (under King Aretas ; cf. 2 Cor. xi. 32) occupied a vast territory around, and at one time including, Damascus, as well as east of Jordan and south towards the Sinai Peninsula (cf. iv. 25). Nothing in Paul's language requires us to believe that on this journey he went far from his base. The picture sometimes drawn of Paul sojourning, as Elijah had once done (1 Kings xix. 8 ff.), in the wilderness of Sinai, and learning there to see how the Law must now give place to the Gospel, is an imaginative reconstruction for which there is no justification. What impelled him to go away into the Arab country ? Was it to avoid persecution from his enraged Jewish brethren ? Or to carry out at once his God-given commission to preach ? Or was it to seek communion with God ? Paul himself has not told us, and critics who assert that the meaning is quite plain claim more than the facts justify. But reasoned conjecture may carry us some distance. However clearly he may have heard the summons to apostleship, Paul would not have felt impelled to answer the call unthinkingly and without preparation. His emphatic disclaimer of consultation with men is itself an indication that his desire at this time was to consult with God. The reason why he left the city, with all its human contacts, was probably that in quietness he might hear what God the Lord would speak. What made the need for prayer the more imperative in his case was that before his conversion he had been securely self-confident in his Judaism, so that the revelation which had now been given him of the Son of God could not be for him, as it was for brethren of the Judaizing type, a mere addition to the old religion, which otherwise remained unchanged. In Paul's case the new wine had to be put into new bottles. And so he went into solitude, following there in the footsteps of Moses and Elijah and of Christ Himself.

How long he stayed in Arabia he does not tell us. All we know is that he returned to Damascus—it is implied, though it is not definitely stated, that it was from Damascus that he had gone away to Arabia ; and not till some two or three years afterwards (verse 18) did he go up to Jerusalem. If there is nothing to indicate that the journey to Arabia was a distant one, there is likewise nothing to indicate that the stay there was prolonged. If Scripture parallels carried weight with Paul, it may have been no more than forty days. His centre at this time was Damascus. It was in a region distant from the Promised Land that the Lord had appeared to him as of old God had appeared to Abraham ; and he was content for a time to remain there. So far there is nothing in Paul's account that essentially contradicts the narrative in Acts ix., except that one would not naturally gather from Acts that his stay in Damascus and neighbourhood was prolonged for three years.

i. 18–24 : *Except for one brief visit to Jerusalem to see Peter, he remained for many years completely out of touch with the churches in Judæa.*

Then, after three years, I went up to Jerusalem to make the 18
acquaintance of Cephas. I stayed a fortnight with him.
I saw no other apostle, only James the brother of the Lord. 19
(I am writing you the sheer truth, I swear it before God!) 20
Then I went to the districts of Syria and of Cilicia. Per- 21-22
sonally I was quite unknown to the Christian churches of
Judæa ; they merely heard that ' our former persecutor is 23
now preaching the faith he once harried,' which made them 24
praise God for me.

After three years Paul went up to Jerusalem. He probably 18
means three years after his conversion, but, if allowance be
made for the inclusive method of calculation, by which part
of a year was counted as a whole year, the total period may
even have been less than two years. Paul knows he must be
careful in his statement of his Jerusalem visits, because his
detractors appealed to them as proof of his subjection to the
Jerusalem ' authorities ' (cf. ii. 6) ; hence he is at pains to
point out that this journey was made only after an interval of
some years, and that it arose from a simple and natural desire
to make the acquaintance of Cephas (i.e. Peter). Paul here
purposely employs a word which is frequently used of travellers
paying visits : he went to *visit* Peter, not to receive instruction
from him. Further, the visit lasted only **a fortnight** ; and
during it he **saw**, besides Peter, **no other apostle**, except **only** 19
James the brother of the Lord. His opponents, he knows, had
published a very different version of this visit, hence he adds
that what he writes is **the sheer truth**, and he confirms this 20
statement by a solemn oath. Of James the Lord's brother
we are to hear more in chap. ii. ; and in the Book of Acts we
see him emerging as the recognized leader of the Church in
Jerusalem (chap. xv.). He generally receives the honourable
designation of ' the brother of the Lord,' and in this way is
distinguished from James the son of Zebedee, who was put to
death in the Herodian persecution (Acts xii. 2). Paul mentions
him here because he was one of the acknowledged 'authorities,'
and to have omitted mention of this meeting with him might
have seemed to Paul's opponents to savour of concealment

or untruth. But Paul's language does not entitle us to argue, as is generally done, that he included James among the apostles. The apostles were men who were ' sent out ' to preach ; and it was probably because their missionary work took them for long periods away from Jerusalem that James, with his gifts for conciliation and administration, rose in their absence to pre-eminence in the Jerusalem community.

There are undeniable discrepancies between this account of Paul's visit to Jerusalem and the narrative given in Acts ix. 26–30. It is not a serious difference that instead of a private visit to Peter we have in Acts a period of open preaching and debate, for these two presentations of the case, given from different points of view, are not irreconcilable. More serious is the fact that in Acts Paul appears in association with Barnabas, and that it is expressly stated that Barnabas brought him to the apostles.

There is, of course, no reason to doubt the essential truth of Paul's statement in Galatians, especially in view of the oath with which he supports it in verse 20. And it is no part of our present task to estimate the reliability of the account in Acts. The differences are not fundamental ; and if we had a fuller account we might find an explanation for them. They may usefully remind us that not every statement regarding Paul in Acts i.–xv. is to be accepted without criticism. But on the other hand they provide no justification for the all too common assumption of critics (of which we shall hear more when we come to chap. ii.) that Acts supplies a quite insecure basis for the reconstruction of the early ministry of Paul.

21   The Jerusalem visit over, Paul departed **to the districts of Syria and of Cilicia.** The order of the names is interesting. Acts tells us that on leaving Jerusalem Paul went on to Tarsus (the chief city of Cilicia), and that later Barnabas took him from Tarsus to superintend the missionary work in Antioch (in Syria). There were close relations between Syria and Cilicia, which were indeed linked together in one Roman province ; and during his prolonged stay there Paul may have frequently passed from the one district to the other.

Otherwise he may have been led to mention Syria first by the fact that Antioch figured prominently in his thoughts as the centre of his later missionary labours.

There he remained for many years (fourteen ?—see ii. 1, and the commentary on p. 35) ; and (here again he asserts his freedom from Jerusalem influence) all that time he remained **quite unknown to the Christian churches of Judæa.** It was 22 not they who were responsible for his going to Syria and Cilicia ; and he on his part was not concerned to report to them or to keep in touch with them. There were, of course, many in the Judæan churches who had known him in earlier days and still remembered him ; but Paul's point is rather that he never went back among them. This being his meaning, there is no need to say, with Lightfoot, that Judæa, in the country districts of which Paul *was not* known, is here used in contradistinction to Jerusalem, where he *was* known. It may be noted that Paul courteously speaks of *the Christian churches*, lit. ' the churches in Christ,' recognizing that the designation ' church ' might still be claimed by Jews *who were not Christians* (see Introduction, p. xlv.).

In a closing sentence Paul emphasizes that the only link 23 the Judæan churches had with him was provided by hearsay. From time to time they would **hear that ' our former persecutor is now preaching the faith he once harried.'** They recalled the destructive activity of his pre-Christian days (on the word ' harried ' see note on verse 13) ; but as they thought how Paul the persecutor was now Paul the apostle, fear and dread gave place to joy and pride, **which made them praise God for 24 me.** What a revelation we have here into the souls of those early Christians, glorying in what the grace of God had accomplished ! And what a revelation also into the soul of the man who could use such words of himself ! It may seem a proud thing for him to say ; yet it was not a vainglorious thing, for the ' me ' for whom praise was given was not Paul the apostle merely, but the persecutor now called to be an apostle. Some such thought as this always qualifies Paul's boasting (cf. 2 Cor. xi. 30, and the pathetic contrast of himself with Andronicus and Junias in Rom. xvi. 7) ; and it enables us to see that whether or not Paul's persecuting zeal caused him any misgiving *at the time*, Paul the Christian always looked back on those days with a sense of deep remorse and even horror, qualified only by a sense of the grace of God who had pardoned his apostasy, and called him to preach the faith he once had persecuted. For the phrase ' the faith ' cf. iii. 23 ; vi. 10.

ii. 1–10 : Paul's Second Visit to Jerusalem

Still seeking to assert his independence of the Jerusalem apostles, Paul tells the story of his second visit to Jerusalem. Though on this occasion he conferred with the so-called ' authorities ' of the church, he did not in any sense take orders from them. On the contrary, they gave their blessing to his work.

Among the points which Paul emphasizes with regard to this visit are the following :

(*a*) It took place after an interval of fourteen years. If three years had passed before he saw the apostles in Jerusalem after his conversion, a much longer period elapsed before he saw them a second time.

(*b*) He would not have gone to Jerusalem even then, if he had not received from heaven a special revelation bidding him go. Hence if it was insinuated that he went up so as to submit himself to the Jerusalem authorities, the insinuation was false.

(*c*) The result of his conference with the Jerusalem ' authorities ' was that his ' gospel ' (though it was a gospel which did not demand from Gentile adherents acceptance of the Jewish Law) was recognized as complete. The authorities did not enjoin any ' additions ' to be made to it. Giving him the right hand of fellowship, they acknowledged that he had been called to be an apostle among Gentiles as Peter had been among Jews.

On the difficult question whether this visit is to be identified with that at the time of the Apostolic Council (Acts xv.), or (as the present writer believes) with that recorded in Acts xi. 30, see Introduction, pp. xxii. ff.

ii. 1–2a : *Paul tells how it came about that he paid a second visit
to Jerusalem fourteen years later*

11.

**Then, fourteen years later, I went up to Jerusalem again, 1
accompanied by Barnabas ; I took Titus with me also. (It 2a
was in consequence of a revelation that I went up at all.)**

Paul continues the narrative of his visits to the ' head- 1
quarters ' of the Church at Jerusalem. The second visit came
fourteen years later. Does he mean fourteen years after the
previous visit ? Or is this visit too, like the other (i. 18),
dated from his conversion ? Both interpretations are no
doubt possible, though it must be admitted that the former is
the more natural. The present visit being, on our view,
identical with the famine-relief visit of Acts xi. 30, its date
falls probably in the year 46. If we allow for the ancient
' inclusive ' method of reckoning (see note on i. 18), *fourteen
years* earlier would be the year 33, and if this be regarded as
the year of the first Jerusalem visit, then the conversion,
three years earlier, would fall in the year 31—not an impossible
date for the conversion if the crucifixion be dated, as it is by
so many authorities, in 29 or 30. It has been suggested
that *fourteen years* is a mistake for *four years*, but in the
absence of manuscript authority the suggestion seems unnecessary and improbable.

If Paul says that he went up **accompanied by Barnabas**
(' with Barnabas ' is what the Greek has), this does not imply
that he claims for himself a priority. He is passing in review
the various occasions on which *he himself* visited Jerusalem :
on this particular visit, he states, he had Barnabas as a colleague. We should certainly gather from Acts that Barnabas,
who was no doubt the senior in years as he was in Christian
experience, had a position of special authority both at Antioch
and in the developments which immediately followed. It was
not till, in the course of their missionary journey, the apostles
had crossed from Cyprus to the mainland that the order of
the names ' Barnabas and Saul ' gives place in Acts to the

inverted order ' Paul and Barnabas ' (cf. the other expression used at that point : ' Paul and his companions '—Acts xiii. 13). We may reasonably infer from the picture in Acts xi. 22–26 that in the development of the work at Antioch Paul was the more aggressive force, Barnabas' contribution being given rather by way of sympathy and support ; and what we know of Paul as a thinker makes it further probable that he would accept the responsibility of thinking out the implications of the gospel which he was presenting to the Gentiles. And so we need not be surprised if, in regard to the talks which take place in Jerusalem, Paul says of himself, without reference to Barnabas, that he submitted the gospel which he was in the habit of preaching (verse 2), and that he should even speak of ' my gospel ' (verse 6). It is even quite possible that in some of his positions he went further than Barnabas was able to go with him. But when all this has been said, it remains true that he was at this time a young man, unknown (as he says) to the churches in Judæa and little known even to the leaders ; and when he went up to Jerusalem accompanied by Barnabas, he knew how much his cause gained in strength from the fact that he had Barnabas as a coadjutor.

Paul adds, **I took Titus with me also,** thereby implying that the responsibility was his for including Titus in the party. The position of Titus (who is a Gentile-Christian, verse 3) is obviously a subordinate one—his name is mentioned merely in view of the important developments to which his presence gave rise. The Galatians need not have known him personally as they knew Paul and Barnabas, but from the way in which he is mentioned here we may infer that his name at least was known to them. What made his name known was the controversy of which we are to read in verse 3—a controversy which had its echo in Galatia. Indeed it is probable, as we shall see, that, in presenting his version of events in verses 3 ff., Paul is refuting another version which his Judaistic opponents had already made current in Galatia.

It is plain from Paul's later Epistles that Titus became one of the apostle's most trusted lieutenants ; but for some reason which it is hard to understand (it has been suggested, with insufficient reason, that he may have been a brother of Luke's) his name is never mentioned in Acts. Whether, therefore, he accompanied Paul and Barnabas to Galatia we do not know. Neither can we tell how, or when, he first became associated with Paul. It is tempting to infer from the present passage that he was a Christian of Antioch, and that it was as a representative of the Gentile-Christian community there that he was invited by Paul to go to Jerusalem. The case for this is strengthened if one of the objects of the present visit was to take to Jerusalem a famine-relief fund from the church in Antioch. We know how at a later period of his missionary activity Paul invited his Gentile churches to join together in a collection for the benefit of the Jerusalem church, and delegates from the various churches accompanied the apostle when the money was finally taken to Jerusalem. On that later occasion Paul was clearly concerned to demonstrate the essential unity of the Jewish and Gentile congregations in the one ' body of Christ,' and the same was true, no doubt, at this earlier date. He knew that in Jerusalem ignorance and suspicion were sure to be rife regarding his policy of the free admission of Gentiles to the Church ; and so, while the relief-fund itself was a demonstration to the Jewish-Christians of Judæa that the Gentile-Christians of Antioch were at heart their brothers (far more truly brothers, perhaps, than the non-Christian Jews of Jerusalem had shown themselves to be since the days of Herod's persecution two years before), the presence of Titus, as the representative of the Antiochians in the handing-over of the money, enabled the Jerusalem Christians to see in the flesh one of their Gentile brethren in Christ.

When Paul adds, by way of parenthesis, that this visit was **2a** paid **in consequence of a revelation** which had come to him, he wants to make it clear that no mere personal motive lay behind the visit. If he did see the Jerusalem ' authorities ' and confer with them, it was not to seek any ruling from them that he went. Revelations meant much in the life of the apostle (cf. 2 Cor. xii. 1)—not merely as mystical experiences but as indications of the divine will. Acts shows how many of the great decisions of his missionary career were taken as

the result of divine ' guidance ' (e.g. xiii. 2 ; xvi. 6, 7 ; xx. 22).
In particular we may recall that on his previous visit to Jerusalem he had received a revelation to quit the Holy City, for his
witness would not be received there and his destined work was
among the Gentiles (Acts xxii. 17–21) ; and it was therefore
natural that he should not wish to return until another
revelation authorized him to do so. And the claim that he
went now in consequence of a revelation is not in the least
inconsistent with the view that this visit was the same as
the famine-relief visit of Acts xi. 30. No description is given
either of the form or of the content of the revelation. We are
not even told that it was given directly to Paul himself—
it may have been the one described in Acts xi. 28 as given to
Agabus, in accordance with which, we are told, the relief-
visit was undertaken. But however the revelation reached the
apostle, it is clearly not impossible, and in view of the narrative in Acts xi. 28–30 it may even be claimed as probable,
that it was *in consequence of a revelation* that Paul reached the
decision to organize a relief-fund and to take it in person to
Jerusalem.

Of the events which took place when Barnabas and Paul
arrived in Jerusalem Acts says nothing beyond indicating that
the money was to be handed over to the presbyters. This
reference to presbyters need not be taken to imply that the
apostles were absent at the time, for the fund, being destined
for local needs, would naturally be handed over to local
office-bearers. At such a time of anxiety the apostles were not
likely to be far away. If therefore they were present at
Jerusalem, we cannot imagine (as some commentators seem
to do) that Barnabas and Paul could have departed without
taking the opportunity of discussing at some length with them
the important developments in and around Antioch. It was
to investigate these developments in their initial stage that
the church in Jerusalem had despatched Barnabas to Antioch,
and, so far as we know, he had not returned to report until now.
Certainly this was Paul's first visit since the work began, the
first visit since those early days shortly after his conversion ;
and it was impossible that he should meet with the Jerusalem

apostles without seeking to inflame them with what was now
the master-passion of his life—the winning of the Gentile
world for Christ.

ii. 2b. : *On that occasion he submitted his gospel to the Jerusalem
authorities*

I submitted the gospel I am in the habit of preaching to the 2b
Gentiles, submitting it privately to the authorities, to make
sure that my course of action would be and had been sound.

Every word in this sentence is significant. Paul does not 2b
say he consulted anyone, as a pupil might consult a master.
His gospel had already been given to him by revelation
(i. 11, 12), and what he did was to tell people about it—he
submitted it. After ' submitted ' the Greek adds ' to them,'
which may be merely an anticipation of the reference to the
' authorities ' later in the sentence, but more probably refers
quite generally to Jewish-Christians in Jerusalem. We may
be sure that Paul would have an opportunity of addressing
a meeting of the congregation, quite apart from his private
meeting with the authorities. And what he submitted to them
was his **gospel**, i.e. he did not content himself, as is sometimes
the way with missionary speakers, with describing the circumstances in which he worked and the results which had been
achieved, but he informed them what the message was which
in those unusual circumstances was being blessed with such
success. Naturally under the term ' gospel ' would come the
question of the conditions on which Gentiles were being admitted ; but beneath the question of conditions lay the more
fundamental questions of the nature of the salvation which was
being offered, the character and purposes of the God who
offered it, and the means which God took to make the salvation
operative. Paul saw that those whose work of evangelization had hitherto lain among fellow-Jews had not exhausted
the meaning of the gospel until they had considered what the
gospel might mean for non-Jews. The full significance of
Christ, in other words, is something which must be grasped

' with all the saints ' (Eph. iii. 18). On this all-important matter Paul believed that he himself had received clear light by revelation ; in its main features, therefore, his gospel remained unchanged from the beginning, and as is shown by his use of the present tense (I am) the gospel which he sub-mitted at Jerusalem was the same as he was still (at the time of writing) in the habit of preaching to the Gentiles.

Paul goes on to refer more particularly to private conversa-tions which took place with the authorities. Who these ' authorities ' were is not stated, though from verse 9 it is apparent that they included Peter, James, and John. The same designation occurs twice in verse 6. Why does Paul use it ? The phrase ' the so-called authorities ' in verse 6 gives a clue to the answer. It is not that the apostle wishes to be ironical—such an attitude would be quite unworthy of him and inconsistent with what we otherwise know of his character and his attitude to the primitive apostles. It is merely that his opponents had grandiloquently made use of the phrase ' the authorities ' in reference to the leaders at Jerusalem, seeking by comparison to depreciate the authority of Paul, and Paul is therefore falling back on a term which had already played a part in the discussion. This being so, the phrase might be printed here in quotation marks as it is in verse 6.

When Paul says ' I wished to make sure that my course of action would be and had been sound ' (lit. ' lest in any way I should be running or had run in vain '), this does not mean that if ' the authorities ' had found fault with his gospel he would have been under the necessity of amending or ampli-fying it. Such an admission would have been a denial of the independence which he sought so resolutely to assert. His concern was not that his gospel to the Gentiles should conform to the requirements of the Jerusalem authorities, but that they should understand and agree with him in his interpretation of the gospel. He wished them to be informed on a situation which was unfamiliar to them, and to secure their approval of the way in which he was attempting to meet it. ' Sound ' is a misleading translation of the phrase which Paul uses. What concerned Paul was whether his whole missionary work, past

and present, should be rendered ' useless,' should be made
' to lead nowhere '—as it would have been had the Jerusalem
church insisted that Gentile-Christians must accept circumcision. Such a demand, being one to which Paul could never
agree, would have ruined all his work, because it would have
separated Jewish-Christianity and Gentile-Christianity into
two camps. How Paul had to face that same issue when it
arose in a new form at Antioch we are to read in verses 11 ff.

ii. 3–5 : *He recalls the difficult situation created by the demand
that his Gentile companion Titus should be circumcised*

But even my companion Titus, Greek though he was, was not 3
obliged to be circumcised. There were traitors of false 4
brothers, who had crept in to spy out the freedom we enjoy
in Christ Jesus ; they did aim at enslaving us again. But 5
we refused to yield for a single instant to their claims ;
we were determined that the truth of the gospel should hold
good for you.

As it appears in the original, few historical passages in the 3
New Testament provide more difficulty than this for the exe-
gete. A more literal translation of verses 4 and 5 would run
as follows : ' (4) but owing to the false brethren surreptitiously
brought in, who had crept in to spy out our freedom which we
have in Christ Jesus, in order that they may enslave us.
(5) to whom not for an hour did we yield as regards the
subjection, in order that the truth of the gospel might continue
with you ' (or ' unto you '). In what follows we shall take this
literal translation as our guide.

The first difficulty comes from the sudden break in the
construction of the sentence at the end of verse 4. Paul
suddenly interrupts himself at this point, and the sentence
proceeds along what is perhaps quite a new line.

A more serious difficulty arises from the uncertainty of the
text. With one exception the main Greek MSS. give verse 5
as we have translated it above. But Codex D, the old Latin
version, Irenæus, and Tertullian omit the two opening words,

the relative and the negative, so that, without any awkward break in the middle, the passage as a whole yields the following sense : ' but owing to the false brethren . . . we yielded for an hour,' i.e. we made a temporary concession. And of these two readings it seems scarcely possible, *on textual considerations alone*, to say which is the more original. There are also other readings which obviously are variants of one or other of the above.

Put concretely the situation is this. A demand was apparently made that Titus, being a Gentile (the word **Greek** here means non-Jew), should **be circumcised.** And involved in this particular issue there would seem to have been raised the more general question of principle—hence the reference in verse 5 to ' claims ' or (as in the more literal translation) ' *subjection.*' But the questions which remain obscure are :

(i.) In verse 5 does Paul admit that, as a temporary expedient, he gave way, or does he deny stoutly that there was the slightest concession ?

(ii.) In verse 4 is it implied that Titus, despite the pressure brought to bear to secure his circumcision, remained uncircumcised, or was Titus circumcised though not as a result of compulsion ? (Another proposed interpretation of the verse according to which it means that ' no pressure was ever applied to get Titus circumcised ' is inconsistent with the Greek, and may be dismissed.)

These two questions are inter-related, but they are not identical. It is possible, for example, that while agreeing in the special circumstances to having Titus circumcised, Paul insisted that the concession made in this one case was in no sense a sacrifice of principle : it was not a case of compulsion, of bowing to a superior authority, of acceptance of a general ruling. And the present writer regards this as the most probable interpretation of the situation, while admitting that there is no room for dogmatism where so much is obscure.

That in any circumstances Paul should have agreed to the circumcision of Titus is a conclusion which, on first consideration, one is inclined to resist. The circumcision of Timothy (Acts xvi. 1-3) is in a different category, for his mother was a

Jewess and he himself therefore was probably only too ready to accept a rite which might normally have been performed on him in childhood. But could the circumcision of Titus (if, as seems probable, he was a pure Gentile) be anything else than a sacrifice of principle ? Many commentators, including Lightfoot, Ramsay, and Burton, hold strongly that he was *not* circumcised. But as finger-posts pointing in the opposite direction we may note the following :

(i.) A difficult expression in v. 10 shows that Paul was accused of ' still preaching circumcision.' On our view of the date of the Epistle this cannot refer to the circumcision of Timothy, which came later, viz. at the beginning of the ' second ' missionary journey.

(ii.) Some of the phrases which Paul uses here, coupled with the passionate vindication of his independence throughout the Epistle as a whole, indicate that he had given his opponents a ' handle ' for their emphatic assertion that he accepted some form of ' subjection.' Some ' concession ' must have been made which they were able to represent as a ' submission.' And from the nature of the case the only likely occasion on which this could have happened was his present visit to Jerusalem.

(iii.) The very incoherence of his language at this point suggests that Paul is dealing with a matter of extreme delicacy. If the issue had been a clear-cut one, if e.g. Paul had positively refused to have Titus circumcised, and the other party had accepted his position, Paul we may be sure would have expressed himself in emphatic and unambiguous language : instead of justifying himself for not yielding to them (on the general question of subjection) he would have said plainly that the yielding was on *their* side. As Professor Burkitt trenchantly puts it (*Christian Beginnings*, p. 118) : ' who can doubt that it was the knife which really did circumcise Titus that has cut the syntax of Gal. ii. 3–5 to pieces ? ' We ought also to remember that while the language is incoherent and ambiguous to us, it would not be ambiguous to the Galatians, who (on our interpretation) had already been told the main facts of this story, though in a form which put a wrong construction on the facts.

It is not difficult to imagine circumstances which might have induced the apostle, without sacrifice of principle, to allow Titus to be circumcised. Titus must have been one of the first purely Gentile Christians whom the Jerusalem Church had had in its midst—perhaps the first to appear at least in a quasi-official capacity. As a Christian he would be welcomed gladly ; but as a Gentile he raised a number of problems which up till now had never presented themselves concretely in the fellowship. With Paul and other fellow-Christians Titus would naturally go up to the Temple-precincts ; but when the others entered the Temple proper, must he be left behind ? More serious still, for it concerned relations *within* the fellow-ship, what was to happen when they sat down at the Lord's Table, or even at a meal in a private house ? Must Titus be asked to sit apart ? In the Church of Stephen, Peter, and Barnabas there must have been many who were perfectly ready to receive Titus on equal terms, and probably at first no difficulty was felt about receiving him ; but there were certainly others who, confronted suddenly with a question of such far-reaching importance, were not prepared to adopt a liberal attitude ; and in the background, forbidding and dis-posed to be hostile, was the Judaism of the Holy City, from which, despite the recent persecution, the Church had no desire to sever herself entirely, and which indeed she did not wish to provoke further.

Faced with this situation, what was Paul to do ? In bring-ing Titus to Jerusalem the apostle must have hoped indeed that his Gentile convert would be received by Jewish-Christians as if he were one of themselves, and when difficulties arose he doubtless tried to overcome them. But Paul too could face facts. He had not come to Jerusalem to force his opinions on others, and by doing so to divide the mother-church and perhaps create a breach which it would be hard to heal between Jewish and Gentile Christianity. Some day the issue would require to be fought out as a matter of principle ; but for that Paul would choose his own time and place. Mean-time he could allow Titus, in view of the special circumstances, to be circumcised, and yet make it plain that there was here no acknowledgment that Gentile-Christians in general must be circumcised. There were even positive advantages in yielding in the present instance. Titus circumcised could do much that for Titus uncircumcised was quite impossible—so long as he was in Jerusalem he could mix freely with fellow-Christians, he could take part in the services of the Temple,[1] and later, as a member of Paul's staff, he would be free to appeal to Jews and to Greeks.

Here, in the case of Titus, we have the first reference to circumcision in the letter. And in Titus' case it was circumcision alone, and not the wider question of his acceptance of the Mosaic Law, which was in dispute. There were those in the Jerusalem church who were prepared to hold, with regard to Titus or any other Christian, that unless he kept the Mosaic Law he was no true Christian and could not be saved. Such a claim Paul could not for a moment admit—his whole ' gospel ' (verse 2) was directly opposed to it. But the question at issue, as Paul saw it, was—not on what terms Titus could be saved, but on what terms a solitary Gentile-Christian could be welcomed in the home of Jewish-Christianity. What he sought was a *modus vivendi*—not an interpretation of the ' gospel,' which to him was not in dispute. And so, as a practical concession, he allowed Titus to be circumcised. Still, there was no compulsion about the matter ; Titus was not ' obliged ' to be circumcised, i.e. the Jewish ' authorities ' did not enforce it on Paul, and Paul's acceptance of it did not imply any subjection on his part to their authority.

The people who provided trouble for Paul were not the 4 Jerusalem ' authorities ' but others whom he now denounces in unsparing language, seeking to show them up in their true colours. What does he tell us about these men ? They were **false brothers**—Christians, that is, whose attitude and conduct showed that they had no right to the name (cf. 2 Cor. xi. 26). The word translated **traitors** ('unawares brought in '—Authorized Version) is in the Greek very similar to the verb ' **crept in** '

---

[1] If the relief-fund, like the later ' collection ' (Acts xxiv. 17 f.) was, as is probable, to be presented in the Temple, Paul would be gratified to have Titus associated with him on that occasion.

45

which follows : in each case it is suggested that they had come in from the outside and (probably) that there was something surreptitious about their motives or behaviour. The references to **spying out our freedom** and **enslaving us again** indicate that, though they had accepted the gospel, they were at heart militant legalists. Where had they crept in to ? Was it the church at Antioch ?—as if already at this early date emissaries from Jerusalem were at work there like those of whom we read in Acts xv. 1 ? More probably Paul is describing developments which took place at Jerusalem at the time of his visit, and when he says of these brethren that they ' crept in,' he does not imply that they now for the first time joined the Christian Church (it can scarcely be suggested that they actually accepted baptism with no higher motives than those which are here ascribed to them) ; he means that, being Christians (although they were at bottom Jews rather than Christians, and had no sympathy with Paul's work among Gentiles), they insidiously presented themselves on some occasion (or occasions) when they sought, as the apostle says, **to spy out the freedom we enjoy in Christ Jesus.** Who are the ' we ' of whom Paul writes, and what precisely has he in mind in his reference to ' freedom ' ? There is, on Paul's view, a freedom from the bondage of the Law which in Christ belongs to every Christian (cf. v. 1) ; but clearly something more definite is implied here. What Paul has in mind here is that freedom from the Law which, according to his gospel, characterized the intimate social relations of Jewish-Christians with Gentile-Christians, as e.g. in Antioch and in the churches of Galatia. He uses the present tense (*we enjoy*) because such freedom is inherent in his gospel and is not limited to any one time or place ; but a special demonstration of that freedom was given at Jerusalem when Barnabas and Paul associated freely with their Gentile-Christian companion Titus, no doubt sharing the same table with him. And it was this ' freedom ' which the ' false brothers' watched with suspicious and malevolent eyes and resolved even to wreck, aiming (as Paul says) **at enslaving us again,** i.e. at compelling us, in all our associations with Gentiles, even Gentile-Christians, to conform to

the demands of the Jewish Law. This contrast between the
' freedom ' that is in Christ and the ' enslavement ' of the Law
comes to fuller expression in chapters iv. and v. of the Epistle.
How far the 'false brothers' were prepared to go in their
enslaving demands we are not told. They obviously insisted
that fellowship with Titus on the part of Jewish-Christians in
Jerusalem could not be encouraged or even condoned unless
Titus was circumcised—and on our interpretation of the
incident Paul decided, for practical reasons, to give way on
the matter, though he is careful also to maintain that he was
not ' obliged ' to do so. But it is probable that the 'false
brothers ' also took up the more general position that all
Gentile-Christians must be circumcised, and it is this or some
such demand which Paul has in mind when in verse 5 he goes
on to say : ' **we refused to yield for a single instant to their** 5
claims.'

Taken literally, what Paul says is : ' we did not yield as
regards the subjection.' The use of the definite article, which
unfortunately is omitted in the Authorized and Revised
Versions, shows that something quite specific is here referred
to. The probability is that we have here a term which has
already been employed in the controversy (translate therefore,
with the aid of inverted commas : *on the ' subjection ' issue*),
and we may even suggest that Paul knew that the Galatians
were already familiar with it. On this view Paul in his statement of the case is consciously controverting a false version
which the Judaizers had spread abroad in the Galatian
churches, according to which Paul had been brought to task
at Jerusalem and had accepted the ' subjection ' which was
imposed on him. What exactly was involved in that alleged
subjection the Galatians would thus already know, while we
are left to conjecture. It may have been that Paul was said
to have bowed to the superior ruling of the Jerusalem ' authorities,' a view of the case which Paul's whole account of the
incident indignantly repudiates ; or the reference may be to
the claim that all Christians, Jewish and Gentile alike, must
acknowledge the authority of the Jewish Law. On this question of principle Paul says ' **we refused to yield for a single**

instant.' The 'we' probably implies that on this matter
Barnabas was entirely with him. We took our stand, he says,
' that the truth of the gospel should hold good for you,' ' you '
referring primarily of course to the Galatians but indirectly to
Gentiles in general. Had we given way on this fundamental
issue, Paul implies, it would have been a denial of the truth
of that gospel which already I was in the habit of preaching
among the Gentiles (verse 2), and the gospel which subsequently I should have had to bring to you would have been a
mere ' distortion ' of the truth (cf. i. 7).

ii. 6–10 : *The Jerusalem authorities cordially recognized Paul's
apostleship, and asked for no modification of his gospel*

6 Besides, the so-called ' authorities ' (it makes no difference to me
what their status used to be—God pays no regard to the
externals of men), these ' authorities ' had no additions to
7 make to my gospel. On the contrary, when they saw I had
been entrusted with the gospel for the benefit of the uncircumcised, just as Peter had been for the circumcised
8 (for He who equipped Peter to be an apostle of the circum-
9 cised equipped me as well for the uncircumcised), and
when they recognized the grace I had been given, then the
so-called ' pillars ' of the church, James and Cephas and
John, gave myself and Barnabas the right hand of fellowship. Our sphere was to be the Gentiles, theirs the cir-
10 cumcised. Only, we were to ' remember the poor.' I was
quite eager to do that myself.

It was not subservience to the Jerusalem ' authorities '
which lay behind his action in visiting Jerusalem on this
occasion and in consenting to the circumcision of Titus—so
much Paul has made plain in the preceding verses. Now he
emphasizes the further point, in continuation of what he said
in verse 2 about submitting his gospel to the ' authorities,'
that they had no addition to make to that gospel, and indeed
gave full and cordial recognition to his authority as a missionary to the Gentiles.

Judaizers had apparently alleged that the Jerusalem 6
' authorities ' had even made Paul modify his gospel. Such
an allegation stirs Paul to the depths, and here, as in verses
4 and 5, his surging emotions play havoc with his syntax (for
a more literal translation see Authorized Version and Revised
Version—he begins with the words : ' but from the so-called
" authorities," ' as if he had meant to say that from them he
had received no addition to his gospel). Even the reference to
' authorities ' cannot be allowed to pass this time without
qualification. ' That is not my term,' he implies ; ' I only use
it because others have imported it into the discussion '—hence
so-called, a qualification which conveys no depreciation of the
authorities themselves, though it does of the arrogant claims
which the Judaizers made with regard to them. This qualification is expanded in a long parenthesis, designed to repudiate
any claim that their authority was in some way superior.
Here the Authorized and Revised Versions translate : ' whatsoever they were ' ; the other translation, what their status
used to be, refers apparently to the association which they had
had with the Lord *in earlier days*, when they had companied
with Him on earth as His disciples. Paul, who bases everything on the reality of his call, denies emphatically that their
past relationship with Jesus puts the Jerusalem leaders in a
superior position ; the Lord calls whom He wills, and in His
presence all earthly differences disappear—God pays no regard
to the externals of men.

Passing on to resume the sentence which his parenthetical
explanation had interrupted Paul now comes to what is his
main contention at this point. These ' authorities,' he says,
had no addition to make to my gospel. Here, as the Greek
verbs show, Paul catches up what he had said in verse 2.
' Being in Jerusalem ' (so his argument runs) ' I took the opportunity of laying my gospel before those who there were accepted
as " authorities "—explaining to them what in my opinion
was the significance of Christ for the Gentile world, and on
what conditions Gentile believers could become heirs of salvation. And they, in turn, accepted my gospel, having nothing
to add by way of correction or amplification.' Thus Paul

disposes of the allegation that the Jerusalem 'authorities' enjoined that Gentile converts should be circumcised or keep the Jewish Law.

7 What the attitude of the Jerusalem leaders really was he goes on now to state more positively. To begin with, he explains, **they saw I had been entrusted with the gospel for the benefit of the uncircumcised, just as Peter had been for the circumcised.** By this is not meant that there were two gospels, but that the task of presenting the gospel to Gentiles differed in practice, and therefore required different workers, from that of presenting it to Jews. That the gospel was meant for the Jews was never doubted, and Peter is here specially mentioned as a representative leader in that department of the Church's missionary work ; but Gentiles too were marked out to receive it, and now, after Paul's exposition (verse 2), the Jerusalem leaders recognized that for that work Paul had been called by God. In no sense was one task subordinate to the other ; both were subdivisions of the one great commission to preach *the gospel of God*. Neither, we may add, was there felt to be any hard and fast division between the two tasks—neither territorially nor in any other way was a rigid division possible. What is stated here is nothing

8 more than a working arrangement, based, as verse 8 shows, on the recognition of the fact that God gives to men varying gifts and varying tasks, and that **He who** had **equipped Peter** for the one task had obviously **equipped** Paul **as well** for the other.

9 Summing up the matter Paul says that **they recognized the grace I had been given**—it was by 'grace' on God's part that the Gentiles should be included in the blessings of the gospel, and more especially it was by 'grace' that Paul should be entrusted with the task of taking the gospel to them. Here Paul introduces the names of the three chief leaders of the Jerusalem church, **James and Cephas and John** ; in calling them '**pillars,**' an appropriate designation in connection with the Church as the Temple of God (cf. 1 Cor. iii. 9 ; Eph. ii. 19–22), he is probably using a dignified title applied to them by the Judaizers. James is not the son of Zebedee, whose

death probably took place shortly before this (Acts xii. 2), but the brother of the Lord, who, besides being the acknowledged head of the Church in Jerusalem, was also a leader of the Jewish-Christian party. In view of his general attitude his action on this occasion was especially significant, and it is perhaps for that reason that Paul mentions him even before Peter. Cephas is of course the Hebrew name for which Peter (Petros) is the Greek equivalent : is the Hebrew name preferred here because it is the cordiality of those *Jewish* leaders towards his Gentile gospel that Paul is eager to emphasize ? This is the sole reference to John we have in the New Testament, outside of the Gospels and Acts (and Revelation ?) ; in the early chapters of Acts (iii. 1 ff.; iv. 13 ff.; viii. 14) he is one of the Twelve who figures most prominently next to Peter, with whom he is always shown in association. An arresting picture here follows of the noble action of these three Jerusalem leaders. Moved by what they had seen of the grace of God, they face their two colleagues who had been working among Gentiles (Paul here associates Barnabas with himself, whereas in the previous verses Peter and Paul were contrasted as *individual* representatives of the two spheres of work) and give them the right hand of fellowship. How Paul's soul must have exulted as he told this tale ! What a travesty of the truth was all the talk of the Judaizers about the ' subjection ' enforced on him by the Jerusalem ' authorities ' ! Here was no ' subjection,' but ' fellowship ' in the work of the gospel ; no enforcement of a superior authority, but mutual recognition by each party of the other's God-appointed sphere of service. Our sphere was to be the Gentiles, theirs the circumcised.

Paul adds an apparent qualification (only) ; but it is a 10 qualification which by its very nature serves to emphasize his claim that the Jerusalem authorities had no additions to make to his gospel (verse 6). The only injunction they gave me, he says, was to ' remember the poor.' This was of course in no sense a limiting condition on Paul's freedom of action ; it was a mere exhortation that in his work among Gentiles he should remember the needs of those who were less fortunate—the reference being to Jewish-Christians. There was

HG   51

evidently poverty among the Christians of Judæa—a famine had been raging, and there was probably also a growing tendency among their non-Christian brethren to boycott them. Apparently too it was believed that Gentile-Christians in those lands which Paul was to visit were likely to be able to help.

With regard to this injunction Paul adds that it meant nothing new for him—*care for the poor was a task to which of his own accord he had devoted himself*. This simple avowal has been subjected to so much discussion that it is well to look into his words with some care. The verb he uses signifies not mere *eagerness*, as in the translation, but *active engagement* in the prosecution of a task. The tense of the verb is aorist (past), indicating probably that the apostle is looking backward—' they were only asking me to do something which had already occupied my attention.' This claim of Paul's accords perfectly therefore with the general interpretation adopted in this commentary, viz. that the present visit to Jerusalem is to be identified with the one recorded in Acts xi. 29 f., when Barnabas and he took to Jerusalem a contribution from the Christians in Antioch. It is no argument against this (*a*) that Paul uses the singular pronoun ' I,' for though he had Barnabas as an associate the point at issue was what the Jerusalem leaders had to say to *him* personally ; or (*b*) that he uses the past tense rather than the imperfect (*had devoted myself* rather than *was devoting myself*), for though it was during the Jerusalem visit that the relief-work came to visible manifestation, the instigation of it lay in the past in Antioch. Paul's point, therefore, is clear. ' Even in regard to the relief of the poor they were not propounding a new scheme of their own to which they asked my adherence. It was a work which I myself had already begun to prosecute, which provided in fact one of the reasons for my present visit to Jerusalem. And they showed their approval of it by asking me to continue it.'

We are now in a position to look back over the whole of the section verses 1–10, and to estimate the significance of this visit to Jerusalem. It had been for Paul a fateful visit. He had gone back to the headquarters of his nation and his nation's faith, to a city which was the scene of some of his earliest successes, but where, since he became a Christian, he was almost unknown save for that brief private visit he had paid many years before to Peter. He was still a young man, who could not count on his name or fame to carry weight with those who had been apostles before him. It might even be that they would refuse to recognize him as a fellow-apostle. When he was there he naturally took the opportunity to tell the leaders of the call which had come to him to preach to the Gentiles, of the success which was attending his work, and of the form which his gospel took. Violent opposition was roused against him by certain extremists, and this reached a head over the question of the circumcision of Titus ; and though he found it expedient to concede this latter point for the sake of peace he took a firm stand in maintaining the truth of the gospel as he knew it. After hearing his exposition the Jerusalem leaders fully recognized his *apostleship*—he had clearly, they saw, been ' called ' by God to this work among Gentiles just as fully as Peter, for instance, had been called to work among Jews ; and so far as his *gospel* was concerned, they made no attempt to ask him to alter or to amplify it in any way. Such a picture shows us that this forward movement among Gentiles was only yet in its infancy ; but conscious now that there need be no breach (verse 2) between this work and the other work which was being carried on among Jews, Paul was able to return to Antioch to prosecute the Gentile mission with vigour. Soon afterwards Barnabas and he embarked on the so-called ' first missionary journey.'

The gospel with which Paul had been ' entrusted for the benefit of the uncircumcised' ('*my gospel*,' verse 6) and which had secured the approval of the leaders in Jerusalem was a gospel of the grace of God in Jesus Christ, and it did not require that Gentiles who accepted it should identify themselves with the community of Israel through circumcision and the keeping of the Law. Accordingly it has sometimes been urged that ' even in content there was an important and far-reaching difference between the gospel that Paul preached and that which Peter preached, the difference, in fact, between a legalistic and a non-legalistic gospel ' (Burton, *Commentary*, p. 92). This is a serious misconstruction of the situation. It is true that circumcision was not to be enjoined on Paul's Gentile Christians, as it was to be on Peter's Jewish ones : but in the latter case it was not Peter who enjoined it, and it was not enjoined *as part of the gospel*. Adult Jews were circumcised already, and even if they became Christians they would (as Jews) wish to have their children circumcised. Paul would have been as ready as Peter to urge that this should be so ; he did not desire to see Jewish-Christians ' denationalized,' cf. the untrue charges brought against him in Acts xxi. 21. The problem was more complicated with regard to the Law. But situations might arise in which the provisions of the Law could not be kept without disloyalty to Christ. Then Paul certainly would have said (and Peter, when he understood the situation, would have agreed with him ; we are to have an example of this in the immediately succeeding verses) that the last word was not with the Law, but with Christ. Thus there were not two different *gospels*, the one for the Jew and the other for the Gentile. There was a difference of soil into which the seed was cast, but the seed itself was the same ; and in each case the same God was at work (verse 8).

In conclusion, we may ask ourselves : what would have happened if the Jerusalem leaders had refused to recognize Paul ? The answer can scarcely be in doubt. He who had received from God Himself both his gospel and his commission to preach it was not likely now to disobey God at the dictates of man. He would have gone on with the work (' Woe to me if I do not preach the gospel,' 1 Cor. ix. 16) ; but he would have gone with a sad heart, realizing that ' Christ was divided ' (1 Cor. i. 13), and that only God Himself could so overrule things that the work would not all be useless (see note on verse 2*b*). Fortunately the ' authorities ' dealt more wisely with Paul than their successors dealt with Luther and Wesley.

ii. 11-21 : DEVELOPMENTS AT ANTIOCH

A new development ensued when Peter visited Antioch. We can scarcely doubt that this visit is *subsequent* to the events in Jerusalem described in ii. 1-10, though this is denied by some critics who wish to identify Gal. ii. 1-10 with Acts xv. On this see Introduction, pp. xxv. f.

Of Peter's detailed movements at this time we know unfortunately next to nothing. It may be debated whether his association with Paul at Antioch came before or after the missionary journey to Galatia. The former is the preferable alternative. The fact that trouble such as is now to be described pursued Paul when he was in Galatia (cf. pp. xxix, 19) suggests that it had broken out in Antioch before the Galatian tour had begun.

ii. 11-14 : *Paul tells of the table-fellowship between Jews and Gentiles at Antioch, and of the public remonstrance he administered to Peter*

But when Cephas came to Antioch, I opposed him to his face. 11 The man stood self-condemned. Before certain emissaries 12 of James arrived, he ate along with the Gentile Christians ; but when they arrived, he began to draw back and hold aloof, because he was afraid of the circumcision party. The 13 rest of the Jewish Christians also played false along with him, so much so that even Barnabas was carried away by their false play. But I saw they were swerving from the 14 true line of the gospel ; so I said to Cephas in presence of them all, ' If you live like the Gentiles and not like the Jews, though you are a Jew yourself, why do you oblige the Gentiles to become Jews ? '

Paul continues to vindicate the claim that his gospel is independent of human authority. So far the claim has been asserted *negatively* : his gospel is not something which he had *inherited*, or which he had been *taught* ; and he had never accepted *dictation* with regard to it from alleged superiors.

He now tells of a development which called him to assert his independence *positively*, viz. by open resistance and remon-
11 strance. The occasion arose **when Cephas (Peter) came to Antioch**, and adopted a line of action in consequence of which Paul **opposed him to his face.** Looking back on the incident Paul has no doubt that Peter was in the wrong, and that the facts of the case **condemned** him.

The point at issue concerned table-fellowship between Jewish and Gentile Christians. Here we have one of those practical problems whose emergence provides so often a serious challenge to the missionary in the organization and development of a primitive Christian church. A congregation united in doctrine will split on some question of custom or ritual. Even those who acknowledged the right of Gentiles to become Christians without the necessity of circumcision were not at one on the practical question how far Jewish-Christians were free to sit down with their Gentile brethren at the same table, whether at a private party or (more particularly) at the celebration of the Lord's Supper.

The question was not altogether a new one—it must obviously have arisen so soon as one Gentile appeared as a member of the Christian brotherhood. When Peter found himself at Cæsarea in the house of a Gentile whom he had baptized, he readily accepted hospitality from him, encouraged thereto by a vision from heaven ; but his action did not escape condemnation from the circumcision party (Acts xi. 2 ff.). The practical difficulty occasioned by the coming of Titus to Jerusalem had been solved, as we have seen, by getting Titus to accept circumcision. The situation, however, was different in a city like Antioch, where Gentile-Christians would seem to have been numerous and may even have been in a majority ; and there the custom had evidently been established, thanks no doubt to the lead given by Barnabas and Paul, that Jewish members of the congregation should join freely in fellowship with their Gentile brethren in Christ. Was it by fraternization of this kind, we may ask, that the believers in Antioch, Jewish and Gentile, so manifested their essential oneness with one another, and thereby their essential difference from Jews, that they earned the distinctive name of *Christians* (cf. p. xxxi.) ?

When Peter came to Antioch, seeing for the first time a church with a large Gentile membership, we can understand how, to the man who had baptized Cornelius, it seemed natural and right that Jewish and Gentile Christians should sit down together. A development occurred, however, when **certain** 12 **emissaries of James arrived** (according to another Greek reading there was only *one* emissary), who forced Peter to recognize a difficulty which in his first enthusiasm he had overlooked.

James was the head of the church in Jerusalem, already mentioned in i. 19 ; ii. 9 ; and we may take it that these men had come with his authority and approval, probably bearing letters of commendation from him (cf. 2 Cor. iii. 1)—had they merely made use of his name to add weight to their pretensions, Paul would have made that plain. This in itself shows that their position, openly at least, was not the extreme one of the 'false brothers' mentioned in verse 4, from whom James, with Peter and John, had quite definitely dissociated himself (verse 9). In other words their ostensible purpose was not to condemn *in toto* the Gentile mission and to demand the circumcision of *Gentile* converts. Rather they had come to remind the *Jewish* members of the Antiochian congregation of the obligations which all true Jews, including Jewish-Christians, must observe in their dealings with Gentiles.

Though eating with Gentiles was not forbidden in the Pentateuch, the tradition had grown up, notably during and after the struggle with Antiochus Epiphanes, when Judaism set itself to remain inviolate in defiance of the menaces of heathendom, that pious Jews should keep themselves scrupulously apart from their heathen neighbours, not merely observing their own regulations as regards articles of diet, methods of cooking, washing of plates, etc., but refusing to sit down with Gentiles at the same table. Thus we read in the Book of Jubilees, xxii. 16, 17 : 'and do thou, my son, Jacob, remember my words, and observe the commandments of Abraham, thy father : separate thyself from the nations, and eat not with them '; cf. also Dan. i. 8; Mark ii. 15 ff. Doubt-less there were diversities of practice. Some Jews might be willing to welcome a Gentile to their own table,[1] where at least the rules about food could be observed ; but fears of pollution would keep a strict Jew from accepting an invitation to dine with a Gentile, especially as, by a practice common in heathen circles, meat bought in the market-place might first have been exposed in a temple as an offering to a pagan deity. It was to overcome this very difficulty that, at the famous Council of Jerusalem, which (on the view adopted in this commentary) was held almost immediately after the writing of this Epistle, James proposed as a *modus vivendi* that Gentile-Christians should avoid certain kinds of food which would make it difficult for a Jewish-Christian to have table-fellowship with them (Acts xv. 20). It may also be conjectured, though we have no direct evidence on the matter, that, previous to this, Paul and Barnabas, in seeking to promote fellowship between Jewish and Gentile Christians at Antioch, had encouraged the latter to have regard for the susceptibilities of their Jewish-Christian brethren.

In the situation at Antioch there was much indeed to cause misgiving to James and to those who shared his point of view. Though they had accepted Christ as the fulfilment of Jewish hopes, they were none the less Jews who could not be disloyal to their past, or look with favour on any developments which, by degrading, as it seemed, the ethical and religious standards of Judaism, could only end by disrupting it. Charity might lead a Jewish-Christian to accept an invitation from a Gentile brother in Christ ; yet was there not a real danger, it was felt, that in this way the Jewish-Christian might unwillingly or unwittingly be led to partake of food which for him and his fellow-Jews was condemned as unclean ? And unreal though such danger might be in a church where the Jewish element predominated, would it not become serious when the Gentile element was so strong as to be able to set up new standards of

---

[1] This was forbidden in the Mishnah; cf. Sanhedrin 6.3*b* : ' Let one not invite a heathen to table, for whosoever does that brings upon his children the punishment of exile.'

its own ? Jewish-Christians of Jerusalem knew, moreover, how fraught with consequence the new development was for the relationships of the Church with orthodox Judaism. If Jews who became Christians were to degrade themselves to the level of Gentile sinners, what hope would there be of winning Israel to an early acceptance of the gospel, and in place of the toleration at present meted out to the Church were not the Jewish authorities likely to be goaded into adopting a policy of repression ?

We can thus understand the opposition of the **circumcision party**—a generic phrase which means more than *converts from Judaism*, as Lightfoot translates it ; it refers to those, both within and without the Church, for whom a fundamental line of demarcation lay between Jews and non-Jews. Is it any wonder that when the situation was so presented to Peter **he began to draw back and hold aloof,** that his fears moreover 13 were shared by **the rest of the Jewish Christians** at Antioch, and that **even Barnabas was carried away ?** His conduct here, as on the occasion when he denied his Master, has caused Peter to be denounced as weak and unstable by those who have not been at pains to understand the severity of the test to which he was exposed. As in his attitude towards Cornelius, so here in his initial readiness to fraternize with Gentile-Christians, his generous sympathies, or, as we may preferably say, his Christian love, had dictated for him at the outset the right course of action. If later he found that his heart had carried him further than now his judgment was prepared to go, he was not guilty of wilful temporizing or weak vacillation ; it was merely that he had been driven to see the implications of his action, and the situation was too involved for him to know what was right and what was wrong. His dishonour was rooted in honour. Paul himself, despite the language in which he describes it, was not blind to the difficulty which the situation presented to those who understood the issues less clearly than he did. Personal regard mingles with anguish and apprehension as he tells how *even Barnabas*, his colleague and loyal supporter in so many phases of the work, had been carried away.

Nevertheless the situation stirred Paul to his depths. With unerring insight he saw what was at stake—nothing less than the unity of the Church and (to go further back) the truth of the gospel. The action of Peter and of those who sided with him he accordingly denounces as **false play**, lit. *hypocrisy*— a strong term to use with reference to men of standing and character such as Peter and Barnabas. Paul has in mind how in the recent conversations at Jerusalem these two great Jewish-Christian leaders had been at one with him on the general question of the admission of Gentiles to the Christian fellowship ; and now they are acting in a way which would make real fellowship impossible. The judgment behind Paul's language is perhaps not so harsh as might appear. He was probably willing to believe that on the fundamental issue of the unity of Jew and Gentile in Christ his two great colleagues were still at one with him, and that what was wrong was that unwittingly they were not acting in accordance with their deepest religious convictions. Not having his insight and vision they did not realize their inconsistency ; it was there- fore the more necessary for him to point it out to them.

14 If Peter and Barnabas were playing false with their con- victions, Paul also **saw that they were swerving from the true line of the gospel** (lit. *were not going straight with reference to the truth of the gospel*). Paul saw here, as in the conversations at Jerusalem (ii. 5), that it was the truth of the gospel that was at stake ; and accordingly he acted with a boldness and defiance such as he would not have felt called on to display had the issue been merely one of practical expediency or personal prestige. He proceeded to remonstrate with **Cephas** (Peter), and to do so publicly. Drawing a contrast between the two ways of life, the Jewish and the Gentile, he recalled how, when Peter first came to Antioch, he was ready, Jew though he was, to be guided in his action by the fact that he was a Christian, and accordingly he associated freely with Gentiles who were his brethren in Christ. By such conduct, so the circumcision party averred, he had begun to **live like the Gentiles and not like the Jews** ; and Paul purposely retains their cynical language so as to add point to the argument that

follows. 'Then you were ready,' he says in effect, ' to forget
that you were a Jew and to adopt what is called the Gentile
way of life. **Why** then is it that now you do precisely the
opposite, and **compel the Gentiles to become Jews ?**

This bold question, with its combination of penetrative
insight and ruthless logic, recalls the question addressed by
Jesus to those who objected to His healing in the synagogue
on the sabbath—' Is it right to help or to hurt on the sabbath,
to save life or to kill ? ' (Mark iii. 6). As the critics of Jesus
might have taken refuge in the retort that they had no thought
of hurting or killing, but were concerned merely to avoid a
breach of the Law, so here Peter might have replied that in
this matter of food Jewish-Christians had no desire to dictate
to their Gentile-Christian brothers, but for themselves they
must remember that they had their Law whose regulations
they dare not break. In other words, their solution of the
problem would have been : let the Gentile-Christians keep
their customs, while *we* keep *ours*. To Paul such a solution was
no solution at all : it emptied the gospel of its truth, and must
in the end disrupt the fellowship. ' Did Peter mean to hold,'
so we can imagine Paul asking, ' that if a Jewish-Christian
received an invitation to dine with a Gentile brother-in-Christ,
he must never accept ? And when the brethren gathered in
solemn assembly around " the table of the Lord," was there
to be one table for Jews and another for Gentiles ? ' In
refusing to accept this division in the Church Paul may have
been influenced by what he knew of the stories of Jesus, who
had defied religious tradition by eating with publicans and
sinners ; but he also saw how such a division cut across the
fundamental conception of the Church as the redeemed family
of God, the fellowship of the Holy Spirit, and would make
impossible the development of the Church as a living society.
He saw too, as Peter at the time did not see, that there were
only two ways by which the unity of Jews and Gentiles in
Christ could be maintained : either Jewish-Christians must,
as Christians, transcend the prejudices and legal restrictions
of Judaism when Christian fellowship so demanded, or else
Gentile-Christians must conform to the ways of the Jews. And

Peter, whose sympathies had led him at the outset to accept the first of these alternatives, was now (Paul argued) acting as if he acquiesced in the second. He was *obliging the Gentiles to become Jews.*

If the situation was to be reduced to these two alternatives, there is no doubt that the conservative party in the Church, with the weight of orthodox Judaism behind them, would have felt bound, in loyalty to their traditions, to choose the latter. Thus what began, on the part of the emissaries of James, in a demand addressed to *Jewish-Christians,* viz. that they should not break the law by having fellowship with Gentiles, might well end (on the part of the more uncompromising representatives of their opinion) in a demand that *Gentile-Christians* must be circumcised. And it was in this form, according to Acts xv., that certain extremists presented the issue, first at Antioch (verse 1), and then at the Council of Jerusalem (verse 5). With regard to Peter, on the other hand, his attitude towards Cornelius, his brotherly recognition of Paul at the time of the Jerusalem conversations (Gal. ii. 7–10), and (we may add) the lead which he gave soon after this at the Apostolic Council (Acts xv. 7 ff.), predispose us to believe that, once he saw the issue clearly, he would allow himself to be guided, not by Jewish Law, but by Christian love.

Critics have not always appreciated aright this incident at Antioch. It has been magnified into a battle-royal between the two apostles, and has even encouraged the belief, which figured so prominently in the presentations of the Tübingen critics, that Peter and Paul represented two opposing parties in the early Church. Such a reading of the situation is completely at variance with the facts. Peter and Paul differed indeed as regards natural endowments and training ; but in simple Christian faith they were at one (compare Paul's statement of their common belief, in verse 16) ; and they were at one also in their general attitude towards the incorporation of the Gentiles into the Church. The right of the Gentiles to full membership in the Church was first vindicated by Peter on the day when he baptized Cornelius and entered into fellowship with him.

On the other hand it is impossible to over-estimate the significance of the incident in its bearing on the development of the Christian Church. We have seen how Paul was driven to compromise at Jerusalem with regard to the circumcision of Titus, and in the circumstances he was probably justified in doing so. But had he compromised at Antioch, inevitably Jewish-Christianity and Gentile-Christianity would have developed as two separate movements, and the ideal of one Church of the Living God, purchased by the blood of Jesus Christ (cf. Acts xx. 28), would have been killed almost at birth. The episode is not without its lesson for the Church to-day. We have our several 'communions,' and Christians of one communion cannot always join with Christians of another at the table of the Lord. In some quarters even the old distinction between Jew and Gentile has asserted itself in violent form within the Church, and Gentile-Christians (now in the majority) are asked to renounce unrestricted fellowship with their Jewish brethren-in-Christ.

ii. 15–21 : *He develops more fully the point of his argument with Peter*

Paul continues his argument, soaring off now into the heights ; and though at the outset he seems still to be addressing Peter, it looks as if in the end Peter is forgotten, and what began as an account of a remonstrance with a brother-apostle changes imperceptibly into a passionate address to the readers. May we go still further and say that, before he reaches the closing sentences, Paul is so carried away by the vigour and fire of his thought that historical situations are transcended, Peter and the Galatians alike are merged for a time in a larger background, and what we have is an out-pouring of a passionate soul, absorbed in the proclamation of its own hard-won convictions ?

We may be Jews by birth and not ' Gentile sinners,' but since [15-16] **we know a man is justified simply by faith in Jesus Christ and**

not by doing what the Law commands, we ourselves have
believed in Christ Jesus so as to get justified by faith in
Christ and not by doing what the Law commands—for by
doing what the Law commands *no person shall be justified.*

17   If it is discovered that in our quest for justification in
Christ we are ' sinners ' as well as the Gentiles, does that
18   make Christ an agent of sin ? Never ! I really convict
myself of transgression when I rebuild what I destroyed.
19   For through the Law I died to the Law that I might live for
20   God ; I have been crucified with Christ, and it is no longer
I who live, Christ lives in me ; the life I now live in the flesh
I live by faith in the Son of God who loved me and gave
21   himself up for me. I do not annul God's grace ; but if
righteousness comes by way of the Law, then indeed Christ's
death was useless.

15   What we have here is a continuation of the argument of
verse 14 ; and the emphatic **we** with which the sentence opens
indicates that this is still part of Paul's reply to Peter. Paul
recalls how he and his brother-apostle are both **Jews by birth
and not ' Gentile sinners.'** Here as often the name ' sinners '
is used with reference to ritual rather than moral delinquency.
In this sense it was applied by devout Jews (i.) to those of
their own nation who were not scrupulous in observing the
Law, cf. the phrase ' publicans and sinners ' ; (ii.), as here, to
Gentiles, who as such were outside the commonwealth of
Israel. By the phrase ' Gentile sinners ' Paul represents not
his own stand-point but that of the self-conscious Jew : it was
a conventional term applied by the Jews to the ' uncircumcised.' As used here it enhances by contrast the pride
of those who could say that they were Jews by birth.

16   Paul proceeds to remind Peter of how little profit to them
had been Jewish birth and Jewish privileges. Even ' we ' came
to **know,** he says (and we remember how often Paul reminds
his readers of the truths on which their religious convictions
are based ; cf. ' we know ' in Rom. viii. 22, 28 ; 2 Cor. v. 1),
that a man is justified simply by faith in Jesus Christ and not
by doing what the Law commands. This is the text on which

all that follows in the Epistle is commentary. Here we have the first mention in the Epistle of that conception of justification which is to play so large a part in the subsequent argument. For an examination of its meaning see Introduction, p. xliii. The question behind it is : How is a God, who Himself is righteous and working out a righteous purpose, to deal with men who are unrighteous and sinful ? Strictly speaking, all men, being sinful, are deserving of God's condemnation. But God, whose righteous purpose includes the salvation of men, is willing to accept even sinful men on certain conditions. That acceptance is ' justification.' Here too we are introduced to the contrast that runs right through the Epistle between the two conceivable modes of justification, (a) by ' faith ' and (b) by what Paul succinctly calls ' works of law.' The translation generally given of the last phrase, viz. ' *the* works of *the* Law,' is perhaps not too precise ; for though the argument is applicable generally to any way of life whose guiding principle is conformity to statute-regulations, still in the present context Paul is thinking primarily of the Jewish Law and its specific demands (cf. p. 92). And even we Jews, he says (he is thinking of course of those who have become Christians like Peter and himself), know that it is not in that way that a man is justified; he is justified *simply by faith in Jesus Christ*. The Revised Version, following too slavishly the Greek in its expression of this contrast, translates : ' a man is not justified by the works of the law (or, works of law; *margin*) *save through* faith in Jesus Christ '—which might be taken to imply that conformity to law is in itself *inadequate* and requires to be supplemented by faith. Such may indeed have been the view of some Jewish-Christians, who believed that faith in Jesus Christ, with the gift of the Spirit which followed on it, enabled them to obey the Law to an extent which formerly had been impossible for them. But it was certainly not Paul's view, and our translation is clearly right in presenting the two methods of obtaining justification as contrasted alternatives, one of which is disowned in favour of the other. We may add that by the phrase ' faith of Jesus Christ ' (which is the literal translation of the Greek ; cf. Authorized Version) what is meant is without doubt ' faith *in* Christ,' and not such faith as Jesus himself made the guiding principle of life.

It is through a recognition of the inadequacy of legalism, Paul continues, that **we ourselves**, true-born Jews as we are, *came to believe* in **Christ Jesus**. ' **Have believed** ' (as in the translation) scarcely brings out the full sense : Paul describes a definite step which was taken when those who formerly did not believe in Christ came to yield themselves to Him. Concerned to emphasize that such a step was a significant one for a self-conscious Jew to take, Paul explains once more the religious situation which made it inevitable. ' We desired to be justified in God's sight : but our past failures when we tried to live by law only bore out the truth of Scripture that in God's sight **no person shall be justified** : hence for justification we turned to faith in Christ.' Paul having stated his position on the relation of legal obedience and faith (and having in fact stated it twice) clinches the matter by an appeal to Scripture. The text which he quotes is from Ps. cxliii. 2. Note, however, that he adds both here and in Rom. iii. 20, where he appeals to the same text, the significant phrase which is not in the Psalm, viz. ' by (the) works of (the) law.' Evidently Paul had no misgiving that, by so adapting the words of the Psalm, he was modifying essentially the meaning ; and from one point of view he was not modifying it, for the preceding sentence in the Psalm, ' Enter not into judgment with thy servant,' indicates that what the Psalmist has in mind is the impossibility of receiving justification on a legalistic basis. It must not be forgotten that the central current in the religion of Israel, such as can be traced in the Prophets and in the Psalms, was as truly evangelical and anti-legalist as Pauline Christianity.

17 The sentence which follows is difficult, and various interpretations have been suggested ; here we shall confine ourselves to the one which seems best to cover the facts.

Throughout this whole argument Paul, still ostensibly addressing Peter, presents his case as sympathetically as possible from the point of view of men who were born Jews. He shows how, in this vital matter of obtaining justification in God's sight, the Jew, for all his privileges (including God's great gift of the Law) discovers himself to be in no better a position than the Gentile, for the simple reason that no one, Jew or Gentile, can so keep the Law as to merit justification. Thus in the presence of a righteous God **it is discovered**, he acknowledges, that **we** who are Jews **are sinners as well as the Gentiles,** and **in our quest for justification** (righteousness) we must seek it, not by conforming to divine regulations, but by faith **in Christ.** Such was the Pauline position. The self-conscious Jew, on the other hand, who valued Jewish privilege and desired to stand fast by Jewish tradition, approached this whole question from an entirely different angle, and all the main terms in the discussion had a somewhat different meaning for him from that which they had for the apostle. To the legalistic Jew all men were *not* equally sinners in God's sight. Rather there were two quite distinct classes, ' the righteous ' and ' the sinners ' (our Lord makes play with this distinction in Mark ii. 17), the line of demarcation being found in the attitude adopted towards God's holy Law ; and Gentiles of course were classed among ' the sinners ' (cf. the phrase ' Gentile sinners ' in verse 15). When a Jew or Jewish-Christian of this rigorous type saw evangelically minded Jewish-Christians such as Peter and Paul so far forgetting their heritage as to rank themselves before God as no better than the Gentiles and to fraternize freely with their Gentile brethren-in-Christ, it seemed to him that they were sinking to the level of the Gentiles, *making themselves ' sinners ' just as the Gentiles were.* And in fairness to the Jew it ought to be remembered that in making this criticism he was not thinking *solely* of ceremonial or legal righteousness ; he was only too conscious how low were the standards of morality in the Gentile world, and accordingly was profoundly concerned lest fraternization should reduce the Jew to the Gentile level. Thus a form of words such as is found in verse 17 could be used by Paul and other devout Jewish-Christians in one sense, as a statement of simple religious faith, and interpreted by their legalistic opponents in quite another, viz. as a measure of the degradation into which Paul was leading Jewish-Christians.

It is this double meaning which explains the point of Paul's argument.

Thus interpreting, or misinterpreting, the Christian position, the rigorous Jewish-Christian (and with him the unbelieving Jew) was tempted to say that what faith in Christ did for Paul and for those who sided with him was to take good Jews and make them ' sinners '—sinners like the Gentiles ! As we have seen, there was a sense in which Paul would readily have accepted such a statement—even though, of course, he would have added that it was only half the truth, for in making men sinners (with a realization of their sinfulness) Christ was taking the first and necessary step towards their ultimate justification. But in the form in which it was presented by his opponents the argument was meant to prove conclusively that *there was something fundamentally wrong with Pauline Christianity.* Paul's doctrine and practice, it was said, was degrading to the Jew who accepted it ; nay more, it was dishonouring to Christ. Surely the work of Christ, who had said He had come not to destroy but to fulfil (Matt. v. 17), was to enable the Jews to rise to the height of their calling, not to make them sink to the level of Gentile sinners. He was an agent of righteousness ; but Paul was making Him out to be an **agent of sin !**

18   Paul knew that such an argument was used by his opponents —he probably knew too that it had been brought to bear upon Peter, and had contributed to his vacillation ; so now he turns to rend it. The emphatic **Never** (*God forbid*, Authorized Version—an expression of indignant repudiation found again in iii. 21, and no fewer than ten times in Romans) is regularly used by him to demolish an argument which according to *human* standards might appear to be logically sound, but whose conclusion is wholly incompatible with the known character and purposes of *God.* Paul has no patience with human disputations which ignore the truths of revealed religion (cf. 1 Cor. i. 17 ff.).

By *all* Jewish-Christians it would have been readily acknowledged that Christ could not be ' an agent of sin.' The deduction therefore which some of them drew (including Paul's

opponents, and Peter during the time of his withdrawal) was
that any policy or behaviour which so operated as to make
Christ out to be an agent of sin stood condemned, and must be
scrupulously avoided.   In other words, Jewish-Christians
must remember always that they were Jews, for whom eating
with Gentiles was forbidden ; and even faith in Christ did
not free them from the necessity of keeping the Law in that
and in other respects.   To Paul, on the other hand, such
reasoning was perverse in the extreme, for if Christ by the
Spirit led His followers to ignore or transcend the commands of
the Law, the resultant conduct could certainly not be called
‘ sin.’   ‘ Sin *does*, however, enter into the matter,’ Paul adds,
‘ and I stand *self-convicted*, if I, for whom the ultimate authority
of the Law has been abolished, begin again to let it dictate to
me how I am to live—setting myself, in other words, to **rebuild
what I destroyed.**’   By the subtle substitution at this point
of a new term in place of the ambiguous word ‘ sinner ’ of the
previous verses, Paul, with a poignant sense of reality, drives
home the plea that conduct such as he now describes is a more
direct and more serious violation of God's Law than that which
the Judaizers call ‘ sin ’ ; it is conscious wilful **transgression.**
If it be regarded as ‘ sin ’ for a Jewish-Christian to eat with
a Gentile, it is sin only in the sense of a technical breach of a
regulation ; but if a Christian allows such a regulation to
stand between him and eating with a brother-in-Christ, then
he is breaking God's Law in a much more heinous sense, for he
is doing violence to the Will of God as clearly revealed in
Christ.   For *transgression*, in this sense of a violation of moral
and spiritual standards, we may compare Gal. iii. 19, and
Paul's references to law-breaking in Rom. ii. 25–27.

In contrast to the plural *we* which he had employed in the
previous verses, when with Peter at Antioch he was examining
the position of Jewish-Christians, Paul has here slipped into
the use of the first person singular—an indication, perhaps,
that he is thinking now more definitely of his personal relation
to his readers.   What once he had said in controversy with

Peter has now crystallized into calm conviction, and in this form he seeks to share it with his misguided converts. Even so, however, Paul in verse 18 is merely stating what he believes 19 to be a general truth. In verse 19, on the other hand, he becomes direct and personal—the I here is emphatic ; and in what is one of the most moving passages in the New Testament he lays bare his very heart. The Galatians may be wayward and senseless (iii. 1), but Paul will keep back nothing if only he can win them again wholly for Christ.

Employing a double contrast between dying and living, law and God, Paul declares : **through the Law I died to the Law that I might live for God.** By dying to the Law he means that he ceased to have any direct and personal relation with it, and he implies that he had passed into a realm where the Law had no hold over him (cf. Rom. vii. 1). When he adds that death to the Law took place *through the Law*, he probably means (though the phrase is undoubtedly difficult) that it was his experience under the Law that revealed to him the Law's ineffectiveness (i.e. as a means by which a man can be ' justified ' in God's sight), and so led him to be done with it, and to seek justification in another way. Here, as in other passages, it may be debated whether ' law ' or ' the Law ' is the preferable rendering. Paul is an opponent of legalism in any form ; but in so far as his thought is concrete it is the Jewish Law that he has in mind.

The real significance of this death to law comes out in the phrase which follows—it enabled Paul to begin to *live for God* (lit. *to God*, i.e. in direct relation to God). How vehemently Paul's opponents have repudiated the implications of this contrast : ' Turning from *law* to *God* : Why, in the Law it is God Himself who speaks to man ; it is an expression of His eternal Wisdom and His eternal Will.' ' No,' replies Paul, ' the Law stands between man and God ; for God is not primarily a Law-giver enforcing His commands ; He is a Father seeking His sons.' Paul emphatically denied the *theological* implications of the Pharisaic teaching on the Law ; but above all he had a profound *religious* sense of the reality of the *life* which the Living God seeks to impart to man, a life apart from which they are dead ; and it was because the Law utterly failed to give life (cf. iii. 21) that it stood condemned, and that he personally died to it.

Paul knows that if he has died to law and now lives to God 20 it is all the result of what Christ has done for him : and this thought he now expounds with deep and tender intimacy. Paul does not encourage the belief that a man who recognizes the failure of his own ideals can of his accord turn and live to God. The old self must *die* if the new self is to *live* ; hence **I have been crucified.** But further the death of the old self and the life of the new are themselves determined by Christ's own sacrifice. *He* was crucified ; **and I have been crucified with him.** It is not that the sense of his own failures has caused Paul to turn in despair to Christ ; rather it is that the contemplation of the redeeming love of Christ has constrained him to be done with self for ever. Many strands enter into this rich thought of being *crucified with Christ.* Paul knew as a matter of religious experience how, after his conversion, the things that characterized his past life—his hopes and ideals, his ambitions and his ways of thought—all fell into nothingness, becoming, as he says in Phil. iii. 8, ' the veriest refuse ' ; and moreover, when they were once dead for him, they could never come to life again—hence the use of the perfect tense, ' I *have been* crucified.' There may even lie behind Paul's words a reminiscence of the actual scene on Calvary, or of some early account of it, and of the story of the malefactors who were ' crucified with Christ ' (Mark xv. 27). More certainly there is a recognition that in undergoing the rite of baptism the Christian shared Christ's death (cf. the fuller expression of this thought in Rom. vi. 3 ff.) before receiving the new life of the Spirit. But undoubtedly the main strand in this conception of sharing Christ's crucifixion is the experimental one. It is altogether unnecessary to appeal to the influence or even the analogy of the pagan mystery-cults.

If his crucifixion with Christ enabled Paul to be done with law, it enabled him also to enter on a life wholly devoted to God ; and this changed life he now explains in the words which follow. The thought is obscured in the Authorized Version, which adds an unnecessary clause ' nevertheless I live,' followed by an adversative ' yet.' Paul's assertion is much simpler : it is that as he (the old Paul) has been crucified, Christ now lives in him instead. It is unfortunate that in English we cannot retain the succinct and stately order of the Greek : ' and live no longer I, there liveth in me Christ.' Here as in all similar attempts to analyse personality we are exposed to the ambiguity of such terms as ' I ' and ' self ' and ' life.' Paul claims that the old life, the life of the natural man, the life that is merely ' in the flesh,' has given place to a life of which Christ has taken so complete possession that he can say : ' it is no longer I who live, Christ lives in me.' Paul, the natural man, Paul the self-assured and self-righteous Pharisee, has gone out, and Christ has come in. How much this means may be gauged from his references to the self-consciousness and pride that characterized his life previous to his conversion (cf. Gal. i. 13 ff. ; Phil. iii. 4 ff. ; 2 Cor. xi. 22). But Paul has learned the lesson which Jesus taught, viz. that the disciple must ' deny himself,' i.e. disown himself ; he must recognize that his life belongs not to himself but to the Master whom he serves. The new life might have been described by reference to the ' Spirit,' for it was because he had received the Spirit that the Christian who had been crucified with Christ could claim to be in possession of ' life ' ; and that the thought of ' life in the Spirit ' is not far from the apostle's mind is made plain by the reference which follows to the contrasted ' life in the flesh.' But at this point what Paul wishes to emphasize is not the spiritual character of the new life but the fact that it is a life which acknowledges a new mastery, a life which has its beginning and its end in Christ. We have here a different aspect of Paul's ' Christ-mysticism ' (on this see Introduction, p. xliv.) from that which is expressed in the conception of the believer's life *in Christ*. The believer lives *in Christ* as a member of a fellowship (cf. note on p. 103) ; but when Paul asserts ' Christ lives in me,' he describes rather a transformation of the personal life.

Paul goes on to express the same thought in a new form—

less epigrammatic, it is true, than the preceding, but no less poignant and no less triumphant. Some of the phrases in this part of the sentence are not without difficulty. Even the believer who has received the Spirit of God and is called therefore to lead the life of the Spirit (cf. v. 16) does not cease thereby to **live in the flesh**. To live in the flesh is to live in a body of flesh, a body subject to all the ills of the flesh, and exposed to sin and death. The Christian is not here and now delivered out of the present evil world ; he is called to go on living in it, and to the outward eye there is no difference between him and other men. But inwardly there is a difference. The difference is that he does not stand alone, but is united by **faith** to **the Son of God**. Literally Paul's words are : ' I live in faith of the Son of God ' (Authorized Version), but they must be taken to imply that he goes through life in trustful and confident reliance on One with whom he enjoys spiritual communion. We have here another instance of Christ-mysticism, for even though the sentence reaches its climax in a reference to Christ's self-sacrificing death, Paul's reliance is not solely on Christ's ' finished work,' but rather on His unseen presence and fellowship. It is noteworthy that the name by which Jesus is referred to is *the Son of God*.[1] The reason no doubt is that the faith Paul has mainly in mind is not faith in Christ as risen and ascended, but faith in one who, ' though he was divine by nature ' (Phil. ii. 6), humbled himself by taking flesh and subjecting himself to all the powers of this world, thereby becoming in all respects like unto his brethren (cf. the use of the term ' Son ' in a similar context in iv. 4, 5). Christ's humiliation and self-identification with His needy brethren of earth has never been more movingly described than in the simple tender words which follow : **who loved me and gave himself up for me**.

Every word here is rich in meaning. A history lies behind the words ' who gave Himself up.' In using this phrase with regard to their crucified Lord the early Christians who knew

---

[1] Another reading, which gives *God and Christ* in place of *Son of God*, is not to be set aside lightly, attested as it is by Codex B and many Western authorities.

Greek doubtless remembered how the same expression was used in the familiar passage in Isaiah (LXX Version) regarding the Servant of Jehovah, ' who poured out his soul unto death.' It was indeed in the sacrifice of Jesus that that prophecy had found fulfilment. The same word was familiar to them in the story of the ' betrayal ' of Jesus by Judas ; but it was not really Judas, they knew, who gave Him up, rather *He gave Himself up*. That death on Calvary was not a mere act of violence on the part of wicked men (Acts ii. 23) ; it was an act of willing surrender on the part of the Son of God. Himself.

Meditating on the death of Christ, His followers were led to see in it (and no one saw this more clearly than Paul) an evidence of divine *grace* ; but analysing it further they saw how it must have originated in divine *love*. *He loved me*. In the Synoptic Gospels Jesus does not once use the term ' love ' to describe His own attitude, or the attitude of God, to men. What was it then, we may ask, which gave the early Christians their unshakable conviction that all things were overruled by ' love ' ? Undoubtedly it was the vicarious death of Christ. ' God proves His love for us by this, that Christ died for us when we were still sinners ' (Rom. v. 8). They were sure that *God* loved them because they saw how by His death *Christ* loved them.

Finally, the love of Christ was real to these Christian believers because it was a love directed to each one of them *personally*. It was not merely that ' God loved the world ' (John iii. 16) or that ' Christ loved the Church ' (Eph. v. 25) ; every man who was redeemed could say ' Christ loved *me*, and gave Himself up for *me*.' Paul, the self-conscious Pharisee, had come to realize the truth of this in his own life ; and if it would help the Galatians he would not scruple to avow it.

21   What does Paul mean when in a closing sentence he says : ' I do not annul God's grace ' ? Ought we mentally to supply the words ' as you say I do ' ? In other words, have his opponents been urging against him that he ignores the grace which God had always shown to Israel, that grace which He

had manifested especially in the great gift of the Law? A preferable explanation reveals the apostle in a mood, not of defence, but of attack. 'I refuse,' he says, 'to annul the grace of God, as the Judaizers and those who follow them are really doing.' He explains his meaning more clearly in the words which follow, the correct connecting particle being not 'but' as in the translation, but 'for.' The orthodox Jewish position, carried forward by the Judaizing party into the Church, was that the Law was given by God for men to keep, and that righteousness (i.e. justification or acceptance by God) was accorded to those who kept it. What Christ does on this view is to help men to keep the Law. Paul trenchantly declares that, if righteousness comes in that way, then indeed Christ's death was useless ; there was no need for Him to die. As understood by Paul, Christ's death was essentially a *redemptive* act ; but clearly redemption is meaningless and unnecessary if we can win acceptance in God's sight by the things which we ourselves do.

III. THE TRUTH OF THE GOSPEL (iii. 1–v. 1)

Having by an appeal to historical facts vindicated his gospel against assaults on its *authority*—he got it by revelation from Jesus Christ, and was in no way dependent for it on those who went before him—Paul now goes on to vindicate it against those who challenge its *truth*. The treatment of this theme, for which he has provided an unpremeditated transition by his sublime argument in ii. 15–21, is to occupy him throughout chap. iii. and iv., where, contrasting his gospel of grace with a legalistic gospel, he appeals successively to experience, to Scripture, and to reason.

iii. 1–5 : *Paul addresses a personal appeal to the Galatians.*
The experience of the past, when they received the Spirit, ought
to guide them with regard to the present

iii.

O senseless Galatians, who has bewitched you—you who had 1
Jesus Christ the crucified placarded before your very eyes ?

2 I simply want to ask you one thing : did you receive the
   Spirit by doing what the Law commands or by believing
3 the gospel message ? Are you such fools ? Did you
   begin with the spirit only to end now with the flesh ?
4 Have you had all that experience for nothing (if it has really
5 gone for nothing) ? When He supplies you with the
   Spirit and works miracles among you, is it because you
   do what the Law commands or because you believe the
   gospel message ?

The argument begins by an appeal to the experience of the
Galatians themselves. Behind all that Paul writes there glows
a passionate interest in the men and women whom he addresses,
and whose salvation he strives to secure against all the
enemies that imperil it. He and his converts are united by
living ties of a rich common spiritual experience. Thus he
reminds the Thessalonian Christians (1 Thess. i. 5 ; ii. 13)
that the gospel came to them not with words merely but with
power ; when he came to the Corinthians (1 Cor. ii. 1–5) the
success of his preaching depended solely on the proof supplied
by the Spirit, and he reminds them later (2 Cor. iii. 2 ff.) that
his converts are the only certificate he needs, written not with
ink but with the Spirit of God. In our present passage the
personal note comes out not merely in the fact of this appeal
to experience, but in the apostle's direct method of approach
to his hearers—he calls them by name, he asks them questions, and appeal is combined with affectionate remonstrance.

1 On the use of the name **Galatians** see Introduction, p. **xxi**.
Paul is deeply stirred when he addresses his readers in this
direct way (cf. 2 Cor. vi. 11). In calling them **senseless** he is
not reproaching them for being devoid of intellectual acumen,
but lamenting their lack of spiritual perception. The same
word is used in Luke xxiv. 25 of men who are ' slow of heart
to believe ' ; one may compare the Psalmist's ' fool '
(Ps. xiv. 1) who says there is no God. So senseless is their
conduct in view of what went before that it looks as if somehow they had been **bewitched**. Without necessarily implying
that he himself believed in magical arts, Paul uses a verb

which suggests the influence of a spell, more particularly perhaps of the evil eye, and which carries with it, as Lightfoot reminds us, the two-fold idea of ' (i.) the baleful influence on the recipient and (ii.) the envious spirit of the agent.' We may recall how, in 2 Thess. ii. 11, Paul alludes to ' an active delusion ' (in that case sent by God) which leads its victims to believe a lie. The words occurring in the Authorized Version, ' that ye should not obey the truth ' have been wrongly introduced into the text here from chap. v., verse 7.

The apostle recalls how in his preaching he had placarded before their very eyes the proclamation regarding Jesus Christ the crucified. The words ' among you ' which follow ' crucified ' in the Authorized Version are no part of the original text. Here the reference to ' eyes ' catches up the previous reference to bewitchment : if only their eyes had been fixed steadily on the great proclamation which had been put before them regarding the Messiah, they would not have fallen so easy a prey to this evil spell.

The significance of the death of Christ on the cross is central in Paul's message of salvation, and in no epistle is it emphasized more strongly than in Galatians ; but in his public preaching, and more particularly in his teaching to his converts, it is clear that besides dealing with its significance he must also have given an account of the event itself as a historical occurrence. The space allotted to the Passion-narrative in each of our canonical Gospels is a reminder that the earliest Christians were trained to know that story as they knew no other. As to the further question whether Paul himself may have seen Christ nailed to the cross, we can of course have no sure knowledge. While he certainly had no direct responsibility for the death of Christ (he accuses himself of having persecuted the Church—Gal. i. 13—but never of having had a share in the death of the Son of God), it is probable that he was at that time resident as a young student in Jerusalem ; and from what he himself tells us of his youthful ardour and abilities (Gal. i. 14) we may infer with some confidence that he would have interested himself keenly in the discussions and developments of that fateful week in Jesus' ministry, and would have found satisfaction as a keen young Pharisee in seeing how the blasphemer had been brought to the death he deserved. There is therefore no inherent improbability in the suggestion that Paul may have been an eye-witness of the scene on Calvary, and so have been able from personal experience to paint an unforgettable picture of that wondrous cross which he called on his hearers to survey.

It has even been suggested that behind Paul's language here there lies the metaphor of a picture, the word translated ' placarded ' being taken to mean ' depicted.' But what the apostle has in mind is rather the familiar practice of making public announcements by means of bills or posters. In this case the announcement read : *Messiah Jesus Crucified*. (The definite article, which appears in the translation before ' crucified,' is not in the Greek.) Had Paul, we may ask, been impressed by the eager concern with which people would stop to read a notice posted up in the street, recognizing in it something which directly affected them—some benefit, e.g., to be conferred, some demand to be exacted ? And when the greatest of all possible announcements was placarded before them, were they to pass it by (or, as the Galatians were now doing, to turn away from it) as if it meant nothing to them (cf. Lam. i. 12) ? It ought always to be remembered that to those who first heard it the announcement of the crucifixion of the Messiah meant something far more arresting and far more terrible than that He had died ; it meant that He had been taken by violence and subjected to the most degrading of deaths. Here in describing that death Paul uses, not the aorist tense, but the perfect : denoting not the *act* but the *state* of being crucified. In other words, what is announced is not the historical fact of the crucifixion but rather the eternal truth which that fact embodies, viz. that the Messiah on whom men are called to believe, and to whose coming as Saviour or Judge they must look forward, is one to whom for ever belongs the reproach, or the glory, of being *a crucified Messiah*. This is an announcement which men cannot afford to read with an empty wonder, as if what it deals with, however wonderful, is something now past and done with ; it is one to which they must give earnest heed, for it has an abiding significance.

In his missionary preaching Paul had placarded this announcement before the eyes of the Galatians, and (as we can see from the Epistle) had trained them to see in it a ' gospel,' a message of deliverance from this present evil 2 world. And, hearing the message, the Galatians had accepted it with ready faith, and in consequence of their faith they had been enabled to receive the gift of the Spirit. Of all this Paul pleadingly reminds them. That coming of the Spirit among them was a reality which, he knows, they fully recognized— he refers to it again in verses 3 and 5 ; and was it by doing what the Law commands that they had received it, or simply by believing the gospel message ? Here question follows question, and in each the thought is so closely packed (note the alternative in verse 2, the antitheses in verse 3, and the condensed expressions translated in the Authorized Version ' the works of the law,' ' the hearing of faith ') that we feel welling up in the apostle's soul more questions than the pen can cope with. Special interest attaches to the difficult phrase ' the hearing of faith,' translated above ' believing the gospel message.' Rom. x. 17 helps us to understand it. There we see that in using it Paul recalls the words of Isa. liii. 1 (LXX Version) : ' Who hath believed our report ? ' (i.e. ' Who could have believed what we have heard ? ') No passage in the Old Testament seemed to the primitive Church (and the same of course is true of the Church throughout all its history) to point forward more arrestingly to the gospel message than the sublime prophecy in which Isaiah tells of the vicarious sufferings of the Servant of Jehovah ; and it was also noted that that same prophecy sounded as one of its opening notes the need for ' belief ' in the message which was proclaimed. (With the Pauline passages we may compare Heb. iv. 2.) Hence Isaiah's phrase about ' believing in what is heard ' suggests to Paul the cognate thought of ' listening in such a way that faith follows.' ' The hearing of faith ' means ' the hearing which leads on to faith.'

From now onwards throughout this chapter we shall see

how much of Paul's argument is built up on an appeal to the Old Testament. There is good reason to think that here, as elsewhere in early Christian literature, we may see the influence of a collection of proof-texts from Scripture which the early Christians used in confirming the faith of the brethren, and in enlisting the sympathy or refuting the opposition of their fellow-Jews.

Verse 2 therefore puts in a nutshell the issue between Paul and his Galatian converts as it presented itself to his clear vision. Did the gift of the Spirit come to you, he asks, because you were already following a course of action prescribed by law, or because, when the gospel message was proclaimed to you, you adopted a responsive attitude, listening to it with eager attention, and believing it, and so opening your hearts to receive what God had to give you ? Presented with irresistible cogency the question admits of only one answer, and 3 Paul does not await for it to be forthcoming ; how can they be such fools (the word is the same as ' senseless ' in verse 1) as to play with the other alternative ? Rushing on, he seeks to put his case in another form, employing a double antithesis between ' beginning ' and ' ending,' ' spirit ' and ' flesh.' Despite the demand which religion always makes for spiritual advancement, is your aim, he asks, to end up on a lower plane than that on which you began, as certainly will be the case if in violation of another fundamental law of the spiritual world you exalt flesh over spirit. In the first of these contrasts (' begin ' and ' end ') Paul is probably facing a contention of the Judaizers that to attain to full salvation the Galatians must not rest satisfied with merely believing the gospel. Just as in some of the heathen religions there were ' stages ' through which the initiate passed on his way to ' spiritual completeness,' so, too, belief in Christ seemed to the Judaizers to provide a useful stage by which pagans could come in the end to full incorporation in God's covenanted people Israel. Paul, too, believes in spiritual advancement, but this for him is not the true line of advance. In violent opposition to the Judaizing view, he insists that the issue, which already he had represented as one between ' doing what the Law commands '

and ' believing the gospel message,' is in the last resort one
between flesh and spirit. To the modern reader this contention may seem rhetorical rather than logical, for ' the
flesh ' in this case is not the seat of the appetites but the
flesh which was marked by circumcision, and ' the spirit '
refers rather to the Spirit of God received by men than to the
spiritual side of human nature. To Paul himself the contrast
is not a mere matter of rhetoric. He knows nothing of the
so-called ' spirit ' of man (with a small ' s ' as in the translation) as distinct from the Spirit which God imparts to men ;
man is ' flesh ' except in so far as he is under the influence of
the Spirit of God (on Paul's view of flesh and Spirit see Introduction, p. xl.). The Galatians might have replied that by
accepting circumcision they were not necessarily resisting the
Spirit. Paul wishes them to realize that they assuredly are
doing so. To attach value to circumcision when the Spirit
has been received without it is to deny the value attaching to
the Spirit, and any such glorying in the flesh (cf. Gal. vi. 3 ;
Phil. iii. 3 ff.) is a sign of spiritual retrogression, and not of
progress.

Dropping argument for quiet appeal, Paul goes on to ask, 4
Have you had all that experience for nothing ? The Galatians
would know to what experiences he was referring ; we on the
other hand can only guess. The Greek verb which Paul uses
(*paschō*, normally translated *suffer*) does not in itself define
the experiences as either good or evil ; it merely denotes that
the people in question are recipients rather than agents.
Some interpreters accordingly take the reference as being to
the *spiritual experiences* of the Galatians following on their
reception of the Holy Spirit. On the other hand it is to be
noted (i.) that in Scripture this Greek verb is not elsewhere
used in a good sense ; (ii.) that in general it is so used only when
the context or some accompanying phrase makes the sense
plain, as is scarcely done here by Paul's vague term ' all those
things ' (lit. *so many things*, or it may perhaps be *so great
things*). Hence it seems more natural to regard Paul as
appealing here to *the sufferings* which the Galatians had en-
dured for the faith. Any attempt to identify these sufferings

more definitely would be precarious, for no matter what
was the precise date or destination of the Epistle, persecution
in some form or another was not likely to be unknown among
those to whom it was addressed ; but advocates of the South
Galatian hypothesis can at least appeal to the hostility manifested against the brethren in Iconium (Acts xiv. 2), and the
persecution which is said to have been directed against the
apostles in the South Galatian towns (Acts xiv. 5, 19, 22) is
certain to have extended itself towards their followers.

Paul's previous appeal therefore to the spiritual benefits
which have accrued to his converts through their attitude of
faith in Christ is here followed by a reminder of the sufferings
which their faith has enabled them to endure. We may recall
how he reminds the brethren in Philippi (Phil. i. 29) that,
great as is the privilege of believing in Christ, it is no less a
privilege to suffer on His behalf. Here, with hope breaking
through, for the issue is not yet lost (cf. i. 6 ; iv. 11), he adds
an ' if ' clause (*if your experience can really be going for nothing*).
Paul calls on them to take note where their senseless behaviour
is carrying them, but suggests that surely it will stop short
before disaster supervenes.

5   Verse 5 sums up this appeal to experience ; in a slightly
different form it is a repetition of verse 2. The fact from which
Paul cannot get his thoughts away, the fact which transcends
in significance everything else for him, is the reality of God's
full and free and efficacious gift of **the** Spirit. That Spirit, as
the Galatians knew without any reminder from Paul, had,
ever since their conversion, been at work in their midst in a
wide variety of ways (for ' spiritual gifts ' see 1 Cor. xii.) ;
but here Paul specially mentions its operation in the performance of works of power, **miracles.** Acts xiv. 8 ff. gives an
instance of such a ' mighty work ' accomplished by Paul
himself on his visit to Galatia ; we are doubtless to infer that
others had been performed by the Galatians since Paul had
left them. The New Testament leaves no room for doubt that,
just as Jesus performed ' mighty works,' so too did many of
the early Christians, and the performance of these ' miracles '
was ascribed to the power of the Spirit. (There is a trenchant

modern discussion of this subject in Principal D. S. Cairns'
book, *The Faith that Rebels.*)

iii. 6 : *Appeal is made to the case of Abraham, who was justified,*
according to Scripture, by his faith in God

Why, it is as with Abraham, *he had faith in God and that was* **6**
counted to him as righteousness.

Paul's summing up in verse 5, with its reiterated contrast **6**
between ' doing what the Law demands ' and ' believing the
gospel message,' is now enforced by an appeal to the typical
case of **Abraham.** With verse 6 serving as a transition Paul
passes from direct remonstrance (verses 1-5) to a long general
argument based on God's acceptance of Abraham, or, as we
may put it, from the personal question : ' How did you
Galatians win your acceptance with God ? ' to the larger and
more general question : ' Who are the people whom God
accepts and on what basis are they accepted ? '

Why does Paul cite the case of Abraham ? It is not that he
is himself here opening up a new subject of controversy ;
rather it is that his opponents have already based their case
on an appeal to the case of the patriarch, and Paul now sets
himself to refute them. It may clarify our thoughts on
this matter if we remember that the case of Abraham, the
founder of the Jewish race, which here (cf. Rom. iv. ; James
ii.) provides a basis of controversy between two different
parties within the Christian Church, is one which appears to
have been frequently discussed in opposing schools of Judaism,
and continued to be a subject of debate between Jews and
Christians. Paul in his days of training as a rabbi may often
have heard the subject discussed and, both then and later, as
a Christian, have taken part in debates on it. The legalistic
section of Jewish opinion, followed by the legalistic section of
the Christian Church, laid stress, as we have seen, on the terms
of the covenant of circumcision made with Abraham. The
evangelical party, whether in Judaism or, as in Paul's case
here, among the Christians, emphasized rather the fact,

Kᴑ   83

recorded in Scripture (Gen. xv. 6), that Abraham had shown faith in God, and that his faith had been counted to him for righteousness.

It is a matter of some significance that, while the story of Abraham's circumcision belongs to that later source of the Pentateuch which we call the Priestly Code, most of the Old Testament stories of Abraham, including the one from which Paul takes his text here, belong to the source (JE) which we associate with the teaching of the early prophets. They reveal accordingly a religious attitude which is not merely different from, but opposed to, the legalism which became so pronounced during and after the Exile. It is therefore not surprising that these stories of Abraham's faith should have exercised a strong appeal for Jews of a later date whose religious sympathies were not with the legalist. Thus Philo, the syncretistic philosopher of Alexandria, refers again and again in his writings to the faith of Abraham, and indeed his whole teaching on faith seems to be moulded in accordance with the Old Testament stories of the patriarch. And from the eleventh chapter of the Epistle to the Hebrews we can see that there was a ready disposition in certain quarters to regard Abraham's whole life as regulated by faith in the Unseen.

For a true understanding of Paul's argument at this point it is well to note the precise connection between verse 6 and the passage which precedes. In the Greek, verse 6 is introduced by the simple conjunction *kathōs* (' even as,' Authorized Version and Revised Version), and this has often led to the mistaken idea that verse 6 is essentially a subordinate clause dependent on verse 5, so that Paul's appeal to the Galatians in verses 1–5 is regarded as clinched and closed by the quotation from Scripture in verse 6 or by the subsequent summing-up in verse 7. Such an interpretation obscures the real point of Paul's argument. The Greek word *kathōs* is regularly used to mark the introduction of a new topic, the statement as it were of a text on which the commentary is to follow (cf. Mark i. 2 ; 1 Tim. i. 3). And so here Paul's expostulation with his foolish converts in verses 1–5 naturally leads him on to appeal to the typical case of Abraham : **Why, it is as it was with Abraham,** and the theme thus introduced really continues to the end of chap. iv., when expostulation, direct and eager, which occasionally finds expression even in the midst of the exposition of the case of Abraham, bursts forth afresh in chap. v.

Bound up with the foregoing is the other and more important question of the strict *relevance* in the present connection of any appeal to the words of Gen. xv. 6. It is one of the tenets of modern Biblical criticism that Scripture passages ought to be studied in their original context ; and the text which is here quoted has reference to Abraham's attitude to God when the promise was made to him that he would yet have a son and that his descendants would be as numerous as the stars. Abraham's **faith in God,** it may be said, was nothing more than reliance on a divine promise ; and what has a simple confident trust to do with the faith that believes in a crucified Messiah, and how can it possibly provide an argument for the superiority of such faith to the performance of the commands of the Law ? Is it not a fatal flaw in the use of Abraham as an analogy that the Biblical story nowhere represents him as a sinner who attains to forgiveness in virtue of his faith ? Such an objection would not for a moment have been admitted by the apostle ; even his opponents, while they denied the validity of his argument, would not have denied its relevance. Hence before assenting to the charge of irrelevance it would be well for us to consider whether we have penetrated sufficiently into the depths of the apostle's thought.

There are two considerations which it is important to keep before us. (i.) There is the fact to which we have just alluded, viz. that the words quoted in verse 6 are not meant, in themselves, and without further exposition, to provide an obvious parallel to the case described in verses 1–5 ; they are the text for an argument, and the question of relevance cannot be decided until we see how the argument is developed. (ii) Faith in God, that trustful attitude to the Unseen which is backed by reliance and obedience, is in essence ever the same, no matter how it is evoked or how it is expressed. That is why Jesus can say of the centurion, whose belief in His power to heal by merely giving the word might have seemed to be mere superstition, that He had not found so great faith even in Israel. That is why the author of the Epistle to the Hebrews can take people like Rahab and Barak and those unnamed fugitives who dwelt in caves of the earth, and set them all in the ranks of the heroes of faith, with Jesus Christ at their head as ' the pioneer and the perfection of faith ' (Heb. xii. 1). To anyone who has himself entered, as Paul had done, into the full experience of a life of faith, with all that it brings of vision and freedom and all its demands for receptiveness and obedience, one of the great dividing lines of life, more clear than that between the ' good ' and the ' bad,' is that between those whose lives are ordered by faith in God and those others whose guiding principle is conformity to imposed standards.

What, it may be asked, is really meant by the phrase ' it was counted to him for righteousness ' ? The verb translated ' counted ' conveys an idea of calculation : thus in 1 Cor. xiii. 5, Paul says of love that it does not reckon up the evil. A false conception of the meaning of righteousness has sometimes caused this word ' counted ' to be wrongly interpreted as equal to ' imputed,' as if the calculation were necessarily fictitious, God counting as righteous something which He really knew was not so. Imputation in this sense ought to have no place in our reading of Scripture ; in the Revised Version the word is found only once, and that rightly, in Rom. v. 13. We may refer to what has already been said (Introduction, pp. xlvii. ff.) regarding the Scriptural meaning of righteousness. God has defined the standards by which a man can be accepted as righteous, and He regarded Abraham, in virtue of his faith, as conforming to these standards.

iii. : 7–9 : *Similarly Abraham's true sons are those who share his faith, and it is by faith that the Gentiles will inherit the blessing which it was promised that all nations would receive in him*

Well then, you see that the real sons of Abraham are those 7
who rely on faith. Besides, Scripture anticipated God's 8
justification of the Gentiles by faith when it announced
the gospel beforehand to Abraham in these terms: *All
nations shall be blessed in thee.* So that those who rely 9
on faith are blessed along with believing Abraham.

Having stated his text in verse 6, Paul proceeds to use it
as a basis for a long and sustained argument. The main lines
of this argument, as we shall see, are laid down for him by the
necessity of refuting the contentions of his judaistic opponents
who had themselves appealed to the case of Abraham; but
even more than his judaistic opponents Paul has in view his
deluded Galatian converts, and his chief aim is not to score
an argumentative success but to build up a strong dogmatic
position which will confirm his converts in the gospel which
he delivered to them.

The first section of the argument extends only to verse 9; 7
and it deals, not with the character of Abraham's faith, but
with the question: Who are **sons of Abraham**? This is
significant. The question of Abraham's sons had obviously
been raised by the Judaizers, whose argument, based on
Gen. xvii., was as follows: (i.) the divine blessings were
promised to Abraham and to *his seed*; (ii.) according to the
covenant between God and Abraham all male descendants of
Abraham were to be circumcised; (iii.) accordingly, if Gentiles
wished to inherit the promises, they must first of all become
members of the family of Abraham by circumcision. But the
question had likewise a vital importance for Paul, and it is
thoroughly in keeping with his own position that it should
be brought to the fore at the outset. Contrasting Paul and
Philo in this regard, Lightfoot (*Commentary*, p. 163) has well
pointed out that the only lesson which the Alexandrian philosopher draws from the story of the faith of Abraham has
reference to the life of the individual. ' Abraham was but a
type, a symbol of the individual man. The promises made
to him, the rich inheritance, the numerous progeny, had no
fulfilment except in the growth of his own character. The

idea of a *Church* did not enter into his reckoning. He appreciated the significance of Abraham's *faith*, but Abraham's *seed* was almost meaningless to him.' It was not so with the great apostle to the Gentiles. At the heart of his missionary enthusiasm there is ever the theocratic ideal of a God who is seeking to win for Himself a people whom He can call His own, and in whom and through whom He can execute His righteous purposes. Paul would thoroughly have agreed with calling Abraham ' the father of the faithful.' Indeed it was in his relation to his innumerable progeny that Paul saw the real significance of Abraham.

The contention of the Judaizers was too securely based on Scripture to be combated directly. Yet all that Paul has learned through Jesus Christ of the purposes of God convinces him that that contention is false. How then does he refute it ? He begins (i.) by giving an interpretation of the phrase ' sons of Abraham ' which, though it is not the literal one, is still to him a perfectly reasonable and natural one—so reasonable and natural that he introduces it with the words **Well then, you see,** which in the Greek may either be an indicative, or else (as in Authorized Version and Revised Version) an imperative. Paul's argument is here based on an idiomatic use of the word ' sons,' which is familiar in Oriental thought and is often found in the New Testament, denoting people whose lives show the characteristic mark of their origin (e.g. ' sons of thunder,' ' children of disobedience ') ; accordingly he argues that **' sons of Abraham '** (in the Greek the expression is generic, without the definite article) need not be taken genealogically, but ought rather, in view of the words just quoted in verse 5, to be interpreted, and interpreted solely, **of those who** like Abraham **rely on faith.** Paul's argument is in no sense a quibble. While he is perfectly in sympathy with the demand of the Judaizers to link up the new religion with the history and religion of the Jewish people, and indeed insists himself on doing so, as his repeated appeal to Scripture shows, still he is equally insistent that the connection must be traced along religious and not along merely tribal or national lines. We may add that the words here translated

those who rely on faith correspond to a pregnant Greek phrase,
literally, *those out of faith,* i.e. those whose lives are ordered
on a basis of faith. No attempt ought to be made to read into
the words of Dr. Moffatt's translation more than they are
meant to convey. Strictly speaking, Paul's position is that,
while Christians live by faith in Christ (cf. ii. 20), it is on
Christ, and not on their own faith in Him, that they *rely* for
salvation. The phrase really implies ' those whose lives are
directed by faith,' ' those for whom faith is a guiding principle.'

(ii.) In developing his next point Paul gets away for a 8
moment from the text of Scripture to the facts of history,
and here he appeals to something which his own experience
in Galatia had convinced him to be a fact, however much
judaizing theorists might deny it, viz. **God's justification of
the Gentiles by faith.** As the order of the Greek words unmis-
takably shows, the emphasis is entirely on the words ' by
faith '—it is in virtue of their faith, so the argument runs, and
not through their acceptance of the covenant-rite of circumcision, that the Gentiles are being accepted by God. Paul
dares to make the statement because he had seen in the case
of the Galatians, as Peter had seen in the case of Cornelius,
that they had received the gift of the Holy Spirit (cf. Acts
x. 45). The justification, we may add, is a present reality ;
but Paul is thinking of a general law of God's working, a
' mystery ' as he calls it with reference to the same theme in
Col. i. 25 ff. (cf. p. xxxi.).

From this established fact of history Paul now argues
backwards towards the true meaning of an all-important passage of **Scripture** : it was, he says, in **anticipation** of this fore-
ordained event that the promise was made to Abraham :
' **All nations shall be blessed in thee.**' The Scripture passage
in question (and by the term ' Scripture ' Paul probably does
imply a *passage* in Scripture) is not taken from the section
(Gen. xvii.) on which the Judaizers mainly built their case,
but is from Gen. xii. 3 (LXX Version), except that instead
of the word ' families ' (Gr. *phylai*) the word ' nations ' (*ethnē*)
is introduced, no doubt because the phrase ' the nations ' had

come to be used by Jews as equivalent to ' heathen nations,' ' Gentiles.' Paul therefore claims that in declaring this promise to Abraham the Scripture (by which he means God whose voice is recorded there) **announced the gospel beforehand to Abraham.** How can Paul possibly make so daring an assertion ? Loisy contends that, even if we regard the promise as actually referring to the divine blessings of salvation (and certainly, whatever the original significance,[1] this was the meaning put upon it in later Judaism, and accepted both by Paul and by his opponents), still, all that can be legitimately deduced from it is that ' the true religion will come to the nations through the medium of Israel.' Paul himself would readily have admitted this ; but he would have flung back at his objector the question, ' What is the religion of Israel ? Is it not essentially a religion of faith in God, free from all nationalistic or legalistic limitations ? ' In the story of God's dealings with Abraham, regarded simply as a story of promise and of faith, Paul saw the same principles at work as later found expression in ' the Gospel.' It is essential for us to see that in Paul's eyes God Himself does not change, whatever advancement or retrogression men may show in their appreciation of Him. His redemptive purpose in Christ was inherent in His purpose before the world began (Eph. i. 3). The gospel of justification by faith was implicit in His Word from the beginning. However much men may limit their vision of God by their mistaken loyalties to tradition or to nation, God by His very nature (so Paul would have argued) has been, is now, and ever shall be, an ' evangelical ' God, seeking to express Himself freely in what He has to *give* to men, if only they will receive it, and ' justifying ' them solely on the ground of their faith. Abraham awoke to that great truth, though his descendants in subsequent ages tended to forget it ; but it is plain, Paul contends, that if men are to be blest ' in him ' (according to the words of the promise), it

---

[1] We need not stay to consider what the words quoted meant in their original context. The contention that in the Hebrew, as opposed to the LXX Version, the meaning was merely that other nations would *bless themselves* in Abraham (i.e. in Israel), in the sense that they would regard themselves as fortunate if they could attain to the same standard of earthly blessedness as the children of Abraham, is not convincing.

can only be in so far as they learn to take their stand before God in the same spirit of faith and receptivity as Abraham did. Even, therefore, though the promise was to Abraham and to his seed, we must expect to find the inheritors of it, not in his ' sons ' according to the flesh, as the Judaizers said, but in those whose guiding principle in life is faith in God.

What then are the conclusions on which Paul would like his 9 Galatian converts to rest ? (i.) In the first place let them be assured that in company with all **those who rely on faith they are blessed.** They have already experienced blessing through the gift of the Spirit : but the reference includes also those future blessings which will be theirs in the new age after the judgment. Only indirectly has Paul referred to their justi-fication ; but his full reasoning is that they have been accepted (justified) on the basis of faith, and in consequence of this acceptance have become eligible for God's promised blessings. (ii.) In the second place they are to remember that by blessing them in this way God has fulfilled in them the promise He gave to Abraham : they **are blessed along with believing Abraham.** If any question is raised about ' Abraham's sons,' they can reply : ' We are sons of Abraham by faith, we are heirs, by faith, of the promise made to him ' ; and they can therefore be confident that neither their sonship nor their inheritance depends in any way on their acceptance of the rite of circumcision.

It is not surprising that Marcion, who sought to distinguish sharply between the doctrine of the New Testament and that of the Old, should (as we learn from Tertullian and Jerome) have preferred to omit the above section (verses 6–9).

iii. 10–14 : *On the other hand, life under the Law entails a curse; and when Christ died on the cross, it was to remove that curse from those who were under it, and to make the promised blessing available, apart from the Law, to the Gentiles*

Whereas a curse rests on all who rely upon obedience to the Law; 10 for it is written, *Cursed is everyone who does not hold by all that is written in the book of the law, to perform it.* And 11

12
13
14

> because no one is justified on the score of the Law before
> God (plainly, *the just shall live by faith,*—and the Law is
> not based on faith : no, *he who performs these things shall
> live by them*), Christ ransomed us from the curse of the
> Law by becoming accursed for us (for it is written, Cursed
> is everyone who hangs on a gibbet), that the blessing of
> Abraham might reach the Gentiles in Christ Jesus, so that
> by faith we might receive the promised Spirit.

As above he had shown that a life regulated by faith leads
on to blessing, so now, *per contra*, Paul argues that a life regulated by obedience to law involves not blessing, but a curse.
10 The key-note is struck in the words with which in the Greek
the section opens—all who rely on obedience to the Law.
Just as above Paul had used the concise expression ' those
out of faith ' to express those whose lives were ordered by
faith in God, so here the corresponding phrase ' those out of
works of law ' denotes those who seek to please God by carrying
out His prescribed regulations. As the Greek speaks not of
' the Law,' but simply of ' law,' it may be argued that at this
stage Paul is thinking generally of that attitude to God which
is called legalism, and of which the demand that Gentile
Christians should be circumcised was itself a manifestation.
Nevertheless, as the argument proceeds, it becomes plain that
in his references to *law* Paul is less concerned with abstract
principles than with historical facts ; it was the Jewish Law
that the Gentiles were being pressed to accept, and it is the
Jewish Law whose place in the divine ordering of history
now comes up for review (cf. pp. 65, 70).
Contrasting therefore with those who live by faith those
others who rely on conformity to God's commandments, Paul
seeks to show that the inevitable outcome of this second attitude to life and to God is not blessing but a curse. In the
story of Abraham there is this contrast between the blessing
and the curse (Gen. xii. 3) ; we may refer also to the catalogue of blessings and curses in Deut. xxvii. and xxviii.,
from which Paul now proceeds to quote in support of his contention. Even in the Mosaic Law itself (Deut. xxvii. 26) it is

written, Cursed is everyone who does not hold by all that is written in the book of the law, to perform it. Here then is a statement of what the Law itself requires of those who come under its authority, and the issue is plain that *they must either find a way of keeping the Law or else come under its curse.*

Paul might have been expected to follow this up by an appeal to personal experience, viz. that apart from divine help no man is able to keep the Law, and no man therefore can escape the curse. This however is not the line which his reasoning takes ; and to assume, as so many commentators do, that such a thought supplies an ' unexpressed premise ' to his argument is to misunderstand the precise point at issue. The point of view of the Judaizers, as we have already seen, was just this, that the divine help which was necessary for the perfect keeping of the Law was available now through Jesus Christ, i.e. through the gift of the Holy Spirit, and this was the belief which in turn they had sought to impress on the Galatians. It would have been useless therefore for Paul to appeal to a fact of experience which might have carried weight in an argument directed against non-Christians, but which neither his Galatian readers nor their judaizing teachers would have acknowledged as being applicable to the present dispute. Besides, it was not on personal experience but on the written Word that Paul knew his case must be built. His opponents had appealed to Scripture and from Scripture he must refute them.

How then does Paul continue the argument ? He asserts on **11** scriptural authority that **on the score of the Law** (this prepositional phrase carries the emphasis in the Greek, just as ' by faith ' does in verse 8) **no one is justified before God.** The strength of this assertion is weakened by the introduction of the word **because** in the translation. The precise syntactical construction is better preserved in the Authorized Version and Revised Version, viz. ' that on the score of the Law no one is justified before God is plain, for *the just shall live by faith.*' The Galatians are invited to keep steadily before themselves the question of *justification* on which their ultimate destiny, *blessing* or *cursing,* will depend. They have already been shown

93

how *faith* leads on to *justification* and *justification* to *blessing;*
will *justification* and *blessing* likewise follow for those who seek
to attain to them by obedience to *law* ? **Plainly,** Paul says,
they will not ; the evidence of Scripture is against it.

We need not be surprised that, in seeking Scriptural
authority for his argument, Paul does not appeal, as he did
in ii. 16, to the words from Ps. cxliii. 2, ' in Thy sight shall
no living man be justified.' As was pointed out in the commentary on that earlier passage, the relevance of the quotation
there depended on the addition of the phrase ' by doing what
the Law commands.' But while the addition was not illegitimate in the point at issue between the two apostles, where
Paul was appealing to a fact of religious experience on which
Peter and he were in fundamental agreement, it would not
have passed unchallenged in a case like the present, where a
closely reasoned argument was being built up against opponents. The Judaizers were as ready as Paul to acknowledge
that, *left to himself,* no man could be justified in God's sight ;
but they would not have agreed to interpret this as meaning
that there was no justification by ' works of law,' for their
fundamental position was that justification could be obtained
in no other way than by conformity to God's Law, and that
Christ enabled men to attain to such a measure of conformity
as would merit justification.

The Scripture evidence to which Paul does appeal is rather
that in which justification is connected (*a*) definitely with
faith and that, too, (*b*) to the exclusion of justification by the
performance of ' works of law.'

(*a*) The first text from which he quotes is Hab. ii. 4,
' the just shall live by faith ' (quoted also in Rom. i. 17, and
in a slightly different form in Heb. x. 38) ; and while in the
original Hebrew of that passage ' faith ' implied ' fidelity ' or
' steadfastness,' and the prepositional phrase ' by faith ' was
connected definitely with the verb ('shall live by faith'), Paul
quotes the words as if the sense were : ' the man who is just
(i.e. justified) on the score of faith shall *live.*' Is he here doing
violence to Scripture ? It must be remembered that for him
the true meaning of any passage was to be found, not within

the narrow limits of its historical context, but in its relation to the eternal truths of divine revelation. Had he been conscious, as almost certainly he was not, that objection could be taken to his interpretation of the phrase ' *by faith*,' we can imagine him indignantly replying that in his analysis of faith he was more thoroughgoing than those who found fault with him ; for (i.) can there be any ' fidelity ' on man's part, such as God can reward with the great gift of ' life,' which does not ultimately have its roots in man's attitude of ' faith ' in God ? and (ii.) if it is ' faith ' which makes the ' just ' man worthy to receive life, what is it but his faith which gives him originally his title to be called ' just ' ?

(*b*) Having thus shown from Scripture that *life*, the sum 12 and substance of God's blessing to the justified man, is definitely promised to the man who is just (i.e. justified) by faith, Paul now argues that the hope of obtaining the blessing is forfeited by those who base their claim to justification on legal obedience, and he gives as his reason that *the Law is not based on faith*. Paul does not mean that faith and the scrupulous observance of ordinances are wholly incompatible *in practice*. In every age the profession of evangelical religion may go hand in hand with a punctilious attention to religious observances. Certainly Paul knew that many a devout Jew who made the Law of God his delight did not cease to rely on the divine promises and trust in the divine mercy ; and it was this combination of *legal observance* and *faith* which characterized the attitude of judaizing Christians in Galatia and elsewhere. What Paul does insist on is that faith and the observance of Law are incompatible as grounds of *justification*. The Law in itself takes no account of the religious attitude of those who are under its authority ; it is concerned merely with the question of performance or non-performance, its own ruling (Lev. xviii. 5, quoted again in Rom. x. 5) being that *he who performs these things shall live by them*. If in true devoutness and humility a man asks God to enable him to fulfil the divine will, that man is justified by faith and inherits life by faith ; but if he believes that his standing before God depends on the extent to which he carries out the divine enactments, if (in other words) he seeks to be justified by what his faith enables him to accomplish, then his attitude of faith does not strictly come into consideration, and he must face the fact that, ' justification ' and ' blessing ' (' life ') being regarded as dependent on performance, non-performance must entail loss of ' blessing,' i.e. loss of ' life ' ; or, to put the same truth otherwise, he comes under the ' curse ' with which the Law visits those who do not keep its enactments (verse 10), and (though this is not expressly stated) his end is not ' life ' but ' death.'

13 Thus we come to verse 13, to many readers one of the most difficult verses in the New Testament. If some of its ideas appear to the modern reader strange and even repugnant, this means that patience and sympathy will be required of those who would understand them. At the same time we must be careful not to rest satisfied with an interpretation which, while it may be acceptable to modern thought, does not do justice to the thought of the apostle. Before seeking to give an interpretation of the verse as a whole, let us look at the expressions which Paul uses.

The connection with what goes before is provided by the expression **the curse of the Law,** which of course refers back to verse 10, where the statement was made (to be elaborated in verses 11, 12) that, for those who live under law, disobedience to law involves a curse. To Paul that curse was not mere metaphor : it was a dire reality, and he now goes on to tell how **Christ ransoms us** (i.e. those who were under the Law, and therefore also, as has just been shown, under a curse) from **the curse of the Law, by becoming accursed for us.**

The sentence is all the more impressive in the Greek because verses 11, 12 form an independent sentence, and verse 13 has no introductory particle to connect the new and contrasted statement with what goes before. Coming after all that has been said about the curse, the abrupt introduction of the name Christ suggests the appearance on the scene of one who alone can deal with so tragic a situation.

' When all was sin and shame
a second Adam to the fight
and to the rescue came.'

Christ ransomed us. Though the Greek verb originally
means ' bought us out ' (cf. the language of 1 Cor. vi. 20 ;
vii. 23), the metaphor of *payment* becomes merged in that of
deliverance. Christ has emancipated us from some form of
enslavement, described in this case as **the curse of the Law.**
For a similar triumphant exclamation about Christ ' setting
us free ' cf. v. 1. This deliverance He achieved for us, when we
were under the curse of the Law, by becoming in the fullest
sense one of us, even to the extent of sharing our curse. In
this He was a voluntary agent ; He ' gave Himself ' (as in i. 4 ;
ii. 20), the sinless for the sinner (cf. ' the just for the unjust,'
1 Pet. iii. 18), the free man for the slave, God's Holy and
Anointed One for those who in the eyes of a holy God were
accursed. It might be said of Him that He became **accursed**
along with us, as if in this respect too ' He had to resemble His
brothers' (Heb. ii. 17) ; but that leaves something still unsaid.
When such a One as Christ voluntarily submitted Himself to
the curse of the Law, it was that He might thereby *remove* the
curse from His brethren—He became accursed **for us.** It is
worth noting that in the Greek it is said that He became ' a
curse ' (not ' accursed '). Paul avoids the implication that in
His own person Christ was actually ' accursed.' He became
' a curse ' in the sense that He allowed Himself to come under
a curse, just as it is said in 2 Cor. v. 21 that He was made to be
' sin ' though He Himself knew nothing of sin.

In what sense Christ became a curse is explained by reference to the Law itself (Deut. xxi. 23). **It is written, Cursed is
everyone who hangs on a gibbet** (lit. a tree). To understand
the issue here we must recall how both those who preached
the gospel and those who controverted it appealed continually
to Scripture texts ; and the text which Paul quotes here in
support of the faith was already a familiar weapon in the
hands of Jewish antagonists. In its original context the text
referred, not to the putting to death by some form of impaling

or crucifixion, but to the barbarous practice of hanging up
and leaving exposed the body of a criminal after death, by
which act it was felt the land was defiled. But the prevalence
of crucifixion in Roman times, and the horror with which such
a form of punishment was regarded, made it easy to include
in the reference of the text those who had been made to suffer
this ignominious fate ; and, in particular, opponents of the
gospel had here ready to hand what seemed a direct word
of Scripture in condemnation of the Christian Messiah—
' accursed by God ' (or, according to another interpretation
of the original Hebrew, ' an insult offered to God ') ' is it for
a man to be left hanging on a gibbet.' Had not Paul himself,
in the days before his conversion, allowed these terrible words
to blind his eyes to the truth as it was in Jesus ? And had
he not, in the years that followed, had to listen to the same
words flung at him by bitter and intolerant revilers—while he
proclaimed ' Jesus is Lord,' their cry being ' Jesus is Anath-
ema ' (I Cor. xii. 3) ? What is more, did not the followers
of Jesus believe that it was of Him that it had been written
beforehand, that He should be as one ' smitten of God '
(Isa. liii. 4) ? And was it not a historical fact—one of those
features in the story of the Cross which added immeasurably
to the heights and depths of its significance—that Christ Himself in His dying agony had cried aloud about being ' forsaken '
by God (Mark xiv. 34), thus revealing how little seemed to
separate His fate from divine rejection ? And, conscious of
all those things, must not Paul, in his personal faith and in
his preaching, have realized how hard it would have been to
interpret the crucifixion of Christ in any other way than as a
curse, were it not for the fact that in His life Christ was the
sinless Son of God, and that after His death on that Cross He
had been raised from the dead ? But the resurrection being a
fact Paul, in common with other Christians, accepted the
challenge of the Cross (cf. the use of the same quotation in
Peter's sermon in Acts x. 39, and the reference to ' the tree '
in I Pet. ii. 24) ; and here he goes further, boldly claiming
for that curse a place in the Christian scheme of salvation.
Christ did indeed become ' a curse,' but He did so by an act

of self-dedication and He did so on our behalf, taking on Himself the curse which really was ours, that we in our turn might be delivered from it.

Who were the people whom Christ ransomed from the curse of the Law ? By ' us ' Paul clearly means all who, like himself (and, we may add, like the Judaizers, who are never far from his thoughts as he writes) were under the Law—all those sons of Abraham who in course of time came under the Law, including the humblest believer who in true piety combined with his devotion to the Torah a trustful reliance on divine grace. There is no reference here to non-Jews, for though Paul might have said that Christ died for them too, Christ did not die to deliver them from the curse of the Law. In other words, Paul is not dealing here with the religious truth that all men are sinners ; He is dealing with the historical truth that, in working out His eternal purpose of blessing the nations in Abraham and his seed, God intervened in Christ to deliver the seed of Abraham from the curse which (again, as part of that purpose) had overtaken them through their subjection to the Law. Indeed there is an emphatic contrast between the ' us ' of verse 13 and ' the Gentiles ' in verse 14, as may be seen from the order of the Greek words in the latter case ; it is by the deliverance of Israel from the curse of the Law that God made it possible for the blessing promised to Abraham to extend to the Gentiles. Thus by Christ's ransom Paul is not to be regarded as referring merely to a spiritual experience in the individual soul ; rather he is describing the central event on which, as on a pivot, turned all God's purpose for the redemption and the blessing of His people.

Surveying now Paul's statement as a whole we must ask ourselves : in what sense can Paul, believing as he does in the Father of the Lord Jesus Christ, dare to assert that a section of God's people came under so terrible a curse that the death of Christ was required to ransom them from it, and that in

Lo

paying the ransom-price Christ Himself became ' a curse ' on their behalf ? Faced with such a question, it is not surprising that many commentators have taken the line that Paul does not here mean all that he appears to say. As regards the curse of the Law, he is not (we are told) presenting a statement of his own religious beliefs ; rather he is forcing his readers to recognize the tragic result which would inevitably follow if it were true (as the Judaizers contended) that God demanded of men conformity to divine enactments. Thus Burton, in his *Commentary* (*ad loc.*), says of the curse : ' This is not the judgment of God. To miss this fact is wholly to misunderstand Paul ' ; and he adds : ' If the curse is not an expression of God's attitude towards men, neither is the deliverance from it a judicial act in the sense of release from penalty, but a release from a false conception of God's attitude, viz. from the belief that God actually deals with men on a legalistic basis.' Similarly, when Paul says that Christ became accursed, this does not mean (it is said) that He became accursed in the sight of God as God really is, but only in the sight of such a God as legalists believe in.

There is obviously a measure of truth in these contentions. The curse of which Paul speaks is called *the curse of the Law*— not the curse of God ; and in the quotation from Deuteronomy the words ' cursed by God' which appear in the LXX. are replaced by the one word ' cursed.' Nevertheless we must not be content with taking out of Paul's language less than there is for us to take. He is saying something far more than that behind legalism there is a false or inadequate *conception* of God. If that were all, the curse of the Law might be evaded by saying: 'Let us lay aside the attempt to live by law and get back to a life of simple faith.' But the situation as Paul saw it could never be met by a mere change of attitude on the part of man. Under the Law God's people had come into such a condition that God Himself had to intervene on their behalf. The curse was, for those who were implicated in it, something so real and inexorable that they required *deliverance*; and in no other way could they be delivered except through the action of One who Himself was under the Law as they were (cf. iv. 4) and who voluntarily took on Himself the curse which was theirs. And if Paul does not say in so many words that the curse was imposed by God, he nevertheless believed, as his subsequent argument shows, that the Law which brought the curse in its train was introduced in order to further the divine purpose of redemption ; and in so far as God was behind the giving of the Law, so far also was He a party to the curse. The Law is certainly not a complete revelation of the character and purpose of God ; but it does have for Paul an essential place in His providential order. Thus the God who put a section of His people under the Law, with all that the Law brought of curse and of blessing, was the same God who in the fullness of time manifested His grace in the gift of His Son. We are doing an injustice to the righteousness of God in face of the world's sin unless we see that in leading men to know His demands He inevitably imposes a curse on their disobedience ; but in so doing He is in no sense violating His own grace, seeing that, in the very imposition of the curse, He has already planned for men a way of escape from it.

Paul does not explain precisely how Christ's taking the curse on Himself accomplished the deliverance of others. No doubt he felt that when the Law, even in one particular, brings God's own Christ under its condemnation it is, as a revelation of the mind and will of God, so thoroughly discredited as to lose its authority and validity. Such a law cannot clearly be accepted as God's last word to men. There must be a higher authority, one which Christ Himself obeyed when He gave Himself to be crucified ; and in leading us to this higher authority Christ has delivered us from the domination and the curse of the lower. We shall not understand Paul's language here unless we read it in the light of the Christological beliefs which filled the souls of the early Christians, viz. that He who died for them was not merely in His earthly life sinless (and therefore immune from the curse of the Law), but was One who by His resurrection from the dead had been declared by God to be the Messiah, the Lord—not merely *a* representative therefore of the people, but *the* supreme representative, and the representative not of the people merely, but of God Himself. We must remember that the men to whom the apostle's argument was addressed (including the judaizing preachers who, even more than the Galatians, were present to his mind throughout this section) were themselves Christians, who believed as he did that Christ had provided a deliverance for those who otherwise were exposed to wrath and condemnation. And this fact must not be lost sight of when we consider the meaning of the passage for our own day. Paul is not here developing a philosophy of history for unbelievers. He is pointing out, with special reference to the Jewish Law, what the significance of Christ's redemption was for those who were themselves under that Law, and who accepted that redemption as a fact. And so, if we would understand the passage for ourselves, we must not study it as an isolated utterance but must bring the Christian faith to the interpretation of it, recognizing that a life governed by regulations or mere ideals rather than by faith in the living God is a life which leads to failure and merits condemnation, and that God in Christ has wrought for us a deliverance which can lead on to victory and blessing.

14 From this long and involved discussion we turn to resume the course of Paul's argument, and now we discover that, despite all the importance which attaches to it, verse 13 is after all little more than a transitional statement leading on to what is Paul's main concern at this point, viz. the question of the ingathering of the Gentiles into the people of God. In His dealings with Abraham, and in His subsequent imposition of the Law, God's aim had been **that the blessing of Abraham might reach the Gentiles,** in fulfilment of the promise of Gen. xii. 3 ; and that aim He never laid aside, even though its consummation tarried. Part of the reason why it tarried was that the sons of Abraham after the flesh so lived as to be incapable of receiving His blessing, and in fact brought on themselves not His blessing but His curse ; hence they could not be a means of mediating God's blessing to others until they themselves were ransomed from the curse, as they were

now ransomed through Christ Jesus. As we are to see when we come to verse 16, the significance of Christ in this connection is a two-fold one : not merely does He ransom the ' sons of Abraham ' from the curse which their disobedience to the Law has brought down on them, but there is a sense in which He and He alone is the true seed of Abraham. It is in Christ Jesus that the blessing promised to Abraham and his seed ultimately extends to the Gentiles.

As a historical statement Paul might have closed his sentence here ; but he adds a subsidiary clause (perhaps to be taken as strictly co-ordinate with the previous one rather than as dependent on it) so as to express the same truth afresh in terms of living spiritual experience. If the blessing promised to Abraham is now to reach the Gentiles, this means, he asserts, two things : (*a*) that it is by faith (as in the case of Abraham) and not by adherence to the Law that the Gentiles are to attain to the blessing ; (*b*) that the only vital way in which God can fulfil His promise and give them blessing is by giving to them His Spirit. The experience of the Galatians had indeed shown that it is in this way (cf. iii. 2, 5) that God was fulfilling His promise among them. Hence, though no mention of ' the Spirit ' had been made in the promise given to Abraham, Paul is only bringing out a latent truth when he speaks of the promised Spirit—a phrase which is doubtless also meant to recall certain words of Jesus (cf. Luke xxiv. 49 ; Acts i. 4).

The phrase ' in Christ ' which occurs in this verse repays study. We have already found it in ii. 4, 17 ; it occurs again in iii. 28 and v. 6. The frequency with which it and its correlative expressions (e.g. ' in the Lord ') occur in Paul—we find over 160 instances—is all the more remarkable in view of their absence from the Synoptic Gospels, Hebrews, and James. In the Fourth Gospel there is a parallel in the expression ' abide in Me.'

Professor Deissmann's earliest published work was a study of this characteristically Pauline phrase ; and he came to the conclusion that the preposition ' in ' must be taken with a certain literalness as conveying a ' local ' significance. ' In Christ ' means more than ' by Christ's agency ' ; it implies that Christ and those who are His are linked together in an indissolvable union. This union, moreover, is not the directly personal one between the individual believer and his Lord. Rather it is implied that Christ and His people form a corporate fellowship, so that to be ' in Christ ' means to be a member of that religious fellowship which draws its very life from Christ. Thus the introduction of the phrase at this point in Paul's argument is significant ; cf. its repetition in the emphatic summing-up of verse 28. Paul is concerned with the question : ' who are members in the fellowship of God's people ? ' ; and his answer is : ' not those who are *in Israel*, but those who are *in Christ*.' Paul, of course, never loses sight of the fact that this fellowship has an essentially spiritual basis ; and it may be that both the form and the meaning of the phrase ' in Christ ' are to be explained by reference to the dominant Christian conviction of being ' in the Spirit.' It is noticeable that in the present verse a reference to the Spirit follows immediately.

Exegetes of a former day tended to do less than justice to this great Pauline conception. The redemption accomplished by Christ's death was conceived too often as completed by the work of the Spirit in the individual soul. Paul's teaching, in continuation of the prophetic hope of the Old Testament, is that Christ's work is the salvation and sanctification of a *people*.

iii. 15–18 : *Paul shows by an analogy from human life that God's free Promise cannot later be conditioned by the demands of the Law*

15 To take an illustration from human life, my brothers. Once a man's will is ratified, no one else annuls it or adds a
16 codicil to it. Now the Promises were made to Abraham *and to* his *offspring* ; it is not said ' and to your offsprings ' in the plural, but in the singular *and to your offspring*

which is Christ. My point is this : the Law which 17
arose four hundred and thirty years later does not repeal
a will previously ratified by God, so as to cancel the
Promise. If the Inheritance is due to law, it ceases to be 18
due to promise. Now it was by a promise that God
bestowed it on Abraham.

Here Paul introduces not merely a new argument but a new 15
type of argument : he turns from the controversial exegesis of
Scripture **to take an illustration from human life.** His phrase
is literally : ' I speak after the manner of men.' Though the
ways of God cannot be *deduced* from the ways of man (cf.
Isa. lv. 8) they can nevertheless be *illustrated* by them. Both
by the character of the illustration and by the introduction
of the word ' brothers ' (cf. i. 11 ; iv. 12, etc. ; he never forgets
that the ' foolish Galatians ' are brothers in Christ) Paul
strikes at this point a more human note than he has done in
the preceding verses ; and he does not here rush on, as in
verse 10, to enunciate the conclusion which he is about to
establish by argument, but takes time quietly to describe the
situation on which he is to base his analogy.

A good deal of doubt exists as to the precise character of
Paul's illustration (cf. Heb. ix. 15–20). The word here translated ' **will** ' (*diathēkē*) certainly would mean ' will ' in the
common Greek of the time, but in the Greek of the Jewish
Scriptures it regularly means ' covenant,' i.e. not a disposition
made by *one* person (such as a man might make in anticipation
of death) but rather an arrangement made by agreement
between *two* parties ; and in particular it is used of a covenant
made between God and man, of which a supreme example
was the covenant of promise which God made with Abraham.
Hence many commentators believe (and the present writer
agrees with them) that the principal, if not indeed the sole,
meaning present to Paul's mind here is the meaning which the
word had in the Greek Bible with which the apostle himself
had been familiar since boyhood, and with which his readers
too were more or less acquainted. Instead of ' a man's will,'
therefore, we should translate ' *a human covenant.*' When

we come to the spiritual interpretation of the illustration, it matters little which of the two renderings we adopt, for from a truly spiritual standpoint a ' covenant ' in which God takes part is as essentially a one-sided proposal as a ' will ' is. It is not that God and man strike, as it were, a bargain, but rather that God makes a gracious offer to man upon certain conditions of obedience, and that man accepts the offer on these conditions ; in other words, it is an agreement made not so much between God and man as by God with man. From the evangelical standpoint a divine covenant is by its very nature a covenant of *promise*. Moreover, just as a man's will is directed to posterity, so is it with a divine covenant (cf. the reference to ' the offspring ' in verse 16) ; God requires future ages for the working out of His promises.

Taking then the meaning ' covenant ' as more strictly in accordance both with Biblical usage and with the immediate parallel of God's covenant with Abraham, we interpret the passage thus : Even in the case of a solemn agreement between one man and another (to say nothing, that is, of the case where it is God and not man who initiates it) the agreement, once it is ratified, holds good between them ; there must be no one-sided attempt either to annul it altogether or to modify its character by the introduction of additional stipulations ('no man disannulleth or addeth thereto,' Authorized Version). Paul of course does not deny that even the most solemn compact may be set aside or altered by mutual consent of the parties, but he is not concerned here with such a contingency. His contention rather is that there must be no wanton action on the part of any one party. If the interpretation ' will ' rather than ' covenant ' is followed, the unjustifiable interference must be conceived as coming *from without*—hence ' no one else ' as in the translation. The fact that there is no word corresponding to ' else ' in the original (the Greek merely says ' no one ') is a further argument against taking the reference as being to a will.

16   The analogy of the ' human covenant ' is to receive its main application in verse 17 ; but first of all we have in verse 16 a sentence which to the modern reader may seem to have the

double disadvantage of obstructing the course of the reasoning, and of introducing an argument which has no validity.
It has indeed been suggested that the verse may be a gloss
added in the margin by a scribe ; but the reference to ' the
offspring ' in verse 19 disproves this, and it was natural for a
man of spiritual insight like Paul to find in an interpretation of
this kind an additional support for his argument. What Paul
has in mind in verse 16 is that, according to his reading of
Jewish history, **the Promises, made to Abraham and to his
offspring** (or ' seed ' ; cf. Gen. xiii. 15 ff. ; xvii. 7 ff.) were not
really fulfilled till the coming of Christ ; and this, he says, is
in line with Scripture, which uses **the singular, ' offspring '** and
not **the plural** : the singular, therefore, can refer only to
Christ. Paul must have known that neither in Hebrew nor in
Greek did the plural of the word in question indicate a difference of meaning from the singular such as he here suggests.
He might even have admitted (cf. Rom. iv. 13 ff.) that other
interpretations of the passage in Genesis were at least possible.
But for Paul the only true interpretation of this or of any
other Scripture passage was one which was in accordance with
the revelation of God in Christ. He is not here *allegorizing*
Scripture, as he does in iv. 22 ff. ; he is *spiritualizing* it, looking
at it in the light of his gospel.

If Paul therefore interrupts his argument as he seems to
do in this verse, it must be because what he has to say has for
him real spiritual significance, and the very strangeness of
his contention ought to make us the more concerned to understand it. The term ' offspring (seed) of Abraham ' obviously
required definition and limitation. Paul's opponents were as
concerned as he was to assert that the Promise could not apply
to every member of every tribe that sprang from ' father '
Abraham : not physical descent but righteousness would in
the end determine the claim to the inheritance. The orthodox
Jew went on to assert that the true seed of Abraham was to
be found in Israel, and that the demand for righteousness
could be satisfied only through obedience to God's Holy Law.
Paul proceeds in verse 17 to show the essential unfairness in
this demand, inasmuch as the Law, by coming later, was a

limitation of the Promise ; but meantime (verse 16) he attacks the position from another angle, viz. from the conviction that there is no true righteousness except such as is found in and through Christ. In other words, the ' seed of Abraham ' was neither Abraham's posterity as a whole, nor Israel as a whole, nor that remnant of Israel which survived the winnowing process of the tests of the Law. The true seed was One who appeared in the fullness of time long centuries after the Covenant of Promise had first been established ; and the real significance of the Jewish people was, not that they were the true seed of Abraham, but that out of them came the true seed, namely Christ.

Hence, in this conception, as in so many others, Paul is true to the prophetic tradition. The language of Isa. vi. 13 is a reminder how, to the prophetic mind, the conception of ' the holy seed ' was linked up with that of a holy ' remnant ' in Israel, through whom God's purposes of righteousness and salvation might be advanced. In the development of Stephen's apologia in Acts vii. we see a similar tendency to associate the promise made to Abraham and his seed with the emergence in God's good time of ' the Just One ' (verse 52). Throughout all his argument in this section Paul likewise is dominated by the thought that the true people of God has at last come into being in Christ. And, as we showed in the note on the phrase ' in Christ ' in verse 14, Christ and His people are not to be separated : the fellowship derives its life from Christ, and Christ would be left incomplete without the fellowship (cf. the development of that thought in Eph. i. 22, 23). The early Christians were justified in maintaining that in the history of Israel the ideal of a holy people, envisaged by the prophets under various designations, remained nothing more than a dream until Christ *in His own person* fulfilled the ideal— He and He alone was ' the Remnant,' ' the Offspring of Abraham,' ' the Son of Man ' of Dan. vii. 13 ; but as a result of the gift of the Spirit they were also convinced that the ideal was now reaching ever fuller fulfilment in the expanding fellowship of those who belonged to Christ (iii. 29). So interpreted, Paul's argument about the Offspring is more than a piece of rabbinical subtlety: it is the expression of deep religious conviction.

Now if what has been said in verse 15 is true as regards a 17 purely human agreement, it is even more certainly true, Paul continues, in the case of a divine one. If there was *a covenant previously ratified by God,* in which God made a promise to Abraham and to his offspring, how can the Law, which came some centuries later, *annul that covenant,* and so cancel the Promise? In stating as he does that the Promise antedated the Law by no fewer than 430 years, Paul adds impressiveness to his argument, but the correctness or incorrectness of the figure has importance in no other way, and in this connection it is interesting to note that while he is here in substantial agreement with the Greek Bible, which in Exod. xii. 40 gives 430 years as the time of the total sojourn of the Children of Israel in Canaan (i.e. until their departure under Moses), the Hebrew text of the verse, which is followed in our English Bible, limits the 430 years to the time of the Israelites' stay in Egypt.

Immediately there looms before the disputants the question 18 of the relation of the Law to the Promise. Paul and his opponents joined issue not merely on the question: 'What is the primary necessity for participation in the blessing promised to Abraham? Is it circumcision or faith in God?' but also on the question of the significance and purpose of the Law (cf. verses 10 ff., and Introduction, pp. xxxvi. ff.). To the legalist, Jewish or Jewish-Christian, the two questions hung inseparably together: while God's first demand, as a preliminary condition of membership in the covenanted nation, was circumcision, He was pleased at a later date through the Law to give to His people a further, and final, revelation of His nature and of His will for them; and by a faithful keeping of the Law they were to 'inherit' the blessings of the Promise. Promise and Law are thus complementary terms in a process of continuous development. Paul, on the other hand, insists on separating the two questions. As regards the first, his reading both of Scripture and of history leads him to the conclusion that the covenant relation between God and Abraham is dominated by the conception of ' promise ' : it is not to be interpreted as a stipulation between two contracting parties, but as a gracious offer made by God in response to an attitude of faith. In whatever way, therefore, the Law might be related to the Promise, it was God's gracious Promise which provided the unalterable basis of the covenant-relationship between Him and His people ; the inheritance thus offered to Abraham and his offspring would come as the result of God's free gift ; and that gift would be robbed of its initial fullness and freeness if it were subsequently made dependent on obedience to the Law. Paul will have nothing to do with the judaizing contention that by keeping the Law it is possible for Abraham's ' seed ' to inherit the Promise. Rising aloft into a general argument, in which the particular cases of the Law given to the Children of Israel and the Promise made to Abraham are seen against the background of two great conflicting principles, law and promise, legalism and evangelicalism, Paul firstly asserts, in forcible and concise language, that **if the Inheritance is due to law, it ceases to be due to promise.** This general statement is followed by a reminder that in the determinative case of Abraham (the reference to Abraham is emphatic in the Greek), legal obedience was not made a condition for receiving the inheritance : **it was by a promise that God bestowed it.** (The inheritance could be said to be *bestowed* on Abraham even though it was only in his ' offspring ' that he received it—he himself died in faith, not having received the promises, Heb. xi. 13.) Paul's point here, following on the major premise in the previous part of the verse, is that as the inheritance originally came by promise it could not now come by law. If in the case of Abraham God took the initiative and of His own free grace *promised* to him the inheritance, why should the sons of Abraham think they are called to *earn* it by a process of legal obedience ? The inheritance ceases to be a free gift from God when men think that their obedience gives them a claim on it.

As with the idea of ' promise ' in verse 14, Paul has suddenly

introduced here another of the key-conceptions of the controversy, viz. that of the Inheritance (for the position of the son
as 'heir' cf. iii. 29 ff.). The Inheritance (note the definite
article) is the substance or concrete realization of the Promise ;
it forms the blessing which was promised to Abraham and his
offspring. Originally conceived of materially as a local
habitation, the 'promised land,' it naturally admitted (so
both parties in the dispute would have recognized) of a spiritual interpretation (cf. Heb. xi. 14 ff.). What his own view is
of the character and content of the Inheritance Paul does not
stop at this point to tell ; he is for the present in the throes
of a great argument, and he does not allow himself to be
diverted from the main issue. He hears a challenge rising to
the lips of his opponents, but he himself has anticipated what
they are to say and he expresses it for them.

iii. 19, 20 : *If then the Promise is fundamental, what place
does the Law have in God's providential order ? Its secondary
and temporary character is described*

**Then what about the Law ? Well, it was interpolated for the 19
purpose of producing transgressions till such time as the
Offspring arrived to whom the Promise was made; also,
it was transmitted by means of angels through the agency
of an intermediary (an intermediary implies more than 20
one party, but God is one).**

The challenge which Paul now faces is as follows : If the 19
Inheritance comes to man solely as the result of God's gracious
Promise and the Law has nothing directly to do with it, what
function then does the Law serve ? Paul is bold in his statement of the problem, and bold in his answering of it. You
imagine, he seems to say, that in the Law you have the full
and final expression of God's will for His people, something
which He purposed from all eternity and which will hold for
all eternity. On the contrary I tell you (i.) that the Law is a
mere addition to the main stream of God's purpose, something
which **was interpolated** ; (ii.) it was designed, not to reveal
fully His will, but to deal with a special necessity, viz. the

necessity of bringing home to His chosen people their sinfulness ; (iii.) its reign, so far from being eternal, is a strictly limited one, ceasing when in the promised ' Offspring,' viz. Christ, the Promise began to receive its fulfilment ; (iv.) so far from coming from God Himself, it was transmitted to men indirectly. Each of these contentions deserves further examination.

(i.) God's primary, as also His final, method of dealing with men is to offer them blessing in response to faith. Whatever its purpose was, the Law was in no sense a natural and continuous development of this method of promise (cf. notes on verse 18). It was essentially subsidiary, an addition or ' interpolation ' ; and the method of promise was not departed from even during the period when the Law held sway alongside of the Promise.

(ii.) The subsidiary character of the Law is seen in the special **purpose** which it was designed to serve, that of **producing transgressions.** Paul does not mean (as might be inferred from the Authorized Version, ' added because of transgressions ') that the function of the Law was to check in some way the prevalence of iniquity, for ' transgression ' and ' sin ' are in Paul always to be distinguished (cf. Rom. v. 20, and the commentary on Gal. ii. 18) : men may *sin* in ignorance, but they *transgress* only when they have a recognized standard of what is right, and it was to provide such a standard that the Law was brought in (cf. Rom. iii. 20 ; v. 20 ; vii. 7, 13). God, then, while not departing from the principle of regarding men's faith as a *positive* reason for accepting them, had to deal with the *negative* fact that in the realm of conduct they were not holy as He is holy, and the Law was ' interpolated ' with the express purpose of making them realize how far short they were falling of the glory of God (Rom. iii. 23), and how fully therefore they deserved (if only God cared to deal with them according to their deserts) not God's blessing but His condemnation.

(iii.) Further, the reign of the Law is essentially temporary, for it was designed to hold only **till such time as the Offspring arrived** who was referred to in the formulation of the Promise.

By the ' Offspring ' Paul primarily refers to Christ in His own
person (cf. verse 16), though with his sense of religious realities
he would have recognized that along with Christ must now
be grouped the Fellowship of those who were Christ's (cf.
1 Cor. xii. 12, 27). Paul therefore implies that the Promise
did not receive its fulfilment, as some of his countrymen
conceived, in such material blessings as the Promised Land,
or even in spiritual blessings such as were enjoyed by those
who made the Law of God their delight ; it did not even
begin to be fulfilled until in Christ the ' Offspring ' arrived.
Evidently Paul regards this fulfilment in Christ as being of
such a character that the necessity (of producing a sense of
guilt) which the Law had been designed to meet now no longer
existed : in the case of Christ, the sinless Son of God, such a
necessity of course did not arise, and in the case of Christians
(' sons of God by faith in Christ Jesus,' verse 26) both the
righteousness of God and their own sinfulness were fully dis-
closed to them by the revelation of Jesus Christ, apart from
the Law altogether (cf. verses 22 ff. ; Rom. iii. 21 ff.). The
Law might still continue to serve, as it had done in Paul's
own case (Rom. vii. 7 ff.), as a useful preparatory discipline,
by bringing home to men its own inadequacy and the conse-
quent necessity for a further revelation (Paul proceeds to deal
with this in verses 22 ff.) ; but as an ultimate revelation of
the relationship existing between God and man it could no
longer be accepted.

(iv.) In a final sentence, designed to rob the Law still
further of the unique dignity with which its upholders invested
it, Paul urges that, so far from being a perfect and direct
revelation from God, it was (a) a mere ordinance of God
which was **transmitted** to men, and transmitted (b) **by means
of angels,** (c) **through the agency of an intermediary.**

Every word here is carefully chosen. What Paul has mainly
in mind may be deduced from the contrast provided in
verse 21, where, over against the Law as it is, there is conjured
up the unrealized ideal of a Law that might produce ' life.'
The Jew, with his sense of spiritual reality, regarded all true
communication from God to man as being directed towards

the communication of *life*. In prophetic circles it was abundantly realized that only by the word of the Lord was it possible for man to live (Deut. viii. 3) ; while in more definitely legalistic circles, where it was accepted that life was connected with right conduct and death with sin, life was thought to be the reward of obedience to God's word in the Law.

Paul, whose religion was essentially prophetic, believed that while the Law came ultimately from God, it did not do so directly. Had it been a direct communication from God, it would have brought *life*, as experience showed that it did *not*. So far therefore from conveying the living voice of God, or bringing men into His living presence, the Law merely transmitted His commands and regulations, while He Himself remained apart. This conception of the Law, which had, of course, a history behind it, naturally led to a reinterpretation of many of the features in the traditional story of the giving of the Law. Thus in Acts vii. 38, when Stephen refers to ' living oracles,' he seems to imply a contrast between those ' living oracles ' which the people might have received through the voice of Moses the prophet if only they had been willing to listen, and the inferior law of ordinances which they finally did receive on tables of stone. In the final transaction Moses ceased to be a prophet speaking to the people in the name of God ; he became a mere intermediary between Israel and the multitude of angels by whom the Law was transmitted. It is significant that neither here nor elsewhere in Galatians is Moses mentioned by name.

But the main reinterpretation was as regards the part played by the angels. The tradition that angels were present at the giving of the Law is preserved in the LXX. Version (not the original Hebrew) of Deut. xxxiii. 2, in Heb. ii. 2, and in Stephen's speech (Acts vii. 38, 53) ; also in the Book of Jubilees, chap. i., and in Josephus, *Antiquities*, XV. v. 3. The orthodox view was that these attendant spirits served, like the thunder and the lightning, to show forth the glory of the divine Presence ; Paul's view is that they indicated that God was not present in person, and that a law which was merely transmitted by angels lacked the glory

of the true life-giving Word. It is to be noted that Paul does
not assert that the angels in question were demons or spirits
of evil. He would have agreed that there were in the universe
evil angels as well as good ones ; but even those who were not
essentially evil might, as on this occasion, exercise an evil
influence by intervening between the worshipper and God,
and by having their activities erroneously accepted as the
activities of God Himself. Undue devotion to the ordinances
of the Law seemed to Paul to imply a worship of angels rather
than of the living God, and thus to have affinities with paganism (cf. the commentary on iv. 8–10, and the note on Elemental
Spirits on p. 134).

Paul closes his depreciatory account of the Law by a 20
parenthetical sentence which is obscure in the extreme—some
300 interpretations are said to have been suggested for it !
An intermediary implies more than one party, but God is one.
Have we here the familiar contrast between the Law and the
Promise, as if the Law, being a contract between two parties,
required a mediator, whereas in the Promise all action came
from God ? More probably the contrast is between God and
the angels—God Himself might have dealt directly with the
people as He did with Abraham ; but as the angels were a
plurality just as the people were, a negotiator was essential.
Whatever its precise meaning, the sentence seems to add
nothing of real value to Paul's argument ; it merely emphasizes that, as contrasted with the Promise, which was primary
and direct, the Law was secondary and indirect.

iii. 21, 22 : *This does not, however, imply that the Law is
opposed to the Promise*

Then the Law is contrary to God's Promises? Never! Had 21
there been any law which had the power of producing life,
righteousness would really have been due to law, but 22
Scripture has consigned all without exception to the
custody of sin, in order that the promise due to faith in
Jesus Christ might be given to those who have faith.

21 But all this line of argument (verses 18, 19), Paul realizes, might in the minds of his opponents be construed as leading to an impasse, viz. that it makes out the Law and the Promises, both of which have issued from the same God, as working in opposition to one another ; and to such a position, of course, no loyal Jew would assent. Paul, as loyal as his opponents are to the principles of Judaism, is as emphatic as they would be in repudiating any such contention. He does so by viewing the Law and the Promise in the light of the final purpose of Him from whom both had come. That purpose was to produce life. Here we have a new and important conception introduced, as with ' promise ' in verse 14 and ' inheritance ' in verse 18. ' Life ' was a familiar conception both to Paul and to his opponents, and no definition of it is required at this point ; Paul has something to say in illustration of his own interpretation of it in chaps. v. and vi. But we can see how Paul's mind worked here. Sin and death are bound up with one another (cf. Rom. v. 21, vi. 23 ; 1 Cor. xv. 56), and one function of the Law, as has just been shown (verse 19), is to reveal to men that they are transgressors, and (if the Law were the full revelation of God) are, as such, accursed (verse 10) and doomed to death. The Promise of God, there-fore, when it is fulfilled, will bring to men not merely acquittal from their guilt, but deliverance from death (cf. Rom. vii. 24) and the gift of life (cf. Rom. vi. 23, and ' the just shall live ' quoted in verse 12), life and death being interpreted now not as merely physical, but as moral and spiritual realities ; and for Paul there is no true ' righteousness ' (i.e. acceptance with God) that does not have as its consummation ' life eternal ' (cf. Rom. v. 21, vi. 22). And, says Paul, **had there** only **been** *given* (the word ' given ' is expressed clearly in the original, and is not without significance; cf. ' given ' in verse 22) a **law which had the power of producing life**—or (to take the particular case in dispute) had the Law (of Moses) been truly (as the Judaizers so proudly claimed) a gift from God, designed to enable God's people to attain to their promised inheritance (and not, as Paul would have preferred to call it, a mere ordinance; cf. ' transmitted ' in verse 19), and, more especially,

had this divinely given Law been the means employed by God
to convey to men the supreme gift of life, then indeed, as the
Judaizers contended, and as Paul, on this hypothesis, would
have freely admitted, **righteousness** (i.e. acceptance by God,
justification) **would have been due to law**, i.e. it would have
been obtainable by means of such a system (or, according to
another reading, within the sphere of such a system). The
Law then would have been seen to be working out in the same
direction as the Promise : by keeping the Law men would
have attained to the blessings which the Promise had set
before them. As it is, however (this is the meaning of the
conditional clause), *no* system of law can quicken in man the
life eternal ; at the most, it can awaken in him a sense of the
need for such a gift at the hands of God. And so, to revert
to the problem with which this verse opened, Paul's contention may be said to be that there is no essential conflict
between the Law and the Promise for the simple reason that
they have entirely different functions and different spheres
of operation. To take a parallel case : the King may pardon
a man whom the law has convicted, but that does not mean
that the law was wrong to convict. Viewing the case quite
generally (not ' the Law,' but ' law,' ' any law '), Paul's point
is that the function of law, within its own sphere, is simply to
lay down its regulations, and in any case that comes up for
judgment to decide on the question of guilt. Provision may
be made, and in God's case is made, for the overruling of the
legal verdict ; a prisoner condemned to death may yet receive
the gift of life ; but law as such is called on to decide, not
whether or not man should be pardoned, but whether or not
he is guilty ; and certainly, if he is truly guilty, deserving of
condemnation and death, no law can impart to him the peace
(Rom. v. 1), and the sense of triumph (Rom. vii. 25), and all
those other spiritual blessings which go to make up ' life,' and
which are the characteristic possession of the man who is free
from all condemnation.

No, life was a gift which the Law could not give. There
were many pious Jews, of course, who clung to the belief that
life was God's reward for keeping the Law, and death His

penalty for its neglect (cf. Deut. xxx. 15–20 ; Ps. i. 2, 3 ; cxix. 174 f.). We know how our Lord read the thoughts of one young man who had failed in this way 'to inherit eternal life' (Mark x. 17 ff.) ; Paul himself had tried this way, and had found not life but death (Rom. vii. 22 ff.). And so, building on his own spiritual experience, and interpreting Scripture in the light of it, Paul begins by taking his stand on the assertion

22 that **Scripture has consigned all without exception to the custody of sin.** There is no adequate parallel to this sweeping assertion in any one passage of the Old Testament— the nearest parallels are Deut. xxvii. 26 and Ps. cxliii. 2, already quoted in iii. 10 and ii. 16 ; and if Lightfoot is right in contending that ' the Scripture ' in the New Testament always means a particular *passage* of Scripture, we can only conclude that in the present instance Paul's recollection was indistinct, and that he was subconsciously influenced by the general doctrine of Scripture on the prevalence and power of sin. Though ' all without exception ' is neuter (' the universe '), Paul is, of course, thinking primarily of human sinfulness. By ' consigned ' is meant that men are shut up *with no apparent possibility of escape*. This sense of a dread impasse is increased by the pregnant assertion that Scripture is responsible for this consigning—it is not merely the power of sin from which there is no escape, there is none from the authority of Scripture. Paul does not say that it is *God* who consigns men to the custody of sin : if he had been concerned to develop that side of his argument, he might have shown how the active agents were the powers of evil. It was on the basis of Scripture that the Judaizers had challenged the apostle, and it is on that basis that he must meet them. In Scripture, of course, God is conceived as being ever at work, intent on His purpose of redemption : and in iv. 5 we are to see how that purpose comes to fruition. But sin, too, is at work, bringing everything under its inexorable sway ; and, in taking account of it, Scripture is like the judge recording his verdict and handing the culprits over to be under its power.

But if we are all without exception brought under the custody of sin, and made to see that of ourselves there is no hope of escape, this is merely a stage by which God seeks to advance the realization of His promise of blessing. What Paul here calls **the promise** is of course the concrete fulfilment of what He had originally promised to Abraham. Every word in this concluding clause is significant. That promised blessing, which may be summed up in the term 'life,' is something to which man of himself cannot attain, for man is a prisoner, under sin, and therefore awaiting death, which is the consequence of sin. If he is to obtain life, life must **be given,** and it can only be given to those who trust the promise which God has so graciously made—to those, in other words, **who have faith.** Paul, however, goes further still. He is arguing, it must be remembered, against men who as Christians acknowledged the need for faith, but who yet believed that 'life' could only be given to those whose faith inspired them towards 'works of law.' Paul, *per contra*, keeps steadily before himself, and before them, the picture of the universal domination of sin, a domination so inexorable that man can do nothing until he is delivered from it ; hence he introduces an additional phrase emphasizing that the faith in question must be **faith in Jesus Christ.** The phrase, which in the translation is connected with the noun ('**the promise due to faith**'), goes rather with the verb—the promise is given *on the basis of faith in Jesus Christ.* The one requirement for justification is faith in Jesus Christ as Saviour.

iii. 23–29 : *Custody under the Law was a stage on the way towards the ultimate realization of the Promise*

Before this faith came, we were confined by the Law and kept 23 in custody, with the prospect of the faith that was to be revealed ; the Law thus held us as wards in discipline, 24 till such time as Christ came, that we might be justified by faith. But faith has come, and we are wards no 25 longer ; you are all sons of God by your faith in Christ 26 Jesus (for all of you who had yourselves baptized into 2 Christ have taken on the character of Christ). There is 28

29
no room for Jew or Greek, there is no room for slave or freeman, there is no room for male and female ; you are all one in Christ Jesus. Now if you are Christ's, then you are Abraham's offspring ; in virtue of the Promise, you are heirs.

23
The implication of the preceding verses that the Law had its own sphere of operation quite distinct from that of the Promise has prepared the way for the definitely positive conception of the Law's function which Paul is now to unfold. The Law, he holds, served as a necessary discipline, so that in due time we might be able to receive at God's hand the promised Inheritance (cf. verses 18, 22). The period of the earlier dispensation is described by the phrase ' **before this faith came** ' —literally, ' *the* faith ' ; the translation ' faith ' (Authorized Version and Revised Version) is misleading, for of course faith in God lay at the basis even of the old covenant made with Abraham, and, as the Epistle to the Hebrews reminds us (chap. xi.), there is a sense in which faith has existed ever since man began to know God at all. Paul is thinking of the faith referred to in the preceding argument (verse 22), i.e. faith in Jesus Christ. He implies that, since the revelation of the Son of God, no other attitude towards God was possible save that of faith, and the faith that was now called for was a faith which admitted of no qualifications, faith *par excellence*. Thus ' the faith ' (cf. i. 23 ; vi. 10) has come, even at the early date of this Epistle, to be practically a designation for the new religion, as ' the Law ' served to designate the old one ; we may compare how, from a different point of view, Christianity came early to be called ' the way.' By his use of the first person (' we ') in this verse and the next, Paul is tracing the Christian religion back to its antecedents in the history of Israel. Catching up what he has just said of the collective *consignment* of the race to the custody of sin, he here repeats the idea (**we were confined**), using the same Greek word as before, but adding to it another which suggests that, in addition to being shut in, we had the Law set over us as a guard on the outside. The custody that he has in mind is

primarily one of enforced restraint rather than of benevolent
protection, for it is a fundamental idea in Paul's thought that
through sin man loses his freedom and requires deliverance
(cf. the ' consignment ' of verse 23) ; yet as the Law no less
than the Promise came from God, the idea of its protective
value ought not to be excluded. Just as God, in fencing off
His chosen nation from their Gentile neighbours by ordinances
which might seem a grievous limitation of their freedom, was
in this very way protecting and preserving them to be to Him a
peculiar people, so too the Law, though it operated primarily
by making men realise their bondage to sin, was still a stage
in the redemptive process by which they were brought to their
freedom in Christ. From this point of view it was God Himself who, with a wiser providence than they knew, had put
them in custody, and set a guard over them. We may compare Paul's thought in Phil. iv. 7—though a prisoner, he could
still rejoice that he was being guarded in heart and mind by
the peace of God, whose deepest purpose is not to confine
but to protect.

Continuing his argument Paul says that in fact the Law 24
came to exercise for us (here again he is thinking primarily
of Israel in the days before Christ came) the same function as
a household servant does who has children under his charge.
He has in mind the figure of a ' pedagogue,' a slave employed
in many families to have general oversight, both disciplinary
and protective, over a boy till he reached the age of maturity.
Paul uses the same metaphor in 1 Cor. iv. 15, where he
compares unfavourably the interest and influence of the
pedagogue with those of the father. The familiar Authorized
Version translation, *the law was our schoolmaster to bring us
unto Christ*, is apt to convey the false impression that the
Law's function was essentially educative, and has been used
to corroborate the modern (but quite unscriptural) conception
of *an evolutionary progress in religion*, as if man naturally
advances from the truths of the Law to those of the Gospel.
Equally erroneous is the idea that, as the pedagogue frequently accompanied the child on the way to school, so men
were led by the Law to the school of Christ, where they could

get, so to speak, superior instruction in religion. It is not as a Teacher that Paul thinks of Christ, but as a Redeemer : the Christian life is not an advanced education, but a deliverance from death into life. The real meaning of the passage is well brought out in the translation : **the Law thus held us as wards in discipline,** a discipline which was designed to last **till such time as Christ came.** Paul adds that the function of this discipline was **that we might be justified by faith.** By this he apparently means that the Law, just because it was repressive in its discipline, robbed us of all faith in human advancement, and left us with no alternative but to cast ourselves in faith on Him who came to emancipate us.

25   By contrast Paul now tells how **faith has come** and **we are wards no longer**—the Greek again is ' *the* faith,' i.e. faith in Jesus Christ ; and the faith has come because in Christ there has come One in whom we can have faith. Instead of being mere wards in discipline, we can now **all** enter on our new life as **sons of God**—a life which is **in Christ Jesus,** and which is made possible **by faith** (it seems better to take these two phrases separately than to link them together as if the one was dependent on the other—*by faith in Jesus Christ*). Here we have one of the many triumphant exclamations of the Epistle—we can imagine the apostle flinging it out as a challenge to the Galatians and to those who were misleading them.

26 And we can see how clearly he has his converts in mind, for he suddenly turns to use the second person (**you** as well as we). Fearful lest the force of his conclusion would be missed if it were couched in too general terms, he feels he must address it directly to the men who are so tragically disregarding it and thus missing the dignity of sonship.

27   His appeal to them is enforced by arguments which serve to remind us what the source of the Galatian trouble really was. The Judaizers had approached Paul's Galatian converts with the old idea of the special regard which God had for Israel; even as Christians, they argued, Gentiles could not win acceptance with God without first becoming, through circumcision, incorporated members of God's chosen people. Paul will have none of it. Circumcision may make a man an

Israelite ; but baptism makes him a *Christ's man*. This is the sole direct reference to baptism in the Epistle (cf., however, note on v. 24) ; but its introduction at this point is a reminder of the significance which Paul attached to it. In baptism the believer on his part professed his faith in Christ ; and God, on His part, accepted his faith and gave him His Holy Spirit. To put the same truth otherwise, at baptism the believer became united to Christ. Paul expresses this thought by saying that those who have been **baptized into Christ have taken on the character of Christ.** The metaphor in this latter phrase is from putting on a garment (' have put on Christ,' Authorized Version) ; but in Scripture it denotes that the wearer becomes in a subtle way identified with what he puts on (cf. the Old Testament thought of clothing oneself with righteousness, with strength, etc., and Paul's use of the same metaphor in Rom. xiii. 12 ; Eph. iv. 24). Thus, when a man is baptized, he becomes so thoroughly identified with Christ that it is no longer he who lives, it is Christ who lives in him. No matter what that person was before, in Christ he is a new creation (cf. vi. 15). Hence, the apostle reminds his Gentile converts that there is no need for them to put themselves right by becoming like the Jews : for the Jew and the Gentile alike become new men when they put on Christ.

The argument causes Paul to recall the contempt of the 28 Jew for all inferiors, not merely for Gentiles, but also for slaves and women. Emmet quotes, in this connection, a thanksgiving, which Paul may have known, from the Jewish Prayer Book : ' Blessed art Thou, O Lord our God, King of the Universe, who hast not made me a heathen. Blessed art Thou . . . who hast not made me a bondman. Blessed art Thou . . . who hast not made me a woman.' But in Christ Jesus, Paul declares exultingly, there is no longer such a thing as **Jew** and **Greek, slave** and **freeman, male** and **female**—or, as we might say to-day, *white man and coloured man, master and servant, capitalist and wage-earner, man and woman.* Such distinctions, of course, exist in the natural world, but they can now no longer be regarded as ultimate. And if we follow the translation given by Dr. Moffatt, it is not merely (as in the

Authorized Version) that these distinctions *cease* to exist, **there is no room** for them—and Paul secures emphasis for his conclusion by a threefold repetition.   In the next sentence the word for ' one ' is masculine and not neuter, the sense being, not that all Christians form a corporate unity, but that in Christ each man stands on the same level as his neighbour ; and this meaning rather than the other is obviously the true summing-up of the preceding argument.   One may note that here again, on reaching a great conclusion which is to form one of his watch-words in the conflict, Paul quite definitely in the Greek emphasizes the word **' you.'**   You Galatians, pagans though once you were, are, he says, one and the same with us

29 once you and we are **in Christ Jesus.**   You are *Christ's men* (cf. the name *Christians* in Acts xi. 26) just as much as we are. Therefore (and this is all-important, both as rebutting the Judaizers' arguments and as confirming by a new line of thought the position taken up in iii. 7) you, who were once Gentiles but who now by faith belong to Christ Jesus, are the true offspring of Abraham (and that without becoming members of Abraham's nation), and as such you are among his heirs, entitled to receive the Promise which was made to him and to his offspring.

iv. 1–7 : *Formerly we were like children, under strict guardianship ; now, through Christ, we have attained to our freedom as sons*

iv.

1 What I mean is this.   As long as an heir is under age, there is no difference between him and a servant, though he is lord
2 of all the property ; he is under guardians and trustees
3 till the time fixed by his father.   So with us.   When we were under age, we lived under the thraldom of the Ele-
4 mental spirits of the world ; but when the time had fully expired, God sent forth his Son, born of a woman, born
5 under the Law, to ransom those who were under the Law,
6 that we might get our sonship.   It is because you are sons that God has sent forth the Spirit of his Son into your
7 hearts crying ' Abba ! Father ! '   So you are servant no

longer, but son, and as son you are also heir, all owing to
God.

Though our familiar division into chapters marks a break 1
here, there is no break in the argument. With the triumphant
vindication of his position in iii. 29 Paul might indeed have
ended this part of his letter. At the mention of ' heirs,' however, in verse 29, following on what he has said in verse 24
regarding the minor and his superintendent-slave, there suddenly occurs to him another point which can be used to
reinforce his argument. His eagerness and irrepressibility are
seen in the ejaculation : **What I mean is this** (lit. ' I say ' ; cf.
' tell me ' in iv. 21). Paul is emphatic that those who are under
law are like children who require to be supervised and controlled, and have no more real freedom than the household
slaves. So far he is merely reiterating the position of verse 24.
His new point is the positive one that even tutelage suggests
a future period of emancipation ; and in putting His children
under restrictive discipline for a period God Himself was
looking forward to a time when they should be of age to enter
into their inheritance as sons.

A good deal of unprofitable discussion has ranged round the 2
precise legal situation which Paul here envisages. It has been
objected that the situation is not strictly in accordance with
what we know of Roman law (at least in the later period of
Gaius, about A.D. 170) ; for in that case the law itself ordained
that a minor whose father was dead remained under the care
(*a*) of a *tutor* or **guardian** till he was 14, and then (*b*) of a
curator or **trustee** till he was 25, so that Paul's reference to a
time fixed by the father is out of place. Ramsay, on the other
hand, argues that in the appointment of both guardian and
trustee by the father we have a trace of the old Seleucid law,
differing in this respect from the Roman, and he even finds in
this a buttress for his view that the recipients of the letter are
inhabitants of *South* Galatia. But dogmatism on such a
matter is out of place. It is probably true that Paul has here
a definite situation in mind, but it may be doubted whether
we have the *data* for interpreting that situation with precision.

May not trusteeship and guardianship go on concurrently, and even be held by the same person or persons, the guardian having a general responsibility for his ward's welfare, and the trustee superintending the management of his estate ? If the father is regarded as dead, may it not be that even Roman law at this time allowed a father to state in his will how long he required his heirs to remain under trustees, a statutory period being fixed only when no will had been made ? Or need it be assumed that the father is to be regarded as dead ? Even during his lifetime a father who was to be away from home might arrange that his son should remain for a fixed period under the care of another ; e.g. we read in 1 Macc. iii. 31 f. how King Antiochus, finding it necessary to go to Persia, ' left Lysias, an honourable man and one of the seed royal . . . to bring up his son Antiochus until his return.' The fact that the son is referred to as **lord of all the property** does not necessarily imply that the father is dead ; ' all that I have is thine,' says the father to the son in our Lord's parable (Luke xv. 31 ; cf. also Heb. i. 2). This phrase, together with the reference to '**a servant**' (cf. the ' hired servants ' in the parable) leads one indeed to believe that Paul may have had our Lord's story in his thoughts as he wrote.

There may be doubts as to the precise legal situation that Paul has in mind, but there is none as to the religious lesson he wishes to draw from it. This lesson, we may note, is concerned with the position of the **heirs,** and only in a quite secondary way with that of the father. In the spiritual sphere the Father cannot, of course, be thought of as dead, though He may be regarded as absent in the sense that other agencies temporarily intervene between Him and His children.

Paul's argument is twofold. (i.) Even the son who is designated to be the father's heir must, so long as he is **under age,** be treated as in the fullest sense a dependant ; he has no freedom of action, and his position is no better than that of a **servant** or household slave. The word here used for ' under age ' corresponds to the Latin *infans* (hence ' child,' Authorized Version and Revised Version), but it covers the immaturity of youth as well as the incapacity of childhood. Paul is

relentless in his assertion that before the faith came (iii. 23)
our position, despite the inheritance which God had marked
out for us, was not that of *sons* in the full sense, but of *children*
who had not yet reached maturity and freedom, and who
might therefore be classed as *servants* rather than as *sons*.
It is to be noted that he uses the first personal pronoun : **so
with us.** It is not only the Galatians who, as heathen, were 3
in their pre-Christian days no better than children or even
slaves ; the same was true of us who were Jews. That Paul,
proud as he was of the traditions of the religion in which he
himself had been brought up (cf. Rom. ix. 3-5 ; Gal. ii. 15),
should *in this regard* put that religion on the same level as
that of the heathen who had never really known God
speaks volumes for his catholicity of outlook and his natural
courtesy towards those who might have been regarded as
inferiors, and also for his profound sense of the revolution
that Christ had made in all previous standards. Yet how
bitterly must the allegation have been resented by his judaizing adversaries ! And not only was that previous life **thraldom,** it was thraldom under the **Elemental spirits of the world.**
The precise meaning of this difficult phrase we shall consider when we come to verse 9, where there is a similar
reference.

(2) Paul is no less emphatic that even by the early stage of 4
tutelage and bondage the Father was looking forward to a
time when men should enter into the full privilege of Sonship.
There is in the spiritual sphere, as there is in the ordinary
affairs of life (verse 2) a time fixed by the Father, when the
divine event to which He has been leading (cf. iii. 19) should
receive its fulfilment. **When the time had fully expired, God
sent forth his Son.** The temporal phrase which Paul uses
(literally, 'when the fullness of the time came'; cf. Mark i. 15)
reminds us how thoroughly the Church from the beginning
saw in the appearance of Christ the supreme event in the
divine plan of the ages. It is natural that we should ask
ourselves how the expiry of the time was calculated. Was it
by the mere passage of a fixed number of years, as in popular
apocalyptic thought on this and on other themes (cf. Dan.

ix. 24) ? Did it mark the peak point in a process of preparation ? Modern historians, for instance, dwell on the *preparatio
evangelica* found in the unifying agency of the Roman Empire,
in the spread of Greek as practically a universal language, in
the renascence of faith implied in the influence of Judaism
and of certain heathen cults. Paul does not help us to answer
our question except in an indirect way, through the emphasis
which he lays on the divine intervention and the ransom
which it effected. It was not man's *progress* which impelled
God to act, but man's *need*. It was not (as on a false rendering
of the 'schoolmaster' passage in iii. 25, where see note) that
man was now educated up to the stage of receiving the gospel,
but that he had now reached a stage of servitude in which
he cried aloud for deliverance.

Paul, however, is quite specific as to the event itself which
marked the fulfilment of the time ; and in describing it every
one of his words is carefully chosen.

God sent forth his Son. The thought is not that Christ left
His home in Galilee to embark on a Messianic mission (as
perhaps in Mark i. 38 ; contrast 'was sent' in Luke iv. 43) ;
rather Paul has in mind the whole of the divine drama of His
pre-existence, birth, life among men, death and resurrection,
and (verse 6) the gift of the Spirit. He is thinking of how the
Son came forth from *God*. It was one of the claims made by
Jesus for Himself that He had been 'sent' (cf. Matt. xv. 24 ;
Mark ix. 37, and the passage from Isa. lxi. 1, quoted in
Luke iv. 18).

Christ's coming was more than that of a prophet sent by
God (cf. John i. 6) ; it was the coming of God's own **Son**
(cf. Mark xii. 6; Heb. i. 1, 2). There is here the same sense of
a pivotal event in history as there was in the statement about
Christ's ransoming work in iii. 13.

Though He was the Son of God He came **born of a woman,**
i.e. He assumed humanity with all its limitations and weaknesses. The phrase means nothing more than that He appeared
as a man among men. It must not be taken as implying on
Paul's part either an assertion of the Virgin Birth of Jesus
(no reference being made to the father) or a denial of it

(through the use of 'woman' rather than of 'virgin'). It does, however, illustrate how, accompanying his exultant conception of the Son sent forth by God, there is a certain reluctance on the apostle's part to describe Jesus unequivocally as *man*, as if He were 'a mere man'; we may compare the circumlocution in Phil. ii. 8, 'born in human guise and appearing in human form.'

In assuming human nature the Son of God also allowed Himself to come **under the Law.** Paul's phrase here is quite general: ' *one who* **was** (or *came*) *under law* '; but there is an undeniable reference to the Jewish Law. Paul's point is that in becoming man Jesus was not born a Gentile; He was born a son of Abraham, a member of the commonwealth of Israel, subject therefore, like His brethren, to the Law. As the Son of God He shared the life of the Father; as the Offspring in whom the Promise was to be fulfilled He was Himself to bring the reign of the Law to an end; yet humbly and willingly He submitted Himself to the rules and regulations which were imposed under the Law for the governance of those who were not yet prepared to inherit the Promise and to enter on the life of Sonship.

In sending forth His Son, God was seeking to accomplish His predetermined purpose, and that purpose is now described. Ultimately it was that through Christ the Son, who by assuming humanity had become one with His brethren of earth, all men should be enabled to enter on a life of **sonship.** But mention must first be made of an intermediate step, viz. 5 that, by coming Himself under the Law, Christ was able to **ransom** His brethren **who were under the Law.** Here again Paul's phrase is literally ' under law,' so that it is possible to argue that he is thinking how humanity as a whole lay under the sway of law (including natural law) until Christ came to set them free. But, in view of the course of the argument, it is necessary to refer the phrase, primarily at least, to the Jewish Law, as is done in the translation. It was part of God's scheme of salvation that one section of humanity, viz. Israel, should be placed under the Law, and then in the fullness of time ransomed from it by One who Himself was under it, and that thus the blessing should spread from Israel to the world in general. That line of Paul's argument had been worked out in iii. 13, 14, where there was an emphatic contrast between 'us' and 'the Gentiles.' Here, on the other hand, Paul is concerned merely to state the position and to pass on to show how the ransom of Israel was only part of God's more general purpose, viz. that **we** (i.e. we all, Jews and Gentiles alike, all for whom Christ was ' brother man ') **might get our sonship.** In this phrase it is best (with the Authorized Version and Revised Versions) to retain the idea of 'adoption as sons.' Christ is the only son of the Father—this idea is conveyed even by the term ' beloved ' in the Voice at the baptism, Mark i. 11. The rest of us are like the youth in the parable— we have cut ourselves off from the Father, and have no longer the right to be called His sons. The Father, however, has never disowned us, and now in Christ He has taken steps to bring us home and to get us installed again in the family. Paul's reference to ' adoption ' here has a purely religious significance, and there is no need to read it back into the illustration of verses 1, 2.

6   Turning now to address his readers directly (he uses the second person), Paul reminds them that sonship implies more than status ; the true son must share the life of the Father. It is not enough, he seems to say, that the Father is willing to recognize you as sons; you on your part must be enabled to rise and enter on this full and free and glad life of sonship. And just as in the fullness of time God had sent forth His Son into the world, so now, having found you ready to be accepted as sons, He **has sent forth the Spirit of his Son into your hearts ;** and, working in you, this Spirit leads you to turn to Him in childlike simplicity and call Him, as Jesus Himself had done, **Abba,** that is **Father.** Perhaps the true Greek reading is not ' *your* hearts ' but ' *our* hearts.' In violation of strict grammatical sequence, though with true Christian courtesy and brotherliness, Paul associates himself for a moment with his readers, as one who shares this spiritual experience of theirs. He too is a lost son who has been redeemed and adopted. It is significant that Paul should

here give both the Aramaic and the Greek word for Father.
Probably the combination has already become liturgical—' a
striking testimony ' (as Lightfoot reminds us) ' to that fusion
of Jew and Greek which prepared the way for the preaching
of the gospel to the heathen.' The earliest Christians would,
of course, repeat the Lord's Prayer in Aramaic ; and if Greek-
speaking Christians, in their form of it, retained the introductory ' Abba,' it was no doubt because a certain sacredness was
felt to attach to the opening word of the original (cf. the use
of Paternoster). As regards the addition of the Greek word
' Father,' there is perhaps point in J. H. Moulton's remark
(*Grammar of New Testament Greek*, Prolegomena, p. 10) that
' Paul will not allow even one word of prayer in a foreign
tongue without adding an instant translation.'

It is noteworthy that in this verse we have an association
of the Father, the Son and the Spirit ; that the Spirit is called
the Spirit of the Son ; and that God, Who had *sent forth* His
Son (verse 4), is said likewise to have *sent forth* the Spirit of
His Son. The phrase, ' the Spirit of His Son,' is not found in
this precise form elsewhere in the New Testament ; but in
Rom. viii. 9 we have ' the Spirit of Christ ' in a passage
which shows that Paul does not distinguish sharply between
the Spirit of Christ and the Spirit of God. Paul's phrase in
our present verse supports the orthodox contention that ' the
Spirit proceedeth from the Father and from the Son.'

Passing swiftly from the plural to the singular, as if he 7
were addressing each of his readers personally, Paul concludes
with a reminder that when the Spirit of the Son comes to dwell
in a man's heart, that man is a son indeed. Even though the
argument has been that sonship for us is attained by adoption,
nevertheless a man who has received the Spirit is in the fullest
sense a son. It is no longer he that lives, but the Spirit of the
Son that lives in him. Freed from all bondage, the son can
now address God as Father ; but no less important is it for
the son to know that the Father can now deal with him as a
son. ' Your position, therefore,' says Paul, ' is this : you are
no longer a servant, i.e. a *slave* ; you are no longer in bondage
either to the Law or to any of the powers of this world ; you

are a **son** of God the Father. Further, **God**, who has intervened to make you a son, means also to treat you as a son. As a son, He has marked you out to be an **heir** : it is your privilege, that is, to share in the inheritance which He promised of old to Abraham and his seed, and in the blessings which are the prerogative of the sons of God. All this is yours **owing to God** ; and God expects you to rise to the height of your calling.'

Paul's language throughout this whole section reveals an acquaintance on his part with some of the sayings and discourses of Jesus, and notably with the parable of the Lost Son. What is even more significant, it reveals how truly he is in accord with the Master's teaching and with His Spirit. Acceptance with God (i.e. justification) is reserved for the childlike, who, in simple trust, can call Him ' Abba, Father ' ; and adoption is equivalent to receiving the spirit of sonship.

iv. 8–11 : *Paul asks why the Galatians should wish to return to the religious bondage from which they have been delivered*

8 In those days, when you were ignorant of God, you were in
9   servitude to gods who are really no gods at all ; but now that you know God—or rather, are known by God—how is it you are turning back again to the weakness and poverty of the Elemental spirits ? Why do you want to
10   be enslaved all over again by them ? You observe days
11   and months, festal seasons and years ! Why, you make me afraid I may have spent my labour on you for nothing !

In the preceding verses Paul has triumphantly reaffirmed the position of iii. 29, viz. that the inheritors of the divine blessing promised by God to Abraham and his seed are those who are Christ's, those who through Christ the Son of God, the one true offspring of Abraham, have come into a relation of sonship to God the Father. The whole section from iii. 6 onwards has been a closely reasoned argument ; step by step the apostle has advanced, fighting every inch of the way, and positions captured by one line of reasoning have been confirmed by advances along another. But at various points in the progress we have been reminded (e.g. by the sudden changes to the second person) that for Paul this is not merely an argument, it is a passionate appeal ; his ultimate concern is not to establish a theological position, it is to save the souls of his converts. And so, having won his way to the assured position 8 of iv. 7, he now turns to his readers with the same note of eager expostulation which had been (iii. 2-5) the prelude to all this subtle and persistent argumentation. How can you think, he asks them, of turning back to the position of bondage which you have left behind ? In your pre-Christian state **you were ignorant of God**—ignorance of God being a description regularly applied in the New Testament to the life of paganism. Paul admits that the Galatians had had **gods of** another kind, but these so-called gods were **really no gods at all** (he means by this, not that they had no existence, but that they were demons rather than gods ; cf. 1 Cor. x. 20), and those who worshipped them stood to them in the relation not of sons but of slaves. On the other hand you have **now** 9 come to **know** the true **God**—an assertion Paul no sooner makes than he corrects himself, not so much retracting what he said as preferring to express it otherwise. It is not really that you have come to **know God,** but rather that now you **are known by God.** In so expressing himself Paul is doing something more than emphasizing the divine initiative (1 John iv. 10 ; 1 Cor. xiii. 12, and verses 4-6 above) : he is operating with a pregnant sense of the word ' know ' as practically equal to ' acknowledge ' (cf. 1 Cor. viii. 3 ; 2 Tim. ii. 19), and his point is that the Galatians have not merely come to know God as Father, but have (by the gift of the Spirit) been brought into such filial relationship with Him that they are acknowledged by Him as sons ; cf. the Voice at the Baptism of Jesus, Mark i. 11, and the thought of God or Christ ' knowing His own,' Matt. vii. 23 ; John x. 15. In view of all that God has done for you, **how is it**, the apostle asks, that you should be **turning back again** to the stage you had left (cf. iii. 3)—you who have attained to the free life of sonship preferring once again to see yourselves enslaved, and substituting for a joyous acceptance of God the Father a worship of **the Elemental spirits,** which in themselves have no *power* (viz. to lift you out of your bondage), and no *resources* (to endow you with the heritage of sons) ?

The Elemental spirits. At this point we must interrupt the exposition to ask what the apostle means, here and in verse 3 above, by the reference to 'the Elemental spirits,' or it may be ' the elements ' (Greek *stoicheia*). The problem is one of great difficulty ; yet it may be that a true interpretation of the phrase will shed a flood of light on the background of religious thought in the Epistle. We may note that the longer phrase of verse 3, *elements* (*Elemental spirits*) *of the world*, is found again in Col. ii. 8, 20 ; and, though parallels are frequent, it occurs *in that precise form* nowhere else in Greek literature.

Originally denoting things which have their place in a row or ordered sequence, and hence used with particular reference to the *letters of the alphabet*, the word in question came to have two main derived meanings, (1) *elements of knowledge* (cf. Heb. v. 12), and (2) *elements of the physical universe*, coming in this latter sense to be applied not merely to earth, air, water and fire, but also to *heavenly bodies* and in particular to the *planets*. An extension of this second use came when *stoicheia* was applied to *angels* or *spirits* associated with the various parts of the physical universe ; and in modern Greek the word is practically equivalent to *ghosts*.

(1) That Paul meant nothing more than the elements of religious knowledge was the view of Tertullian and Jerome, of Erasmus and Calvin, and more recently of Lightfoot and Burton, and this interpretation is adopted in the Revised Version (' rudiments '). ' Rudiments of the world ' would thus refer to the elementary truths of natural religion, as distinct from the truths conveyed by divine revelation. Similarly Goodspeed, in his *American Translation*, renders the phrase in verse 3 as ' material ways of looking at things,' and in verse 9 as ' the old crude notions.' The reference to the

period of childhood in verse 3, and the contrast with the true knowledge of God in verse 9, would seem to favour this interpretation. On the other hand, the emphatic reference in both passages to enslavement is decidedly against it.

(2) The second interpretation, in one form or another, was adopted by most of the early Fathers, and is supported by the weight of modern scholarship. There is no good reason to doubt that it is the correct one. In various Eastern cosmogonies room was found for the belief that angelic or demonic powers, operating perhaps under a supreme God, controlled the forces of nature ; and, passing over into late Judaism, this conception was combined with others (e.g. the ' principalities and powers ' which Paul mentions so often in his later Epistles) to yield a hierarchy of cosmical agencies. Some of these may have been regarded as actively evil (cf. Eph. ii. 2, 3) ; but the *stoicheia* were not so much ' powers of evil ' as ' powers of this world,' belonging to Nature rather than to super-Nature. As Edwyn Bevan reminds us in his *Hellenism and Christianity* (p. 77), ' The fear of these world-rulers, particularly the Sun, the Moon and the five planets, lay heavy on the old world. The Mysterious Seven held humanity in the mechanism of iron necessity.' Men who knew no higher Power could be described, in Paul's phrase (Eph. ii. 12) as ' without hope and without God in the world.'

The pious Jew of the Hellenistic period, viewing these Elemental spirits not merely as parts of a cosmological theory, but as active powers for good or evil, was prone to trace their influence notably in heathendom, where, as inferior ' gods ' or angels, they interposed (it was felt) between man and the true God. But Paul's position was that, until the Redeemer came, the whole world, Jewish and Gentile alike, was under the dominion of these ' powers of the present age,' and as we saw in the commentary on iii. 19 he definitely connected even the giving of the Law with angels rather than with the living God. Hence he could urge that, in accepting Jewish ritual as a necessary part of their religion, the Galatians, so far from advancing in their new faith, were actually *turning back to serve the Elemental spirits* from which Christ had delivered them.

This verdict raises interesting issues. (1) It implies that for Paul the religion of Israel under the Law had affinities with heathenism. It, like heathenism, lacked knowledge of the living God (cf. Rom. x. 3). (2) It does not follow that 'bondage to the Elemental spirits,' the description which Paul gives of the pre-Christian religion in Galatia, could be applied *simpliciter* to the religion of Israel, or that he equates these Elemental spirits with the angels who gave the Law. Nevertheless it is noteworthy that the features of Judaism which he specially selects for repudiation in verse 10 are not circumcision and food restrictions, but the observance of days and months and seasons and years, all of which were under the control of the heavenly bodies. There is a similar line of thought in Stephen's speech, where after their rejecting of the 'living oracles' the Israelites were, it is said, abandoned 'to the worship of the starry host' (Acts vii. 42). Without therefore equating them, Paul recognizes a close affinity between the 'angels' of the devout Jew and the 'Elemental spirits' of the pagan. Both belong to the present age, and both have been robbed of their power by Christ.

10 That men who in Christ have come to know themselves as sons of God should burden themselves with the legalistic obligations of Judaism is, in the apostle's eyes, so retrograde a movement that he dares to describe it as not different from 11 a reversion to heathenism, and he expresses his fear (for note that the position is not yet regarded as irretrievable) that if they persist, all the **labour** he has **spent** in redeeming them from heathenism will be found to have gone **for nothing**. He specially mentions here their zealous celebrations of **days** (sabbaths and other holy days), **months** (i.e. new moons ; Num. x. 10), **seasons** (i.e. the set feasts of the Passover, etc. ; cf. 1 Chron. xxiii. 31 ; 2 Chron. viii. 13), **years** (referring probably to the New Year celebrations : it is not likely that the Galatians can have yet adopted the celebration of the sabbatical year ; cf. Lev. xxv.).

Paul's statement of observances here is significant for what it omits no less than for what it contains. Why, e.g., no reference to circumcision ? The answer sometimes given is that, in their approach to the Galatians, ' the Judaizers had pursued the adroit course of presenting to them at first a part only of the requirements of the Jewish Law and had begun with those things that would be least repulsive ' (Burton). In other words, they had first persuaded the Galatians to adopt the Jewish festivals, and were now engaged in trying to get them to adopt circumcision. Such a reconstruction is obviously a reversal of the true order (in the eyes of men like the Judaizers, circumcision was the first and most important of their demands), and the hypothetical character of Paul's reference to circumcision in v. 2 cannot be cited in support of it. The clue to the answer is rather to be found in those references of Paul's to the Elemental spirits which the Galatians worshipped in those days before the gospel came to them. Paul selects those elements in the Jewish ritual which have obvious affinities with pagan worship ; and the very enumeration of them, he hopes, will bring home to the senseless Galatians the truth of the contention which has come to the surface more than once in the preceding verses, viz. that for the Christian the adoption of Judaism partakes of the character of a relapse into paganism.

iv. 12–20 : *Argument for a moment gives place to appeal, as the apostle recalls to the Galatians the cordiality and happiness of his early relations with them*

Do take my line, brothers, I beg of you—just as I once took 12 yours. I have no complaint against you ; no, although it 13 was because of an illness (you know) that I preached the gospel to you on my former visit, and though my flesh 14 was a trial to you, you did not scoff at me nor spurn me, you welcomed me like an angel of God, like Christ Jesus. You congratulated yourselves. Now, what has become 15 of all that ? (I can bear witness that you would have torn out your very eyes, if you could, and given me them.)

16   Am I your enemy to-day, because I have been honest
17   with you ? These men make much of you—yes, but for
      dishonest ends ; they want to debar you from us, so that
18   you may make much of them. Now it is fine for you to
      be made much of honestly and all the time—not simply
19   when I can be with you. O my dear children, you with
      whom I am in travail over again till Christ be formed
20   within you, would that I could be with you at this moment,
      and alter my tone, for I am at my wits' end about you !

Once again, as in iii. 1 ff., argumentation gives place to open-hearted personal appeal. Nothing in all that Paul has written, unless it be certain verses in 2 Corinthians (e.g. vi. 11–13), illustrates as fully as this passage does the anguish that the apostle suffered through any kind of estrangement (whether the estrangement of friends from himself or, what to him was even sadder, their estrangement from God) and the passionate desire of his soul to get the roots of such estrangement removed. It is not that he is ashamed of the fury of his previous out-bursts : how easily it might break out again we can see from the language of verses 16–18. But though the passion is still there, it is the passion of a man who is concerned not to beat down his opponents but to win them ; it is the passion not of polemic but of Christian love.

12   Paul begins by calling on them (as in 1 Cor. iv. 16 ; xi. 1 he calls on the Corinthians) to take his line ; and again we see how the spirit of appeal expresses itself in the introduction of the word ' brothers.' When he adds as I once took yours (both Authorized Version and Revised Version here translate by a present tense, *for I am as ye are*) he possibly implies that he himself, though a proud Jew, had voluntarily sacrificed his scrupulous observance of the Law so as to identify himself with them—becoming, as his Jewish opponents would have said, no better than a ' Gentile sinner.' To the Greeks he had become a Greek that he might win them for Christ ; (cf. 1 Cor. ix. 21). But all through this section the very intimacy of the appeal, so self-revealing to the original readers, who knew all the inner history of the case, leaves the modern

reader guessing at the precise point of some of the references. Why, for instance, in the opening sentence of verse 13 (which 13 taken literally means ' you did me no wrong ') is there the enigmatic reference to a complaint ? Are we mentally to supply the thought : ' you did me no wrong *until now*,' carrying with it the implication that he does unfortunately have reason to complain of their *present* conduct ? This is not likely : had there been a contrast between ' then ' and ' now ' the Greek would have made it plain. Rather he is seeking with his whole soul to assure his converts that, despite their having turned away from his gospel and despite the tone he has had to adopt in this letter, he nurses in his soul no rankling sense of injustice. There is no reason why he and they should not once again take the same line, understanding and trusting one another as fully as they have done at the beginning.

Such is the apostle's plea : and in support of it he becomes reminiscent. Here again we wish we could understand the references as clearly as the Galatians would have done. Does the reference to a former visit mean that he had visited them *twice* ? (see Introduction, p. xxii.). Does he imply that on the occasion of his earlier visit he had not intended to evangelize the Galatian cities until illness drove him there, and are we therefore to explain the difficult and dangerous crossing of the Taurus Mountains from Perga to Antioch (Acts xiii. 14) by the necessity of his getting to higher altitudes ? And what was the nature of his illness ? Was it malaria ? or does verse 15 suggest that it was eye-trouble ? The last is a doubtful assumption. The reference of verse 15 to ' tear out their eyes ' may be amply explained metaphorically : ' at that time your devotion to me would have stopped short of no sacrifice.' It is tempting to connect this illness with the chronic affliction referred to in 2 Cor. xii. 7 as ' a thorn in the flesh,' which in its turn is generally explained as some form of epilepsy. Though this is denied by some commentators, the Greek probably implies that illness supplied a *reason* for his visit (because of an illness, and not merely *in illness*), and the illness was apparently one which might have 14 evoked among the Galatians contempt and even revulsion. The

word ' **spurn** ' means literally to ' spit out ' : is there behind
this the idea that they might have regarded him as possessed
by *an evil spirit* (which again might point to epilepsy) ? If
so, all the more significant is Paul's proud and grateful recollection that they had **welcomed** him rather as **an angel of
God.** There may be in this a reference to the story recorded
in Acts xiv. 12, how at Lystra Barnabas and Paul were hailed
as Zeus and Hermes (cf. the legend which told how these gods,
disguised as travellers, visited the humble home of Philemon
and Baucis in Phrygia) ; if so, the Galatians soon came to
connect the apostle, not with a heathen deity, but with **Christ
Jesus** whom he proclaimed, and they welcomed him, despite
his illness, as if, in the place of the apostle, Christ Himself had
come to dwell among them. ' No wonder,' says Paul, ' that
15 **you congratulated yourselves,** seeing in all this a sign of the
favour of Heaven. Why do you not do so still ? '

In verse 16 unsuspected difficulties again lurk under the
16 surface. When was it that Paul had shown to them that
honesty which might be construed as *enmity* ? Is the reference
(cf. note on i. 9) to a previous visit ? or to an unrecorded
letter ? Neither of these assumptions is necessary. The
' honesty ' is that of the present letter. Paul is afraid (cf.
note on verse 13) that the strong language he had found it
necessary to adopt may be construed by the readers as
evidence that he has turned against them. ' Far from it ' he
seems to say. ' You once regarded me as a heaven-sent friend,
and took me to your hearts : do not cease to think so of me
because I have had to use such frankness in writing to you.
17 I could be like those others (here of course Paul is thinking
of his opponents and detractors, though he does not name
them) whose only concern is to **make much of you,** to curry
favour with you, whose motives however are **dishonest** and
whose ambition is to " exclude " you.' Exclude from whom ?
Our translation says : **debar you from us ;** but there is nothing
corresponding to ' from us ' in the Greek. Is the reference
to exclusion from the Church ? or, as in the translation,
exclusion from intercourse with Paul himself ? A much better
sense would be got if, despite the weakness of MS. support,

we read 'exclude *us*' : by shutting us out from you these men would get all the more honour and attention for themselves. 'But surely,' Paul continues, 'the right thing to look 18 for in friendship is that it should be both *honourable* and *unchanging*—a claim I can make for myself, for I am as truly your friend when in absence I write to you a letter of stern remonstrance as **when I can be with you** and find myself welcomed as an angel from heaven.'

Here Paul breaks out into language of the tenderest affection. 19 **My dear children,** he calls them. And just as in 1 Thessalonians he regards his relation to his converts as that of a nursing-mother (1 Thess. ii. 8) or a father (ii. 11), so here he likens himself to a mother in childbirth, who must endure **over again** the pangs of **travail** with children who will not be ready to be brought to the birth until **Christ** is **formed** in them. This latter phrase does not of course suggest that the Galatians in turn are like a mother in whose womb Christ is being formed ; it merely means that they themselves are not ready to be born into the Christian life until it is true of them that it is not they who are to live, but Christ who is to live in them (cf. ii. 20). The metaphor may not be applicable in every detail, but it certainly conveys the love and yearning and pain which the apostle feels for his weak and wayward converts. Those same feelings come to expression in the words which follow. He laments the fact that he cannot be near 20 them : ' if only **I could be with you,** with my children, then I could **alter my tone ;** for how easy it would be for us to understand one another.' As it is, what can he do but write to them in a mingled paroxysm of pleading and authority, sorrow and expostulation, anxiety and rebuke, grieved and baffled to know how to deal with them. **I am at my wits' end about you.**

iv. 21–v. 1 : *A further argument, based on the story of Abraham's household. Sarah and her son prefigure a religion of freedom, Hagar and her son one of bondage. The section closes with an eager appeal to the Galatians to maintain their Christian freedom*

21 Tell me, you who are keen to be under the Law, will you not
22   listen to the Law? Surely it is written in the Law that
      Abraham had two sons, one by the slave-woman and one
23   by the free-woman; but while the son of the slave-woman
      was born by the flesh, the son of the free-woman was born
24   by the promise. Now this is an allegory. The women are
      two covenants. One comes from mount Sinai, bearing
25   children for servitude; that is Hagar, for mount Sinai* is
      away in Arabia. She corresponds to the present Jerusalem,
26   for the latter is in servitude with her children. But the
27   Jerusalem on high is free, and she is ‘ our ’ mother. For
      it is written,

> Rejoice, O thou barren who bearest not,
> break into joy, thou who travailest not;
> for the children of the desolate woman are far more
>   than of the married.

28 Now you are the children of the Promise, brothers, like Isaac;
29   but just as in the old days the son born by the flesh perse-
30   cuted the son born by the Spirit, so it is still to-day. How-
      ever, what does the scripture say? *Put away the slave-*
      woman and her son, for the son of the slave-woman shall
31   *not be heir along with the son* of the free-woman. Hence
v.   we are children of no slave-woman, my brothers, but of
1   the free-woman,* with the freedom for which Christ set us
      free. Make a firm stand then, do not slip into any yoke
      of servitude.

* On iv. 25 and v. 1 see notes on p. 195.

21   The apostle does indeed alter his tone, as he had expressed
      a desire to do (verse 20). A fresh idea occurs to him, and he
      turns again to his readers with a reasoned appeal based on
      that very **Law** of which they make so much. In speaking of
      them as being **keen to be under the Law** (or possibly *under law*
      in a general sense) he indicates again (cf. notes on i. 6; iii. 4;
      iv. 11; v. 10) that the situation is still in process of develop-
      ment: all is not lost. There is no irony in the phrase—there
      could be no place for irony in a situation of such gravity; rather
      it indicates the apostle’s anxiety to stand alongside his ‘ dear

children ' instead of merely attacking them, and to help them to realize for themselves the retrograde character of the path they are pursuing. In asking them to **listen to the Law**, he means by ' the Law ' the five books of Moses, or it may be the Old Testament as a whole interpreted from the stand-point of the Judaizers.

In this passage we come to one of the most remarkable instances in the New Testament of the allegorical method of interpretation. One method of expounding Scripture, developed especially at Alexandria (e.g. by Philo, who uses this very passage to prove the superiority of heavenly wisdom to merely worldly knowledge ; and later, in the Christian Church, by Origen) was to interpret the characters and events of Scripture as essentially *types* of spiritual realities. To us to-day, with our emphasis on the *historical* method and our eagerness to arrive at *historical* truth, such interpretations often appear fantastic and even misleading : but to Paul and many of his contemporaries, the learned no less than the simple, religious truths secured their surest and strongest corroboration if they could be represented as foreshadowed, allegorically or otherwise, in Scripture. Here Paul, still glowing with a passionate eagerness to save his converts from their waywardness, seeks to show them that, if they *will* go back to the Law, the Law itself will teach them that the true children of Abraham, the true inheritors of the Promise, are not those who have their bond of union in the Law, but those who have attained to spiritual freedom in Christ.

It is interesting to note that Paul's Galatian readers, pagans though they so recently were, are assumed to have a knowledge of the main outlines of the Old Testament history. Evidently even in preaching to Gentiles the Christian missionaries presented the Christian salvation as something that was not to be understood save as the culmination of a great ' plan of the ages,' whereby God sought through His dealing with an elect people to win at last in Christ a family of ' sons.' The story 22 that is here cited is that of **Abraham** and his **two sons**, Isaac and Ishmael—a story with which, from its very contrast between legitimate and illegitimate descent, every Jewish child, as a true son of Abraham, would have been proudly familiar from his earliest years, and one to which Jewish preachers and controversialists must often have turned as a divine proof of the superiority of their nation to lesser breeds who were outside the covenant. Paul too had from boyhood known the story, but now in Christ he has learned to read its 23 implications in an altogether new sense. In the story of Abraham and his two children (one of whom, born to him **by the slave-woman** Hagar, was a child *only* in a physical sense, while the other was in the fullest sense a son, born **of the free-woman** in accordance with a God-given **promise**) Paul sees 24 **an allegory** of the **two covenants** in which the ' seed ' of Abraham participated, viz. the covenant of the Law, and the earlier and more fundamental covenant of the Promise which was now fulfilled in Christ. By an *allegory* he means something more than an *illustration* : it is a spiritual truth embodied in history, a shadow from the eternal world cast upon the sands of time. Strong in his conviction that the Law entails servitude (cf. iv. 1–7) he has no difficulty in finding an allegorical connection between the covenant of Law and **Hagar,** who was herself a slave-girl, and whose **children** could only be born and grow up in a condition of **servitude,** unless of 25 course the father cared to adopt them as sons. The argument is enforced by a supplementary clause which hints that, besides the connection of the Law with **mount Sinai,** there is some connection also between Hagar and Mount Sinai, and goes on to say that **mount Sinai is away in Arabia.** The reference is obscure. Even the text is uncertain : some MSS. read ' this Hagar is Mount Sinai in Arabia.' The point may be (*a*) that being in Arabia, Mount Sinai lies outside the Promised Land : in other words, when the Law was given Israel herself had not entered into her inheritance. In their arguments with the Jews the early Christians liked to insist that God even under the old dispensation did not confine His revelation to one holy land or one holy place—we may compare how in Acts vii. Stephen contends that God appeared to Abraham ' in Mesopotamia before ever he stayed in Haran ' (verse 2), that He was with Joseph in Egypt (verse 9), that

He spoke to Moses on Mount Sinai (verses 30 ff.), and that He had His ' church ' in the desert (verse 38). Or (*b*) the implication may rather be that just as Hagar herself was a slave-girl, so Arabia is a land of slavery, being the home of an inferior tribe, the Hagarenes (Ps. lxxxiii. 6) whom the Jews as true ' sons of Abraham ' linked up with Hagar and Ishmael. Whatever the point of the addition, it is subsidiary to the main argument, viz. that Hagar, the slave-girl, is a type of the covenant of Law, and of the enslaving religion that makes that covenant its foundation.

We may note how here the allegorical interpretation cuts quite adrift from the historical facts (cf. note on iii. 16), but is regarded as being no less authoritative on that account. Paul does not dispute that as a matter of history the Jewish people are the sons of Abraham, descendants of his first-born son Isaac ; but he insists that when we learn, as is far more important, to see in that simple domestic story of Abraham's household a reflection in time of the eternal relation of the Father in Heaven to His children, then it becomes plain that the Jews, for all their pride of descent (and Paul himself shared that pride, cf. 2 Cor. xi. 22 ; Phil. iii. 4 ff.) are rather to be classed as—Ishmaelites How every word in this argument of Paul must have lashed his Judaizing opponents to indignation.

The argument, however, is not yet completed. Paul has already shown how the two *mothers*, the slave-girl and the free-born wife, represent respectively the two covenants of Law and Promise, and he has drawn a conclusion regarding the *children*, viz. that the children of the former are naturally born to servitude, while those of the latter are born to be free. He now views the allegory from another aspect, and introduces what is virtually a comparison between the two *homes* to which the children belong. The word translated ' **corresponds** ' suggests an arrangement in rows, and the idea may perhaps be represented as follows :

Hagar	Sarah
(=the Covenant of Law)	(=the Covenant of Promise)
corresponds to	*corresponds to*
the present Jerusalem.	the Jerusalem on high.

Corresponding to **Hagar**, says Paul, is **the present** (i.e. the earthly) **Jerusalem,** the centre and home of a religion of bondage, which shuts up God Himself in a Temple made with hands, and substitutes for His spiritual worship a scrupulous observance of legal enactments. Those who acknowledge such
26 a religion are really ' sons of Hagar.' On the other hand, we who acknowledge as our Lord the risen and exalted Christ know that our home is not on earth but in heaven ; by contrast therefore we may claim that **our mother** (the ' our ' is emphatic) is **the Jerusalem on high ;** and she, like Sarah, **is free.** Here the Authorized Version (' mother of us all ') is based on an inferior text which is quite misleading—Paul is definitely contrasting the two types of religion, the Jewish and the Christian, and showing how the children of the one are in bondage, while the children of the other are free. The apostle expresses the Christian position somewhat similarly when in Phil. iii. 20 he says : ' We ' (again the pronoun is emphatic) ' are a colony of heaven.'

This conception of a Jerusalem on high was one which already had a place in pre-Christian Judaism. It was partly the outcome of the spirit of disillusionment so prevalent both in Jewry and in the world in general ; and in its development it was aided by Hellenistic speculations traceable in their origin to the Platonic theory of ideas. But at bottom it was in accordance with the highest spiritual ideals and longings of the Jewish religion. When the Messiah should appear to set up His Kingdom its centre was to be an ideal Jerusalem. The thought finds expression in the Book of Enoch (xc. 28 ff.) ; and in the Apocalypse of Baruch (iv. 2–7), following a verse in which there is a reference to ' the evils of my mother ' (i.e. Jerusalem), there is a notable passage where by contrast the praises are sung of the heavenly Jerusalem which has existed eternally in the mind of God, and which Adam, Abraham, and Moses were privileged to behold in vision. In the New Testament we may refer to Heb. xii. 22 ; Rev. iii. 12, xxi. 2, 9 ff. It was natural that the conception should be adopted as their own by the Christians, who in their mission preaching claimed that the ideal was one which would receive its fulfilment when Jesus Christ set up His Kingdom, and in their apologetic with the Jews insisted that Judaism, by its literalism and its nationalism, grasped at the shadow and lost the substance. In the present passage the very suddenness with which at one leap, so to speak, and with no attempt at explanation, Paul carries his readers on to this thought of the ' Jerusalem on high ' is an indication of the extent to which this conception of a super-natural and supranational Kindgom, with its ideal city, figured in his own thinking and in his missionary preaching. At the base of all his appeal in Galatians is the thought of redemption from the present world (Gal. i. 4).

Paul does not say that this heavenly Jerusalem will be established as a visible entity on earth ; it is for him essentially a heavenly city. Here on earth, however, those who are Christ's are already fully conscious that they are members of it, and already they share its glories, its liberties, and its obligations. And so, pressing home the contrast (with all its 27 far-reaching implications) between the earthly and the heavenly Jerusalem, Paul now appeals exultingly to the language of Isa. liv. 1. To understand the original significance of this quotation we must go back in thought to the time of the exile.[1] Jerusalem is desolate ; the holy places, where Jehovah dwelt in the midst of her, are in ruins ; her children have been carried away into captivity ; Israel in exile is like a lonely woman, with neither husband nor family. And yet it is Isaiah's triumphant assurance that out of this desolation there will arise, on the exiles' return, a new Jerusalem, or rather a new Israel (he is thinking less of the restored city than of the redeemed community that is to dwell in it) for which Jehovah has far greater glories in store than were ever realized in the days of earlier prosperity. Though in Isaiah's vision there is ultimately only one woman, viewed under two

---

[1] Professor Torrey, in his noteworthy book on *The Second Isaiah*, attributes that work to a prophet of Jerusalem, about A.D. 400, representing an opposing tendency to the narrow nationalism of Ezra and Nehemiah. He interprets the present passage as an exhortation to Jerusalem to expand on every side ; the God of Israel ought to be the God of all the earth. Paul's use of the Isaiah passage is of course unaffected by the view taken of its original context.

different aspects, it is possible (cf. li. 2) that he has in the background of his consciousness the relations of Hagar and Sarah—the latter, after a long period of barrenness, finally outstripping the temporary triumph of her rival. But whether this be so or not, we can understand how Paul, following up the allegory of the two women, would see in the prophet's language a sublime corroboration of the truth for which he has just been contending. Judaism, with its visible centre at Jerusalem, was for Paul a religion which had enjoyed at God's hand countless privileges but had not known how to use them aright ; Israel, which had claimed in her pride that she was God's elect people, the very bride of Jehovah, had not won the Gentiles to accept Him as their God. By contrast the fellowship of those who were Christ's was now, after a long time of waiting, seeing the fulfilment of the Promise made to Abraham ; as the true bride of the Lord she was bringing forth children to the glory of His name, and the Gentiles were coming from afar to take their place in the family of God.

28 Turning now directly to address his readers (though according to some MSS. which read ' we ' instead of ' you ' the statement is meant to apply to Christians generally) the apostle asserts in one short sentence that it is to them that the second half of the contrast applies which was outlined in verse 23 ; **you are the children of the Promise, like Isaac.** In all this study of Abraham's domestic life Paul has not forgotten what is the ultimate question, viz. *Who are the true sons of Abraham ?* Abraham, he argues, had not one son merely, but two; further, Scripture itself has established the fact that, for all the vaunted pride which the Jews had in their legitimate descent, the spiritual prototype of the Jewish nation was not Isaac, but Ishmael, the son born merely after the flesh. For these reasons it is now urged that, inasmuch as the Christians are the true inheritors of the divine promise (cf. iii. 7–19), so it is they and not the Jews who can claim to stand towards Abraham in the same relation as Isaac did—it is they alone who are his legitimate sons, born according to promise. Here

again we have a claim that must have evoked the bitterest resentment in the hearts of Paul's opponents.

Especially if we read, as in our translation, the second personal plural ('*you* are the children of the Promise'), we may trace in this verse a confidential undertone (note again the introduction of **brothers**), suggesting that allegorizing is about to give place to a more personal type of appeal ; and this change does indeed begin in verse 31, where again the address is to '*my brothers.*' But meantime the passion of the apostle's soul wells up again. For all his exultation (verse 27) he is conscious of a wound that smarts, and, stirred by the pain of it, he turns again to the old Jewish story, to find in it material for a Parthian shaft.

What follows is apparently based on a Jewish *Haggadah,* 29 i.e. a rabbinical interpretation of a Scripture narrative ; Paul's earlier training had made him familiar with such expositions, and we may note how in his picture in 1 Cor. x. 4 of the Rock that accompanied the Israelites in their wanderings he goes back to a similar source. In Gen. xxi. 9, where the English versions tell how Sarah saw the son of Hagar *mocking*, the LXX. takes a more innocent view of Ishmael's conduct ; it represents him merely as 'playing,' an interpretation quite as consistent with the Hebrew as 'mocking' is. But the necessity for explaining Sarah's anger (which does, indeed, suggest some stronger provocation than mere playing ; it may be that the Hebrew text has suffered mutilation) opened the door to legendary accretions—e.g. a sixth-century Midrash, founding on the adult Ishmael's skill in archery (Gen. xxi. 20), depicts the two children going out to the field, when Ishmael, as if in fun, turns his bow and arrow against his younger play-mate. The story appealed to Paul because, whether or not it was historically true, it foreshadowed a fact which, as he saw, was now in his own day ('**still to-day**') receiving tragic fulfilment, when **the son born by the Spirit** (i.e. the Christian community) was being made to suffer at the hands of **the son born by the flesh** (i.e. the Jewish nation). Had not Christ, the true 'Offspring' according to the Promise, been nailed to a cross by His unbelieving fellow-countrymen, Peter and John been accused before the Sanhedrin and ordered by ecclesiastical authority to cease their testimony, Stephen been stoned as of old the prophets had been stoned, not to mention those others who had suffered during the persecution that arose about Stephen, including those whom Paul himself in his days of apostasy had sought out to deliver to the high-priests? And all this sorrowful story of persecution was already, says Paul, prefigured in Scripture, when it told how the child of Promise was persecuted by the son of the bond-woman. Nor can the apostle forget how he himself had experienced the enmity of his compatriots (cf. Acts ix. 29), and even *to-day* that enmity was manifesting itself in the persistent attempts of the Judaizers to ruin his God-given work among the Gentiles. So is it ever. A legalistic religion cannot be other than a persecuting religion, for it knows that it cannot endure unless its regulations are kept in the letter.

30   With soul deeply stirred Paul asks that as between the contending parties **Scripture** shall be the judge, and he confidently appeals for it to give its verdict. This he finds in the words of Sarah ordering Hagar's expulsion (Gen. xxi. 10), which, quite apart from the guarantee in verse 12 of that passage that the words have the divine approval, is for him an authoritative pronouncement, just because it is a word of Scripture whose validity is being demonstrated by experience ; and this verdict Paul promulgates as if it were full and final, revealing not a trace of that passionate longing or that illimitable hope which at other times (cf. Rom. x. 1, xi. 26) constrained him to dream of the ultimate salvation of Israel. In quoting the words from Genesis he is true in all essentials to the LXX., substituting, however, for ' my son Isaac ' the phrase ' **the son of the free-woman,**' which besides being a more forcible contrast to the phrase that precedes, provides a natural transition to the appeal which is to follow for the exercise of Christian freedom.

By this decree of expulsion, Paul is not descending to the level of that persecuting spirit which in the preceding sentence he had deplored. The persecutor, if he cannot secure submission from the persecuted, sets out to secure his extinction.

In expulsion, though it may seem more terrible, the attitude is rather : ' Your ways may be appropriate in another environment, but they are not so here ; hence you must go.' The house of prayer, for instance, must not be made a den of robbers. In this sense there cannot in the end be any compromise between the Gospel and the Law. When legalism invades the domain of evangelical religion, the alternatives for the latter are to decree expulsion or to accept corruption. There are spiritual dangers even in comprehensiveness and toleration.

What then is the lesson which the Galatians must learn 31 for themselves from the preceding allegory ? Succinctly and sympathetically (' **my brothers** ') Paul seeks to bring it home to his misguided converts. It is that if the question is raised regarding ' the sons of Abraham,' we who are Christ's can claim to be His true and freeborn sons, born not of *a* **slave-woman** (the phrase is quite indefinite, not as in the Authorized Version, ' children of *the* bond-woman ') **but of the free-woman.** In this latter case the phrase is definite ; there is only one true wife, and her children alone are legitimate and freeborn. Whether this free-mother is to be identified in the allegory with the covenant of Promise (verse 24) or with the Jerusalem on high (verse 26) we need not enquire. The important fact is that Christians are born to be free.

Now this conclusion has cogency for Paul just because it is so thoroughly in line with what his whole Christian experience has taught him to be true, viz. that what Christ has done for men is to set them free (cf. the note of ' deliverance ' sounded at the opening of the Epistle ; i. 4) ; and those two aspects, the scriptural and the experimental, of the one religious truth are now, in v. 1, linked on one to the other. As to their precise *syntactical* connection there is a good deal of uncertainty. Perhaps it is best (*a*) to regard the second idea as expressed in a new and separate sentence—in that case the thought is either : ' *with* this freedom Christ set us free,' i.e. *by winning for us* this freedom ; or it may rather be ' *for* this freedom Christ set us free,' i.e. *in order that we might exercise* this freedom. On this view ' this freedom ' (lit. ' *the* freedom ') would refer back to the freedom which, as indicated in the allegory, belongs to those who are not born into bondage to the Law, but are children of the Promise. Or we may (*b*), as in the translation, make the second clause dependent on the

v. former : **we are children of the free-woman with the freedom**
1 **for which Christ set us free.** A third interpretation (*c*), which links the new clause not with what goes before but with what follows (thus Authorized Version, ' stand fast in the liberty wherewith Christ hath made us free ') is based on a MS. reading of obviously inferior value. Our choice must be between alternatives (*a*) and (*b*) : and while (*b*) is 'adopted in the translation on grounds which Dr. Moffatt explains in his footnote, the present writer is strongly in favour of (*a*). On this view the lesson of the allegory is summed up in the words : ' Hence we are children of no slave-woman, my brothers, but of the free-woman ' ; and this is followed by a word of assurance and appeal : ' For (this) freedom Christ freed us—i.e. it was in order that we might live in freedom that Christ set us free. Make a firm stand, then.'

Having thus stated his case, Paul rounds it off with a simple direct appeal that the Galatians, realizing their freedom in Christ, will **make a firm stand**, and not again put their necks under a **yoke** (not ' the yoke,' Authorized Version). The Greek has the word ' again ' which is omitted in the translation : ' be not entangled *again.*' As we saw in iv. 9, Paul is ready to regard Jewish bondage to ordinances as analogous with heathen superstitions and fears. It seems best to regard this exhortation as the conclusion of the argument that began in iv. 21 rather than as the beginning of a new section. The chapter-divisions in our Bibles, it will be remembered, are not older than the twelfth century and are often misleading.

IV. PRACTICAL IMPLICATIONS OF THE GOSPEL
(v. 2–vi. 10)

Paul has now concluded the argument on which he embarked in chap. iii.—the vindication of the *truth* of his gospel. And he has ended on a note of triumph—the note of the freedom of the gospel. With that note still resounding, he passes now to exhort his converts (*a*) not to sacrifice that freedom wantonly (verses 2 ff.) ; (*b*) to realize what that freedom involves for them in daily life (verses 13 ff.), and more especially in their social relationships (v. 25–vi. 10).

Paul's teaching on Christian *freedom* is based on his doctrine of *redemption*. He believed that, apart from redemption from the powers of evil, there is no real freedom for man. Hence much that passes for freedom in our modern world would have seemed to him an inadequate ideal, and indeed to be a false and dangerous ideal. On the other hand he teaches that the redeemed man is called to freedom, and must not relapse into slavery. The danger of such a relapse presents itself in a variety of forms. Not having lost the slavish spirit a man may think he is called to perform the divine requirements rather than live as a son with the Father. Or it may be that, being set free, he regards himself as free to do as he chooses, in which case the Spirit of the Father gets no chance to come in and take possession.

v. 2–12 : *The Christian life is a life of freedom, and that freedom must not be sacrificed*

Here, listen to Paul ! I tell you, if you get circumcised, Christ 2 will be no use to you. I insist on this again to everyone 3 who gets circumcised, that he is obliged to carry out the whole of the Law. You are for justification by the Law ? 4 Then you are done with Christ, you have deserted grace, for it is by faith that ' we ' wait in the Spirit for the righ- 5 teousness we hope for ; in Christ Jesus circumcision is not 6 valid, neither is uncircumcision, but only faith active in love. You were doing splendidly. Who was it that pre- 7 vented you from obeying the Truth ? That sort of suasion 8 does not come from Him who called you ! (A morsel of 9 dough will leaven the whole lump.) I feel persuaded in 10 the Lord that you will not go wrong. But he who unsettles

you will have to meet his doom, no matter who he is.
11   I am ' still preaching circumcision myself,' am I ? Then,
brothers, why am I still being persecuted ? And so the
stumbling-block of the cross has lost its force, forsooth !
12   O that those who are upsetting you would get themselves
castrated !

There are few passages in Scripture more moving than
this personal appeal of Paul to his misguided converts. We
may set it alongside that of our Lord to His wavering followers in John vi. 66 ff. : ' will ye also go away ? ' Paul
realizes that they have come to the parting of the ways. He
will speak to them now, not as a controversialist, not even as
an apostle, but rather as man to man : ' listen to Paul ' (he
uses this same Greek phrase, lit. ' I, Paul,' not infrequently ;
cf. 2 Cor. x. 1 ; Eph. iii. 1).

2   At the outset we are met, rather abruptly, by a reference to
circumcision. Nothing has been said so far in the Epistle
regarding the acceptance of this rite by the Galatians. Yet
this is the issue that lay behind all the controversy regarding
the true ' sons of Abraham.' The Judaizers urged that, if they
wished to inherit the full blessings of God's chosen people, the
Galatians must, besides accepting Jesus as their Lord,
agree to become corporate members in the commonwealth of
Israel, the initiatory rite for which was circumcision. Paul
expresses himself hypothetically : **if you get circumcised**—an
indication, we may take it, that developments are still at a
stage where they may be arrested. The demand that they
should be circumcised must often have proved a stumbling-
block to adult Gentiles who otherwise were disposed to accept
the Jewish faith, and liberal-minded Jews were sometimes
willing, in special cases, not to enforce it.[1] But it would be
a mistake to imagine from Paul's language here, or in iv. 10
(where see note), that the Judaizers in Galatia had begun by
pressing on Paul's converts a certain measure of Jewish ceremonial, and only held circumcision before them as something
to which they must ultimately attain if they were to be

---

[1] There is an interesting illustration in Josephus, *Antiqu.* xx. ii. 4.

' complete ' in their religion (cf. iii. 3, note). The Judaizers in Galatia were certainly not liberal-minded on such a matter. By accepting circumcision, they held, the Galatians would become incorporated into God's holy people Israel ; without it, they remained outside, and could not inherit the Promise. Paul knew that they put this demand in the forefront ; and when in verse 3 he says : ' I insist on this again,' he probably indicates that the danger of such propaganda was present to his mind even when he was in Galatia, and that he had warned his converts at the time against it.

Against the contentions of the Judaizers Paul has said all he wants to say by way of detailed argument drawn from history or from Scripture. Now, as in iii. 2 ff., he proceeds in a few short sentences to put the issue before his readers in its simplest and most vital form. In the first place, he says, if you accept circumcision, **Christ will be no use to you.** As he states it here, Paul's assertion is a sweeping one, and we can imagine many Jewish-Christians, however sympathetic to his general position, taking strong exception to this. Yet his contention is clear and unanswerable. So far as *Jewish* Christians are concerned, he approves whole-heartedly of their continuing the rite of circumcision, and that he ever advocated its abandonment was a slander (cf. Acts xxi. 20 ff.) ; but that Gentiles who had accepted Christianity should afterwards undergo circumcision as a means of making their salvation *sure*, was to annul God's grace, and to make Christ's death ' useless ' (ii. 21). They must choose between the two systems of incorporation into God's family, not superimpose one on the other.

In the second place, Paul goes on, no man can acknowledge 3 the obligation of circumcision without acknowledging in principle the obligation **to carry out the whole of the Law.** This contention again would have provoked dissent among some. Jews as well as Jewish-Christians, and it would have been a shock to the Galatians, who, we may be sure, had no desire to incur such an obligation, and had probably never had its possibility put before them. But for Paul, just because he revels so thoroughly in the freedom that comes to those who are not under law but under grace, it follows with relentless logic that to admit the validity of legalism in this one particular is to admit its validity as a whole. Sacrifice freedom in one essential, and you sacrifice it altogether.

4 Turning again solemnly to address the Galatians direct, Paul expands the thought of verse 2 regarding the incompatibility of the two systems. Seek to win acceptance with God on a legalistic basis, and thereby you have both rendered Christ's work superfluous for you, and (what is more terrible) *you have cut yourselves off from Christ*—cut yourselves off, i.e., from that union with the Son of God which is the very basis of your incorporation into His holy people, so that you have rendered yourselves *outcasts*. Paul pictures the ' outcast ' condition of Gentiles in Eph. ii. 12, and for himself he can imagine no more terrible fate than to be ' banished from Christ ' (Rom. ix. 3). What Paul is here depicting is not schism within the Christian fellowship, but a definite separation from it, an apostasy or ' falling away.' And in depicting it he dwells, not on the sin, but on the tragedy of it. ' By this apostasy,' he asserts, ' you have fallen away from the sphere of God's **grace** (such as is revealed in Jesus Christ), sacrificing all those blessings and promises which belong to those who live in it and which are still *ours*' (such seems to be the implication of the sudden transition to the first person :

5 **we**). ' Why, while *you* turn to the flesh, *we* live in **the Spirit** ; *you* set yourselves to keep God's law, *we* turn to Him in **faith** ; and thus, while *you* bring yourselves under His condemnation ' (cf. iii. 10), ' and find yourselves without hope of satisfying His demands, *we* who still live under grace **wait** with confidence for the fulfilment of the **hope** that we shall yet stand before Him and be acknowledged by Him as righteous.' Though the believer is ' accepted as righteous ' (' justified ') here and now, he relies on Christ to complete the good work that has been begun in him, and to ' make him righteous ' so that he can be accepted on the day of judgment.

6 And so, rising again to one of his great heights of vision, Paul proclaims, in words that to the Galatians must have rung out as a rallying-cry as they have done to succeeding

generations, that when once a man is **in Christ Jesus,** his standing before God (such a God, i.e., as he knows in Christ) is not affected one whit by the question whether he is *circumcised* or not (note that there is as little room for the Gentile to exalt his claim over the Jew as for the Jew to exalt his over the Gentile). With the God and Father of our Lord Jesus Christ, distinctions of this kind cease to carry any weight at all, and the only thing that avails for salvation is **faith** in Him—*a faith which works through love,* or, it may be, *which is set in motion by love.*

The addition of this last qualifying phrase is full of interest —it is unexpected ; and nowhere, not even in I Cor. xiii., has Paul expressed so succinctly the interrelation of faith and love. But its precise meaning leaves room for doubt, largely because of the difficulty attaching to the Greek verb that forms the connecting link between the two nouns—a verb which, according to some commentators, is always *intransitive* in the New Testament, denoting that a thing *operates* or *expresses itself*, while others assert equally emphatically that it is always *passive*, denoting that a thing *is set in motion*. If we take the former view, which is adopted in the translation, Paul means that Christian faith will of necessity show itself **active in love,** and the reason why he introduces that thought at this point is that, having already dealt fully with the general question of *faith* as contrasted with *law*, he is now about to remind his readers (vi. I ff. ; cf. Rom. xii. 7 ff.), much as St. James does in his Epistle (ii. 14 ff.), that true faith in God must issue in love of the brethren. But apart from the fact that a very strong case can be made out for regarding the verb as invariably passive in the New Testament (cf. Armitage Robinson, *Ephesians*, pp. 241 ff.), it seems right that we should read the present verse in the clear light of Gal. ii. 20, where, lost as here in wonder at the splendour of the Christian gospel, Paul declares that what brought him to rest exclusively on *faith* was the revelation of a Saviour who *loved* him. It is preferable, therefore, to take *love* here primarily of God's love to man, rather than of the Christian's love for his neighbour, and to see in the sentence a declaration that when God comes to judge us He will ask, not whether in obedience to His law we have been circumcised or not, but whether, in view of the revelation of His love, we have turned to Him in faith. The one thing that can make a man right with God is a faith that is quickened into life by a sense of God's love. The best commentary on this verse is to be found in Rom. iii. 21–26 ; v. 1–11.

7 Remonstrance now takes the form of a series of short passionate ejaculations, almost all introduced suddenly without any connecting particle. Verse 7 is literally : ' you were running well '—a favourite metaphor with Paul (cf. ii. 2 ; I Cor. ix. 24 ff.) ; it is implied that there was a well-defined goal ahead, and the Galatians, who had had **the Truth**, i.e. of the Gospel (ii. 5 ; cf. ii. 14), set before them, knew that only by following the line so marked out could they arrive there. Why then this tragedy of a race broken off ? The apostle does not blame his converts ; in a sharp question, uttered more by way of expostulation than from desire for an answer, he implies that *someone* must have stopped their progress along the true line (the metaphor behind ' **prevent** ' suggests that the road had been torn up or otherwise obstructed).

8 Certainly in adopting the line they had now done, they were not following the leading of Him (i.e. God) who had **called** and was still calling them, i.e. to salvation (cf. i. 6 ; I Thess. ii. 12). The implication is, as in the parable of the Tares, that

9 ' some enemy hath done this ' ; and, quoting a familiar proverb, which he uses again in I Cor. v. 6, Paul reminds the Galatians that evil influence, insignificant in its beginning, can work in the end a vast amount of harm.

10 Paul refuses, however, to despair—' I am confident in the Lord about you.' Every word here in the original has its own emphasis. Both pronouns are stressed, as if to suggest : ' we know one another, **you** and **I**.' By inserting the words ' **in the Lord** ' (cf. the note on ' in Christ,' iii. 14), Paul indicates that instead of regarding life from a purely human standpoint, which must often lead to pessimism and dismay, the believer, in virtue of his union with the Lord, now looks at life as one who belongs to the Lord, and faces it in the strength of the

Lord ; cf. the ground for rejoicing in Phil. iv. 4. Hence in the present case Paul can express *confidence*. **I am persuaded that you will not go wrong.** This last phrase is literally : *that you will not take any other view*—a vague expression which probably means that they will yet recognize the truth of what he has just been saying, viz. that the path they are now pursuing is not the one that God was inviting them to take. We are back where we were at i. 7 : ' certain individuals are unsettling you ' ; and **he who unsettles you** will have to answer before God for it, **no matter who he is.** The apostle's language at this point is purposely indefinite : it is unnecessary to see in it a veiled reference to some *individual* who was a leading spirit in the Judaizing movement. What Paul has in mind, no doubt, is that these Judaizers were all Christians like himself, and some of them were perhaps men of honour and prestige ; yet in the end no such consideration will save a man who causes one of the little ones to stumble (cf. note on verse 12).

There follows here a sudden outburst, dealing with a very 11 personal matter (the first personal pronoun is emphatic). Paul's opponents had evidently been saying that he himself was still **preaching circumcision,** i.e. making membership in the Jewish people a precondition of salvation. This sentence raises many problems. (*a*) What foundation there can possibly have been for such an allegation would have been clearer to Paul's readers than it is to us. While denying that circumcision was obligatory for Gentiles, Paul certainly held that Jewish-Christians, like other Jews, should continue the rite, and, as regards the offspring of mixed marriages, we have in Acts xvi. 1 ff. an instance (occurring shortly after this, if we date the Epistle before the Council) of his arranging, in view of public opinion, to circumcise even an adult. In other words, he was eager that Jewish-Christians, so far as was possible without compromising the Christian position, should not denationalize themselves or give unnecessary offence to their brethren. Such a position, of course, offered abundant occasion for dispute (cf. the case of Titus, ii. 3), and lent itself easily to misrepresentation (cf. the accusation of ' man-pleasing ' in i. 10) ; but it provided no **real basis for a charge** of inconsistency. Circumcision, for Paul, had value as a national bond ; it had none as a precondition of salvation. (*b*) The allegation took the form that Paul was *still* preaching circumcision. Why ' still ' ? This does not imply (as is sometimes urged in view of the succeeding phrase, ' still being persecuted ') that there was a period after his conversion when Paul's position was a narrowly Jewish-Christian one ; the comparison is rather with the preaching of his pre-Christian days, when in his zeal for Judaism he refused to allow the possibility of salvation outside its pale. (*c*) Quietly claiming the sympathy of his converts (' brothers '), Paul answers the charge by indignantly asking them why he is still being persecuted. Again, we may ask, why ' still ' ? Paul's point would seem to be that his opponents are not consistent in their attacks on him. ' They began by persecuting me for not demanding that Gentile converts should be circumcised. Now they insinuate that at heart I recognize the necessity of circumcision, and sometimes enforce it. They cannot have it both ways. If they themselves believe that I do preach circumcision, why do they go on persecuting me for not preaching it ? '

Paul follows this up by an appeal to the stumbling-block of the cross. In two ways the cross was a stumbling-block to the Jews. In the first place a crucified person was ' accursed ' (iii. 13), and that God's Messiah should be crucified seemed too monstrous to be believable (cf. 1 Cor. i. 23). But this eccentricity of Christian belief might have been ignored if Christians had not gone on to declare that through the death of the Messiah on the cross there had been opened up, even to those outside Judaism, a new way of salvation which entirely abrogated the old demand for circumcision and obedience to the Law. It is in this second sense, viz. that faith in a crucified Saviour provides an alternative to the rigid demands of the old covenant, that Paul employs the phrase here. The translation interprets Paul's language as ironical : ' Do you mean to tell me that I have dropped from my preaching the element in it that most of all provoked opposition ? ' But it is preferable to regard it as severely logical : ' If I am preaching the necessity for circumcision (which, of course, I am not), then the old objection raised against me, viz. that my preaching of the cross makes circumcision no longer necessary, has entirely lost its force.'

The charge has stirred Paul to the depths, and now there 12 bursts from him one of the bitterest and coarsest expressions to be found in all his letters. The word which he uses (lit. ' cut themselves off ') conveys a far deeper significance than that those troublers should cut themselves off from the Church (cf. Authorized Version, Revised Version). As the ancient Greek Fathers recognized, it carries with it the idea of *castration* —a practice which, as Gentile converts knew full well, was enjoined in certain heathen religions (e.g. for the priests of Cybele), but which, as Paul meant to remind the Judaizers, was abhorrent to the God of Israel, so that anything approaching to it involved *exclusion from ' the congregation of the Lord '* (Deut. xxiii. 1). If these men, he argues, think that God is well pleased with the use of the knife, why do they not make a thorough use of it and get themselves castrated ? It is just possible that Paul, in giving vent to this terrible thought, has been influenced by the recollection of a no less terrible word of the Lord against those who cause one of His ' little ones ' (i.e. believers in general) to stumble, which is followed in the gospel-tradition by a stern injunction that whatever is a cause of *stumbling* to oneself is ruthlessly to be *cut off* (Mark ix. 42 ff.). But however his mind worked, we can see here again (cf. notes on iv. 9 ; v. 1) how for Paul there were certain elements in the Jewish religion which might indeed have value as disciplines or national customs, but which deserved, when they were interpreted as necessary for a right relation with God, to be classed as heathenish. And with regard to circumcision we may set alongside this passage the equally brutal language of Phil. iii. 2 ff., which suggests that while the Christians have spiritualized circumcision, the Jews (by limiting it to a physical act) have made it no better than ' incision,' mutilation.

v. 13–15 : *True freedom will manifest itself, not in selfish indulgence, but in loving service*

13 Brothers, you were called to be free ; only, do not make your freedom an opening for the flesh, but serve one another
14 in love. For the entire Law is summed up in one word,
15 in *You must love your neighbour as yourself* (whereas, if you snap at each other and prey upon each other, take care in case you destroy one another).

13 **Brothers, you were called to be free.** This is in essence the same emphatic declaration as (following the interpretation of that verse given in the commentary) we found in verse 1. In each case it is the summing up of a position already established, which becomes in turn the text for a practical appeal. As in verses 1 ff. the appeal had been that those who have been set free should not relapse into the bondage of legalism, so here it is that they should realize the true nature and implications of Christian freedom.

Freedom is not to be made **an opening for the flesh.** The word translated ' opening ' (lit. a place for jumping-off or running out, and hence used in military language as a ' base of operations ') is a favourite with Paul, who alone of New Testament writers uses it. He recognizes that, if freedom be interpreted merely as the removal of restraint, ' the flesh ' will immediately seize the opportunity to break out. Paul is to have more to say on ' the flesh ' before this chapter ends (cf. p. xl.). As may be seen from the contrast which immediately follows, it is characteristic of the flesh to be *selfish* ; whereas where *love* reigns, she ' seeketh not her own ' (1 Cor. xiii. 5). The lengths to which the flesh will go if an opening is provided are to be described later in verses 19 ff., where we shall see that not all the deeds of the flesh are what we would call fleshly indulgences ; but here Paul is dealing rather with the general principle that Christian freedom, so far from implying lack of restraint, is the acceptance of a new but glad and willing servitude, according to which, with love as a motive power in our hearts, we seek not to please ourselves but to serve one another.

The line which Paul's argument follows here is interesting and significant. He does not develop, as he might have been expected to do, the theological argument that for the Christian Christ takes the place of the Law, so that there is still a law for him to keep, viz. that ' law of Christ ' of which he speaks in vi. 2. His concern is rather with the processes which go on in the Christian soul—the door of liberty has been opened, not that through it the desires of the flesh may break out in a riot of selfishness, but that through it there may enter in a new power (to be described later as ' the Spirit ') leading us in love to a life of mutual service. Apart from a phrase in verse 6, there is nothing in the immediately preceding context to prepare the way for this reference to love ; and we must recognize therefore that what Paul is here appealing to is that common basis of faith and practice on which *all* Christians ought to be united (cf. the introduction of the word **brothers** at the beginning of the verse), viz. that God in Christ has shown His redeeming love for men, and that those who are Christ's ought therefore to love one another. The Greek speaks of ' *the* love,' i.e. that love which is the unifying bond among Christians : we may bring out the force of the article by the translation ' Christian love.' The prepositional phrase (similar to what was used in verse 6—see the commentary on that verse) implies the motive power which urges to service rather than the spirit in which the service is rendered, ' *through* Christian love ' rather than ' *in* love ' ; the spirit of love having been quickened in their hearts, Christians are impelled to serve one another. And when Paul speaks of ' serving one another ' he means more than ' helping one another,' as would have been implied by the Greek verb *diakonein*. The verb which he uses is derived from *doulos*, a bond-servant, a word which Paul so often uses of himself as a servant of Christ (cf. the commentary on i. 10) and which in Phil. ii. 7 he uses even with reference to Christ Himself (' taking the nature of a servant '). This strong verb, implying not merely *service* but *servitude*, is of course purposely employed because of the emphatic assertion of *freedom* which immediately precedes ; and the implication is that, free as we are, we are not our own

masters ; our life, like that of our Lord, must be a life spent
in the service of our brethren ; for if the binding force of law
is no longer operative, there has entered into our lives the
new constraining force of Christian love.

14   This last thought is expressed forcibly in the verse which
follows. Some doubt may be felt regarding the precise meaning. Is it that, regarded as an expression of the mind and will
of the legislator, **the entire Law** can be comprehensively
summed up in one word, or that, from the stand-point of those
who have to keep the Law, there is one provision by fulfilling
which we may claim to have fulfilled the whole ? Probably
the latter is what Paul has in mind. In any case there is an
emphatic contrast between **the entire Law** and the **one word.**
The word to which Paul appeals is found in Lev. xix. 18, the
context of which shows that in its original reference it merely
enjoined love towards brother-members of the community
of Israel. But Jesus, who saw in the text one of the two great
commandments on which all else depended, naturally opened
the door to a wider interpretation (cf. the story of the Good
Samaritan, Luke x. 29 ff.) ; and among His followers it is
probable that the Judaizers, while not disposed to accept
Paul's interpretation of Gentile freedom in relation to the
Law as a whole, would have agreed with him in interpreting
this word as enjoining the love of Gentile no less than of
brother-Jew.

The sentence is a significant reminder that for Paul there
is a Law which Christians can and must keep (cf. vi. 2, and
Introduction, p. liii.).

15   The positive injunction to love and service is enforced by
a closing word of warning against exhibitions of the contrary
spirit. If instead of loving one another as Christians we
' bite ' and ' devour ' one another like wild animals, the result
is not mutual helpfulness but mutual destruction. Paul tactfully puts the case hypothetically, but we may be sure that
he believes that these conditions actually exist ; and no doubt
he is thinking, not merely of petty and personal rivalries
between Christian neighbours, but of the *odium theologicum*
which he hears is rending asunder his Galatian churches. If

so, we have fresh evidence that the Galatian controversy was more than an academic one between Paul and the Judaizers ; it had already let loose tides of passion and vindictiveness among the Galatians themselves. For these results Paul does not blame one party more than another : the Christian law of love is binding on all, and all alike must be concerned to see that it is honoured and be grieved when it is forgotten or disobeyed.

v. 16–18 : *The flesh must be brought into subjection to the Spirit*

I mean, lead the life of the Spirit ; then you will never satisfy 16 **the passions of the flesh. For the passion of the flesh is** 17 **against the Spirit, and the passion of the Spirit against the flesh—the two are at issue, so that you are not free to do as you please. If you are under the sway of the** 18 **Spirit, you are not under the Law.**

Having urged in the preceding section that Christian love 16 forbids the turning of Christ-won freedom into licence, Paul now assures his readers that they will be secure against this temptation if they **lead the life of the Spirit,** i.e. if they allow their conduct to be regulated by the Spirit of God. There has been no reference to the Spirit since verse 5, so that clearly this new appeal does not follow from the other by a process of logic ; rather Paul is emphasizing the same religious contention as before, only he approaches it now from a new angle. The ejaculatory **I mean** is a reminder that he is not writing a logical treatise, but addressing a passionate appeal to living men and women.

The emphatic note in the new appeal is **the Spirit**—this is made very clear by the order of the words in the original ; and the place of the Spirit in the Christian life, especially in relation to the flesh, is to be Paul's theme from now till vi. 10, which practically closes the argument of the Epistle. Those whose daily life and conduct is controlled by the Spirit **will,** he says, **never satisfy the passions of the flesh.** Though the Greek might be interpreted as an emphatic command (' and see that you do not satisfy '; so Authorized Version margin, ' fulfil not '), it is far more naturally taken (as in the translation) as a confident declaration—the flesh will assert itself, but its desires will never reach fulfilment. The phrase ' passions of the flesh ' ought not to mislead the reader into thinking that Paul refers here specially to sensuality—just as ' the flesh ' means more than the body, including all that belongs to the natural man, so too the word translated ' passions ' means something far less than ' lusts ' (cf. Authorized Version), denoting in fact any kind of desire, good or bad (passion belongs even to the Spirit, verse 17), though it comes to be associated more particularly with what is evil.

Throughout this passage it is important to remember that Paul is writing to Christians, i.e. to men who have received the Spirit of God ; and in every reference to the Spirit it is the divine Spirit that is thought of. It is true that in the experience of Christians the Spirit becomes so real a possession that it is accepted as part of their very being, a far more intimate part of themselves than the flesh in which they still live (cf. ii. 20) ; but even so it always in the New Testament implies the divine Spirit, given by God as an endowment to those who are able to receive it, never merely the human spirit in the sense of something which belongs to man as man. Paul wishes the Galatians to remember that, as Christians, they have received the Spirit of God, which is now for them the supreme energizing and regulative force in their lives. There is therefore no danger of their Christian liberty degenerating into libertinism if they lead the life of the Spirit.

17 So long of course as the Christian is in the flesh there is bound to be in his soul a conflict between flesh and Spirit, and with this conflict Paul proceeds now to deal. It is well to note that from the very nature of the case the conflict here referred to falls into a different category from that which goes on in the soul of the natural man, who finds that, even when he wills the good, he cannot adequately perform it (cf. Rom. vii. 14 ff.). In the Romans passage Paul is dealing purely with human psychology, and with the helplessness of mere idealism divorced from the saving power of God. There

is no reference in that passage to ' the Spirit.' Here, on the other hand, the power of the Spirit is the dominant idea, and what Paul is concerned with is not human psychology as such, but the divine work of sanctification.

The precise reasoning in verse 17 has been much disputed, especially as regards the concluding clause. Is Paul here describing, quite objectively, first one side, then the other, in this dire spiritual conflict ? Is his argument, in other words, that, as the Spirit has desires of one kind and the flesh desires of a wholly contrary kind, the Christian himself, in whom these two forces strive for mastery, is pulled first in one direction, then in the other, but is never free to advance along either line, the flesh checking him when he seeks to obey the Spirit, the Spirit likewise checking him when he seeks to obey the flesh ? Such an interpretation leaves something to be desired. Even though the phrase ' to do as you please ' means literally ' to do as you will to do,' it is a forced interpretation to deduce from these concluding words a twofold meaning, as if they implied ' you are not free to follow the dictates *either* of the flesh **or** of the Spirit.' But a still more serious objection is that if Paul·had meant to depict flesh and Spirit as waging an indecisive battle in the soul, he must surely, in a context like the present, have gone on to say something about the final issue. The very dogmatism of the previous assertion : *You will never satisfy the passions of the flesh,* ought to remind us, if reminder were needed, that Paul could not describe flesh and Spirit (the latter being the divine Spirit imparted to man) as if they were waging war on equal terms, with no assurance that the Spirit would emerge triumphant. To Paul the very fact that his converts have received the Spirit is a guarantee that (unless, of course, they deliberately turn against it and drive it out) they will be perfectly able, in the power of the Spirit, to check and subdue the passions of the flesh. What, therefore, we have in v. 17 is not the description of an equal and indecisive combat, but a bold and confident declaration that, though the flesh asserts its desires in opposition to the Spirit (this is admitted, but only as the statement of a preliminary and subsidiary truth), nevertheless (and here follows the main contention) the Spirit asserts its desires in opposition to the flesh, **the two** being in each case **at issue** one with the other. And what now follows is added, not as applying to both clauses equally, but with definite reference to the restraint which the Spirit exercises on the flesh. The Spirit, says Paul, sets itself against the flesh, *with the result that* (or the sense may be, in accordance with a more literal interpretation of the Greek, *so as to secure that*, as if to denote the *purpose* of the Spirit's action rather than the *result*) **you are not free to do as you please.** By ' doing as you please ' Paul means ' acting as you would act if you considered merely the dictates of the flesh.' Such freedom of action is debarred for you if you live in the Spirit. And so, looking back over the whole sentence, we see that it is not intended to give merely a vivid picture of the action and reaction of two contending forces in the soul (such a picture, while natural in Rom. vii., would have required something more to complete it in the midst of an eager personal appeal) ; it is introduced rather as a justification of the assertion which had been so confidently made in v. 16, that if men walk in the Spirit they will never satisfy the passions of the flesh.

In all this, however, Paul does not forget how terrible the menace of the flesh may be even in the lives of believers : the struggle may be a long and indecisive one, may even be one in which the flesh achieves supremacy, unless the believer, into whose life the Spirit has come, yields his life fully to the 18 Spirit's domination. He must come **under the sway of the Spirit,** lit. be *led by the Spirit.* Paul uses the same phrase again in Rom. vii. 14. Similarly in verse 16 he speaks of *leading the life of the Spirit* ; cf. also verse 25. And this thought of being *led by the Spirit,* implying that the Spirit is a living, active and personal power, is here especially appropriate in view of the contrast which immediately follows between the Spirit and the Law. *If you are led by the Spirit,* **you are not under the Law.** In this characteristic utterance Paul sums up this section of his appeal. And the sudden introduction of a reference to the Law, like the other reference

in verse 14, is a reminder that even in this more practical part
of the Epistle the old issue is still the dominating one. The
Galatians had been led by the Judaizers to believe that, as
God demands moral conduct from His worshippers, their one
safeguard against becoming slaves to the flesh was to order
their lives according to the ordinances of the written Law.
Paul, equally concerned about morality, asserts that believers
are called by God to order their lives in accordance with the
guidance of His living Spirit, and that those who do so have
a perfectly adequate safeguard afgainst satisfying the passions
of the flesh (verse 16). If you know the life of the Spirit with
its safeguards, you neither require nor recognize the safeguards
of the Law.

As in various other dicta in which he sums up a position
(e.g. iii. 7, 29 ; iv. 7), Paul expresses himself in this verse
with singular force and conciseness. In the Greek neither
Spirit nor *Law* is preceded by the definite article, so that while
the particular case of the Galatians is still in view, Paul rises
above it into the statement of a general proposition. When
you attain to a relation with God which is truly spiritual, you
pass into a sphere in which legalism in any shape or form no
longer holds sway. As has been argued in chaps. iii. and iv.,
law is for servants ; but if we know ourselves no longer
servants, but free-born sons, our relationship must express
itself not in legal obedience but in spiritual affinity. As Paul
says in Rom. viii. 14, ' those who are guided by God's Spirit
are God's sons.'

v. 19–24 : *How life differs in practice according as the flesh or
the Spirit is dominant*

Now the deeds of the flesh are quite obvious, such as sexual 19
vice, impurity, sensuality, magic, idolatry, quarrels, dis- 20
sension, jealousy, temper, rivalry, factions, party-spirit,
envy, [murder], drinking bouts, revelry, and the like ; I tell 21
you beforehand as I have told you already, that people
who indulge in such practices will never inherit the

22   **Realm of God.** But the harvest of the Spirit is love, joy,
23   peace, good temper, kindliness, generosity, fidelity,
      gentleness, self-control : there is no law against those
24   who practise such things. Now those who belong to
      Christ* have crucified the flesh with its emotions and
      passions.

* On v. 24 see note on p. 195.

19 Paul's argument now becomes concrete. He gives a catalogue illustrating what he calls the deeds of the flesh—i.e. evil
practices in which man indulges when, without any regard
to God, he is swayed merely by his own passions and desires.
We shall look first at the list itself, and then consider how it
is related to Paul's argument as a whole.

The list need not have been constructed according to any
very definite principle, yet apparently it falls into four divi-
sions. (i.) First come **sexual vice, impurity, sensuality**—all
three no doubt referring to sexual sin. Sensuality (' lascivious-
ness,' Authorized Version and Revised Version) implies conduct unrestrained by any considerations of propriety. (ii.)
20 **Idolatry** and **magic** (' sorcery,' Revised Version ; ' witchcraft,'
Authorized Version) suggest practices characteristic of heathen
religion, and incompatible with the pure religion of the Spirit.
The Book of Acts gives various instances of religious sorcery
(viii. 9 ; xiii. 8 ; xix. 13). (iii.) **Quarrels, dissension, jealousy,**
temper, rivalry, factions, party-spirit, envy, [murder]. Here
we have sins of self-assertion and strife, at variance with the
spirit of brotherhood. In the Greek all these words except
the second and third are in the plural, denoting repeated
exhibitions of the evil in question. The word translated
rivalry is difficult. Originally connoting the conduct of a
hireling, it acquired the meaning of ' working zealously for
one's own interest.' Lightfoot traces in the words in this
section a gradation in intensity, ' envyings ' being ' a grosser
breach of charity than any hitherto mentioned, the wish to
21 deprive another of what he has.' **Murder** would provide a
natural climax to such a list—it is mentioned after ' envying '
in Rom. i. 29, but the best MSS. omit it here. (iv.) **Drinking**
bouts, revelry—sins of intemperance, in which the spirit of

conviviality is carried so far as to involve conduct that is degrading.

Lists of vices occur frequently in Paul's Epistles, e.g. Rom. i. 29 ff. ; 2 Cor. xii. 20 ff. ; Eph. v. 3 ff. ; Col. iii. 5 ff. Such lists have an interesting history, going far back before the rise of Christianity ; and Paul was already familiar with them. Judaism in the Dispersion looked with horror on the depravity of the heathen world ; and while it taught its own adherents to abstain religiously from certain forms of conduct current among their Gentile neighbours, it also, both by its preaching and by its literature (as e.g. in the Book of Wisdom, a writing with which Paul shows familiarity), proclaimed its belief that the moral degradation of the world had its root-cause in the world's ignorance of the true God and of the Law which He had given for man's moral guidance. In various ways the moral standards of Judaism came to influence pagan ethical thought, and denunciation of certain types of vice became part of the stock-in-trade of popular moralists and preachers. But in so far as they denounced vice at all, pagan thinkers tended to do so because of its anti-social character rather than because it violated any God-given sanctions. Hence fornication, to take one example, seemed as little to be condemned as self-indulgence in regard to food or drink—like these, it only became a vice when it was practised beyond moderation. To Paul, however, and to Jewish thinkers in general, vice was not an offence against society but an offence against God ; and the godlessness which gave rise to it could be seen not merely in the life of the individual but in the whole structure of the social, political, and religious life of the heathen world. He knew, for example, how much the communal life of a pagan city suffered from outbursts of faction and party-strife ; its very religion, he saw, encouraged idolatry, magic, and even, alas, prostitution. But saddest of all to him were the sins which he puts first in this list, and against which he issues so many warnings in his Epistles—sins in which man, to whom God is ready to give His holy Spirit, uses his body as if he were merely ' flesh.' In nothing did early Christianity so thoroughly revolutionize the ethical standards of the pagan world as in regard to sexual relationships.

Trained in the knowledge of God and of His holy Law, good Jews had learned to look on certain ' deeds of the flesh ' as essentially evil, and they avoided them ; but Gentiles, who knew not God, fell an easy prey to them. Hence such sins were often regarded as peculiarly Gentile sins. Hence too, earnest Jewish Christians saw here a practical reason why Gentiles, when they embraced Christianity, should be asked to keep the Jewish law—only by stern discipline, it was felt, would they attain to higher ethical standards, and they must be trained to recognize that certain practices in which they formerly indulged without concern were now forbidden to them by the Law of God. Perhaps this explains why Paul, in continuation of his teaching on flesh and spirit, goes on to say : **Now the deeds of the flesh are quite obvious.** Under the influence of judaistic propaganda the Galatians, we may believe, had been led to imagine that, if they were to rise to standards of conduct worthy of their new religion, they ought to know clearly what was expected of them, and more particularly what was forbidden to them ; and explicit directions on these matters, they were told, would be found in the Law of Moses as it had been interpreted by the Jewish Fathers. To Paul, on the other hand, no formal statement of law-giver or of scribe is necessary in order to make plain to the Christian what sins of the flesh are ; and, quoting a list of such sins—a list which, of course, is not meant to be exhaustive, as we see from the addition of the words **and the like**—he claims that the sinfulness of such conduct is self-evident. If a simpler explanation of the phrase ' quite obvious ' is looked for, it may be that Paul implies that one has only to look around to see how rife these sins are : their very prevalence among those who live only the life of the flesh is itself a warning that those who have received the Spirit must avoid them.

With regard to these vices Paul pronounces a stern warning, and as we read it we feel how concerned he is to vindicate his gospel from even the suspicion of antinomianism. **I tell**

you beforehand as I have told you already (this latter phrase referring, we may be sure, to his missionary preaching), **that people who indulge in such practices will never inherit the Realm of God.** The Realm of God, though the New Testament teaches that it may be anticipated even amid the conditions of the present evil age, will only be established in its full reality in the age that is to come. When it is asserted that unworthy behaviour in this life will be sufficient to debar a man from entry, this is in no sense a violation of the doctrine of justification by faith. For the Realm of God is something which men gain, not by merit, but through inheritance—and they **inherit** it if they are truly sons (for the association of ' sons ' and ' heirs ' cf. iv. 7). But if instead of living the life of the Spirit they are swayed by the dictates of the flesh, then obviously they have renounced their sonship. There is an emphatic contrast between ' people who indulge in such practices ' and ' the Realm of *God.*'

How different it is when men live the life of the Spirit ! 22 Then Christian character and conduct develop naturally : they grow like **the harvest.** Paul's conception of the ' harvest ' of the Spirit (Authorized Version ' fruit,' often quoted wrongly as ' fruits ') ought to be distinguished clearly from the other conception of spiritual ' gifts ' (Greek *charismata*) in 1 Cor. xii. 8–11. The ' gifts ' are powers or capacities with which the Spirit of God endows men for special service, and they naturally differ in different men. The ' harvest ' of the Spirit on the other hand refers to the natural expression in character of the divine life which is within. The tendency in current thought, as Paul well knew, was to associate the Spirit's working merely with extraordinary manifestations of activity and power ; but here he emphasizes that, as the Spirit is life, it works no less powerfully and surely according to the principle of secret growth. Paul had apprehended the lesson which his Master had taught, that ' each tree is known by its fruit ' and ' the good man produces good from the good stored in his heart ' (Luke vi. 44, 45). The peaceful growth of the Spirit's ' harvest ' contrasts also with the ' deeds ' of the flesh, which are outbursts of undisciplined passion. And it is not for nothing that Paul uses the singular ' harvest ' or ' fruit ' rather than ' fruits,' for while the passions of the flesh are many and varied, the life of the Spirit is a harmonious whole, and is in essence the same wherever it is found. Where the Spirit is truly dominant, there cannot, e.g., be such a thing as love without fidelity, or joy without self-control.

Paul explains in what forms the harvest of the Spirit will manifest itself. His list of virtues, like the preceding list, makes no claim to completeness : no catalogue can exhaust the infinite variety of the Christian life. If we look in the list for any principle of classification, we may perhaps say that **love, joy, peace** describe how, in the strength of the Spirit, the Christian is enabled to face life's mysteries and trials ; the next five qualities illustrate his attitude to his fellows ; while the concluding virtue, **self-control,** is a reminder that in his own person he must discipline and finally ' crucify ' (verse 24) the passions of the flesh. But no rigid classification ought to be looked for. The Christian life is a unity, and cannot be dissected ; and the believer's attitude to God determines, and cannot be separated from, his attitude to his fellows, and to himself.

Love naturally heads the list—love is a summing-up not merely of the law, but of all true spiritual life. Christian **joy** (cf. Phil. iv. 4 ; 1 Pet. i. 6, 8) has always put to shame the hollow joy of the pagan. **Peace,** like joy, may result primarily from that sense of confidence which the Christian has in his God (cf. Phil. iv. 7), but if so it enables a man also to be at peace with his fellows, and thus it is akin to the qualities which follow next in the list. **Good-temper** (' longsuffering,' Authorized Version) implies ' endurance ' of the ills of life, or ' forbearance ' in the face of insult and injustice. **Kindness** (' gentleness,' Authorized Version) similarly follows good-temper in 1 Cor. xiii. 4 ; ' love is very patient, very kind.' Next comes **generosity** (Authorized Version, ' goodness '), a virtue to which Paul again refers in 2 Thess. i. 11 ; Rom. xv. 14 ; Eph. v. 9. More general perhaps in its range than ' kindness,' it expresses the Christian attitude to all that is worthy of sympathy and commendation. The Greek word

translated 'fidelity' is *pistis*, generally rendered 'faith' (so
here, Authorized Veision and Revised Version) ; but clearly,
as the context shows, the reference is not to that 'faith in
God' which earlier in the Epistle has been shown to be a pre-
requisite of salvation, nor to that energetic 'faith' which has
a place among 'spiritual gifts' in 1 Cor. xii. 9. What is meant
is either a spirit of 'trustfulness,' such as the Christian, who
is 'always eager to believe the best' (1 Cor. xiii. 7), exhibits
in his relations with his fellows, so different from the attitude
of suspicion and fear from which the pagan never escapes ;
or else the reference is to the steadfast fidelity which the
Christian shows in his own life, and which leads others to
place reliance on him, i.e. 'faithfulness,' 'trustworthiness.'
Gentleness (Authorized Version, ' meekness '), the attitude of 23
the man who in his dealings with others is ' never rude, never
selfish ' (1 Cor. xiii. 5), is a quality praised even in heathen
literature, but it receives its truest appreciation in Jewish
and in Christian ethics, where its springs are traced back to
the spirit of 'meekness' (i.e. trustful submission) with which
the truly religious man waits upon God (cf. Ps. xlv. 4 ;
Matt. v. 5). As such it is never a merely passive virtue : by
consideration for others we can often overcome opposition
when by self-assertion we would only intensify it. ' Gentleness ' and ' consideration ' were among the outstanding
qualities of Christ (2 Cor. x. 1) ; Moses was the meekest of
men (Num. xii. 3) ; and it is interesting to find ' faithfulness
and meekness ' (the same two words as here) conjoined in the
description of Moses in Ecclesiasticus xlv. 4. As the preceding
list culminated with a reference to 'drinking bouts and
revelry,' so the virtue which closes the present list is **self-
control**—a virtue praised by Plato (a sister-quality ' temper-
ance ' has a place among his cardinal virtues), but which has
special significance for the Christian in view of the truceless
warfare which is waged between the flesh and the spirit.

What does the apostle mean when, having closed the list,
he adds : ' **there is no law against those who practise such
things**,' or, more simply, ' *against such things there is no law* ' ?
He has in mind the argument of those who say that law is

necessary for the regulation of human conduct. Law *is* necessary, he admits, if men are governed merely by the passions of the flesh—for the deeds of the flesh are such that law must interfere against them. But when men live the life of the Spirit, their conduct is such that no law can condemn it, no law is required to keep it in check. Paul's argument is that a life under law is not the only alternative to a life of self-indulgence ; another and preferable alternative is life in the Spirit, and where this better life is truly lived, the regulative force of law is no longer necessary.

A question, however, naturally suggests itself here. Is Paul not shutting his eyes to the fact that even in the most truly Christian life sinful tendencies still remain operative ? So long as the Christian remains in the flesh, will not tares mingle with the harvest of the Spirit ? Paul is too much of a realist ever to ignore this dread fact : he is no spiritual romanticist. But for him the right method of dealing with the lusts of the flesh is not to regulate them by law but to 24 ' crucify ' them. And this is what **those who belong to Christ** (on this phrase see pp. xxxi., xliv.) have as a matter of fact done : **they have crucified the flesh with its emotions and passions.** This thought deserves closer examination.

The root causes of the deeds of the flesh have their secret origin in man's unspiritual dispositions and desires, and these must be dealt with before the Spirit can hold effective sway. When Paul speaks however of crucifying the flesh, he knows that the flesh can never be effectively put out of action : so long as the Christian is in the flesh, the flesh will make its presence felt, in opposition to the Spirit. But the *coup de grâce* may be administered to the flesh even though for a time its passions remain operative ; the act of crucifixion is to be distinguished from the death to which it is the prelude ; and it is to that initial act of crucifixion that Paul alludes in his statement in verse 24. The tense of the Greek verb makes it plain that he is there referring, not to a process of spiritual ' crucifixion ' continued throughout life, but to an act consummated at a definite moment in time. In short, he is referring to what took place at baptism. It is in baptism, as has already been said in iii. 27, that the believer takes on the character of Christ ; and in Rom. vi. 3 Paul emphasizes, as a truth which every Christian must surely know, that baptism into Christ means baptism into His death. So here baptism is thought of as implying the crucifixion of the old self, the flesh with its emotions and passions ; and (continuing his argument that Christians do not require the Law in order to discipline the flesh) Paul reminds his converts that for them, as for baptized believers in general, the flesh is 'dead.' Not that it is ever robbed altogether of the power to assert its claims ; but however it may seek to do so, the Christian refuses to allow it any determining voice whatsoever in the instigation or control of his conduct. And in a truly Christian life, where the spirit given at baptism is allowed to hold sway, the flesh is not merely treated as dead, but becomes as a matter of fact as good as dead. How different it is with the non-Christian, as we see him, e.g., in the modern novel or play, a creature who apparently never expects to be able to do anything except what his lusts and selfish ambitions dictate for him.

v. 25–vi. 10: How the Spirit governs Life in its Social Relationships

If baptism marks the beginning of the victory, it is nothing more than a beginning. The crucifixion of the flesh enables the Spirit to enter in and take possession, but the task of establishing possession is one which continues as long as life lasts. Above all, the Spirit's supremacy must be established in that most difficult of all spheres, the sphere of social relationships.

v. 25 : *In our relations to one another the Spirit must be our guide*

As we live by the Spirit, let us be guided by the Spirit.

Paul appeals to his readers that, as they have entered on the life of the Spirit, living, as he says, **by the Spirit** (or perhaps *to the Spirit*), they should allow themselves to **be guided by**

the Spirit. The verb which Paul here uses expresses the
thought of walking in a row, and for that reason, as well as
in view of the words which follow, his injunction in this verse
probably refers less to individual conduct (as in verses 16
and 18) than to the relations of Christians to one another.
As members of a brotherhood let us, he urges, come all together
under the Spirit's direction. If our individual lives are lived
' by the Spirit,' let us also allow the Spirit to marshal us in
our corporate relationships. It is too readily forgotten that
in the New Testament the sphere of the Spirit's working is
thought of primarily as the Christian Fellowship and not the
Christian individual ; and though Paul does not yet give
expression to his conception of ' the Body of Christ,' the
thought of the Church as ' the fellowship of the Spirit ' is
present in Galatians as truly as in any other Epistle (cf.
p. xxxi.).

v. 26–vi. 10 : *Under the leadership of the Spirit we must find*
practical ways of helping one another

26 Let us have no vanity, no provoking, no envy of one another.
vi.   Even if anyone is detected in some trespass, brothers, you
1   are spiritual, you must set the offender right in a spirit of
    gentleness ; let each of you look to himself, in case he too
2   is tempted. Bear one another's burdens, and so fulfil the
3   law of Christ. If anyone imagines he is somebody, he is
4   deceiving himself, for he is nobody ; let everyone bring
    his own work to the test—then he will have something to
    boast about on his own account, and not in comparison
5   with his fellows. For everyone will have to bear his own
    load of responsibility.

6 Those who are taught must share all the blessings of life with
7   those who teach them the Word. Make no mistake—
    God is not to be mocked—a man will reap just what he
8   sows ; he who sows for his flesh will reap destruction
    from the flesh, and he who sows for the Spirit will reap
9   life eternal from the Spirit. Never let us grow tired of
    doing what is right, for if we do not faint we shall reap our
10   harvest at the opportune season. So then, as we have

opportunity, let us do good to all men and in particular to the household of faith.

The injunction that in their relations with one another Christians should walk under the direction of the Spirit now receives practical illustration. The familiar division between chapters v. and vi. is unfortunate, obscuring the essential continuity of thought at this point. But while, in Dr. Moffatt's translation, verse 26 is closely linked with verse 25, it seems preferable to put a full-stop after verse 25, and to regard verse 26 as the first of the series of practical counsels. It does indeed differ from the others in that it is expressed as an exhortation in the first person—' *let us have* no vanity ' is what the apostle says, rather than ' *see that you have* no vanity ' ; but Paul, the Christian gentleman, often slips into this way of writing (aligning himself with his readers, or applying words to Christians in general), when what he has to say is a warning or a rebuke.

It is noteworthy that the apostle's first warning should be : **no vanity, no provoking, no envy of one another.** Though 26 these words are capable of more general application, it is probably the relation of Christians to fellow-Christians that the apostle has in mind : such conduct, when practised within the Christian fellowship, is in obvious contradiction to the dictates of the Spirit. Has this warning been made necessary by the controversies in the Galatian congregations—as if, for example, Jewish-Christians in their pride challenged the Gentiles to become as they were, while Gentile-Christians envied the religious heritage of their Jewish-Christian brethren or despised it because the Spirit had come to them without it ? A spirit such as the apostle here deprecates is indeed readily bred in controversy ; but its manifestations are not to be limited. Experience of the mission-field and of religious ' revivals ' reveals how prone it is to arise where emphasis on the life of the Spirit has not yet led to a realization of its ethical implications. Paul has often to warn his churches against it (cf. notably Phil. ii. 1 ff.).

vi.

The apostle takes a concrete illustration—it deals with an 1 extreme case (hence ' even '), and one which he feels delicacy in mentioning and which the brethren must show sympathy in handling (hence the introduction of ' brothers,' cf. i. 11 ; v. 11). It is the case of an erring brother—despite the generic **anyone,** Paul is certainly thinking of an offence on the part of a member of the fellowship. ' Trespass ' is literally a ' falling aside,' implying perhaps a failure to keep the straight line indicated in verse 25. As an alternative to ' **detected in some trespass** ' a possible rendering is ' overtaken by some trespass,' the reference then being to what goes on in the man's own soul —he is the victim of a sudden temptation which produces an unexpected lapse. In either case the main suggestion is not the sinister one of a secret which has been brought to light, but the surprise which the trespass has occasioned.

How is such a case to be dealt with in a Christian community ? Paul's first reminder, in continuation of his teaching in chap. v., is that as Christians are **spiritual,**[1] acknowledging the Spirit's domination both in their individual lives and in their corporate relationships, their duty towards an erring brother (one in whose life, that is, the flesh has been allowed to assert itself as against the Spirit) is to **set the offender right.** The verb used here is an interesting one : it can be applied to setting a bone or mending a net (cf. Mark i. 19), and in Heb. xiii. 21 we have the thought of God Himself ' setting His people right ' in the sense of bringing them to spiritual perfection. The case will further demand **gentleness,** such as naturally reveals itself where the Spirit is truly operative (cf. v. 23, and the note there). The Christian will never imagine that anything worth while is accomplished by mere denunciation or rebuke ; his duty is not to attack or condemn, but to see that the fallen brother is set upon his feet and that the ranks of the brotherhood are re-established. How nobly Paul himself practised this precept is nowhere better illustrated than in this Epistle. It opened, as we saw, not with vituperation but with surprise (i. 6) ; from first to last it

[1] It is quite beside the mark to trace in Paul's language here a reference to a party of ' spiritualistic radicals,' as is done, e.g., by Ropes in *The Singular Problem of the Epistle to the Galatians.* See the Introduction to the present Commentary, p. xxxiii.

hopes the best, believing that the situation can be retrieved, and peace and unity re-established; and even in its most passionate passages Paul is not the offended master but the agonizing mother (iv. 19). In support of his appeal for gentleness Paul adds a pertinent warning, made more pointed here by a sudden change from plural to singular ('each of you'): each man ought to remember that what has happened to his brother may equally well happen to himself. The tempter does not cease his attacks merely because of the incoming of the Spirit: the flesh goes on 'lusting' against the Spirit (v. 17).

The injunction to **bear one another's burdens** doubtless arose 2 in Paul's mind from association with what has immediately preceded. When one brother falls, the whole brotherhood is involved. Thus, besides the primary duty of setting a fallen brother on his feet (verse 1), Christians have the further duty of helping one another to stand, and not to fall. Apart from the burdens occasioned by his own wrong-doing there are of course many other burdens to weigh a man down, burdens of circumstance and of sorrow; and Paul's language covers burdens of every kind. His next words are a reminder that to bear one another's burdens is not a mere counsel of perfection; it is the carrying out of a law, **the law of Christ.** Paul apparently knew, as part of the Christian tradition, that Christ had given His disciples a command that they were to love one another, and had found in love the root-principle of all the law of God (Matt. xxii. 37–40; cf. Gal. v. 14, and the commentary there). Here as in v. 14, Paul teaches that, in redeeming men from the curse of the old Law, Christ nevertheless imposes on them a new law of His own (cf. 'a new command,' John xiii. 34). In the association of 'burdens' and 'law' in this verse Lightfoot sees a reference to the readiness of the Galatians to burden themselves with the Jewish Law, and he gives Paul's meaning as follows: 'These are the burdens I would have you bear—not the vexatious ritual of the Law, but your neighbour's errors and weaknesses, his sorrows and sufferings.' But it is doubtful whether Paul meant to stress such a contrast.

3   Verse 3 in turn carries on the thought of verse 2. So far from evoking sympathy and help, the sight of a weak and burdened brother may merely inspire in a man a sense of his own superiority.   Such a man is **deceiving himself.**   He **imagines he is somebody ;** in reality, **he is nobody.**   Doubtless Paul is here contrasting the false conception of merit with the Christian realization of human helplessness and divine grace ; what are any of us but ' sinners for whom Christ died ' ? Paul, like his Master, knew how characteristic an element self-esteem was in Pharisaic morality ; and the canker of Pharisaism may invade even the lives of those who have received the Spirit.

4   Paul adds a word of practical advice.   Instead of indulging in vain imaginings, let a man **bring his work to the test.**   It is **his own work** he must look to, not that of his fellows ; he may think that he is better than they are, but that is an irrelevant issue.   If he is to **have something to boast about** (or, perhaps better, ' some cause for self-satisfaction and pride ')

5 it must be **on his own account.**   For every man stands on his own feet : he has **to bear his own load of responsibility.**

Paul expresses himself in verses 3–5 as if he were uttering a mere piece of worldly wisdom.   Nothing in his language is specifically Christian, as is the case in the verses immediately before and after.   Yet it is his Christianity, and not merely his insight into human nature, that lies behind his teaching here as elsewhere.   It is in the presence of a transcendent God that a man sees most clearly that he is nobody.   It is just because he knows that whatever good there may be in his life is the work of the Spirit of God within him that the Christian will never take credit for being better than his fellows.   And nothing brings home to a man the sense of individual responsibility more than the knowledge that the God who is his Saviour is also his Judge.   That the true ' test ' of a man will be found in his ' work ' is not a denial of, but rather an inevitable corollary from, the doctrine of justification by faith (cf. 2 Cor. v. 10, and the teaching of Jesus in Matt. xxv. 40, 45).

In verse 5 the Authorized Version translates : ' Every man

shall bear his own burden,' which is an apparent contradiction to the injunction of verse 2. The Greek however employs a different expression in the two cases, the noun in verse 2 (*barē*) being a generic one for ' burdens,' while that in verse 5 (*phortion*) suggests a pack. We may perhaps say that the former refers to burdens which come to a man he knows not how, and which therefore can be shared, while the pack is part of his own equipment. But it is from the context rather than from the words themselves that the difference in meaning in the two verses is to be deduced.

It seems preferable to take this verse closely with what 6 goes before rather than as the beginning of a new section. There is a gradation in the several duties of which the Galatians are reminded—(i.) to those of their brethren who have fallen ; (ii.) to those around them, all bearing their various burdens ; (iii.) to those who preside over them (cf. 1 Thess. v. 12) here described as **those who teach them the Word.** This apparently simple verse raises many interesting points for consideration.

(i.) In the first place, what does it mean ? Does it deal primarily, as the translation might suggest, with the duty of ministerial maintenance ? Such a reference may possibly be included. But the phrase ' **share all the blessings of life** ' is in the original quite indefinite (lit. ' share in all good things '), so that both the words themselves, and their relation to the preceding and succeeding verses, suggest that Paul's horizon of thought is here much wider. Continuing the thought of a spiritual fellowship referred to in verse 1, he insists that the spiritual relationship between the man who is taught the Word and the man who teaches it (the Greek uses the singular in each case) ought to express itself in the most complete ' partnership '—it is on the ' sharing,' as expressing actively real communion of Spirit, that the emphasis of the Greek falls. He who is being taught the Word is not to be a merely passive recipient : he has something to give back to his teacher, e.g. from the fruits of his experience ; and by his interest and sympathy and helpfulness he must do all he can to further, and nothing to impede (hence ' in all good things '), the good work which is going on around him.

(ii.) *The Word* itself, which is being communicated from teacher to taught, makes the spirit of partnership imperative. For it is not a mere word of human wisdom which a man may teach, if he is so disposed, to those who happen to enrol themselves as his pupils ; it is the living Word of a living God— in fact the Word is God Himself in His self-expression and self-communication towards men ; and those to whom the Word has come cannot keep it to themselves but must pass it on to others. It is interesting to find the simple expression ' the Word ' (cf. ' the faith,' iii. 23) already established in the Christian community. Used frequently in the Old Testament with reference to something *spoken*, the Word of God comes to denote in the fullest sense God's revelation of Himself, such as the Church claims to have received through the life, death, and resurrection of Jesus Christ, and the communication of the Holy Spirit.

(iii.) The Word, therefore, requires to be proclaimed and taught ; and God, Who gave the Word and the Spirit, gave to the Church also apostles and prophets and teachers (cf. 1 Cor. xii. 28). Teachers did not necessarily differ from apostles and prophets as a separate ' order ' ; the different terms denote rather different aspects of ministerial work, and in so far as a man was a teacher his work would be to train enquirers and catachumens, and to give to the brethren who had been baptized further instruction in the fundamentals of the faith. He would deal, e.g., with the basis of the faith in the Old Testament ; with the sayings and doings of Jesus, and the story of the death and resurrection ; with the ' plan of salvation,' judgment and the age to come ; and with the Christian way of life. It would be interesting to know how far, at the early date to which we assign the Epistle, there had already developed a Christian ministry in the churches of Galatia. Acts xiv. 23 tells of the early appointment of presbyters in the various churches and some of these would be men with the gift of teaching. How much of their time did they give to the work ? The present passage sheds little light on the matter, at least if we believe that Paul's words are *not* to be limited to the question of ministerial support ;

and the very simplicity of the description ' *he who teaches the Word* ' may perhaps be taken to suggest an elementary stage of development. Nevertheless all that we know of the Pauline churches, where evangelization and edification were recognized as primary duties, leads us to believe that it would not be long before some of the brethren came to devote most of their time to the work of propagating and establishing the faith.

(iv) In such conditions the question of financial and material support was bound to arise. Paul taught that the responsibility for evangelization must be shared by the whole Christian community, and in his later Epistles he makes it clear that the Christian apostle has a moral right to receive a maintenance allowance (1 Cor. ix. 4–17), and that material contributions provide one way of acknowledging spiritual indebtedness (1 Cor. ix. 11 ; Rom. xv. 27). It is therefore not impossible that in the present passage he may wish to remind the Galatians *indirectly* of the duty they have to support their teachers in material ways. But even if this be so, we must still note that the matter is approached delicately, and from a highly spiritual standpoint, and that the lesson which is enforced is capable of a much wider application. Christian giving, for Paul, is never a mere payment, but is an essentially spiritual act in which it is a privilege to be allowed to share (cf. 2 Cor. viii. 1–6), one way among many in which Christians can show their fellowship in the gospel (cf. Phil. i. 5).

It is the spiritual standpoint of this whole section (verses 1–6), and not merely the injunction in verse 6, which explains the sudden interruption in verses 7 and 8. Here Paul recalls a fundamental principle of the Christian life regarding which there must be **no mistake**. He quotes the proverbial expression that **a man will reap just what he sows**, thereby reminding his converts that those to whom God gives His Spirit are required to live by the Spirit and not according to the flesh ; and such a God, he adds, is **not to be mocked**, i.e. men cannot hoodwink Him, the laws according to which He governs the universe are not such as can be evaded. All through these last six verses Paul has been reminding his readers that by His gift to them of His Spirit God has given them a new standard and a new motive-power for Christian conduct, especially in their dealings with their fellows ; the selfishness of the unregenerate life is therefore incompatible with the fellowship of the Spirit. The proverb of verse 7 receives a more particular application in verse 8. Contrasting ' *his* ' flesh (i.e. man's) with ' the Spirit ' (i.e. God's gift to man),

8 Paul can speak of a man sowing **for his flesh** and **for the Spirit** (in the Greek ' for ' is literally ' into ') because the flesh and the Spirit are as it were the soil from which the man may expect a harvest. But beyond the more immediate results to be reaped (in the one case the enjoyments and profits of the flesh, in the other the fruit of the Spirit) there is the real harvest which comes at the end (cf. the parable of the tares, Matt. xiii. 30, 40–42) ; and while those who have sown for the Spirit will **reap life eternal from the Spirit,** those who live as if the flesh were all can as a result, i.e. **from the flesh,** reap nothing but **destruction.** It is no part of Paul's thought at this point to define the processes by which these results are attained. Probably he implies that for *all* men there is a resurrection, followed by the judgment at which ' life ' or ' death ' is meted out (cf. Christ's picture of the ' sheep ' and the ' goats,' Matt. xxv. 46). The New Testament knows nothing of man, *qua* man, being immortal in the sense of inheriting eternal life ; that is a gift which is guaranteed only to those who have received the Spirit which itself is life, viz. the Spirit of God. The phrase ' eternal life,' so frequent in John, is not common in Paul : contrasted with ' destruction ' or ' death ' (cf. Rom. v. 21 ; vi. 22 f.), its original significance is not so much ' life that knows no ending ' as ' life that will go on into the age (or ages) to come.' This ultimate goal of life is in accordance with the divine Promise. If in sowing and reaping for the flesh we learn that we cannot deceive God, in sowing and reaping for the Spirit we learn that God does not deceive us.

9 The spiritual life is one of growth rather than of anxious human endeavour ; nevertheless we can put hindrances in

the way of our spiritual development, and apart from the temptation to yield to the flesh and so do what is evil, there is the more insidious temptation to **grow tired of doing what is right.** Paul here employs a subtle play on words which occurs again in 2 Thess. iii. 13, suggesting that it is possible to fall into *evil* ways even in doing what is *good.* Believers are to remember that, in the life to which they have been called, the conditions have been set by God, and His is the ultimate responsibility. Hence, if they on their part **do not faint,** He on His part will not fail to give the **harvest** in their lives **at the opportune season.**

Paul carries the same thought further in his closing exhor- 10 tation. The phrase he uses for '**do good**' is literally '*work at the good.*' The good life comes as a gift from God and is not the result of man's 'works'; nevertheless, man must work if the harvest is to come. When Paul adds '**as we have opportunity,**' his thought is clearly not 'on such occasions as are opportune,' but rather 'so long as we have opportunity to do so.' We have our season for the sowing just as God has His season (verse 9) for the harvest. And in his doing of good the Christian is to recognize no limitations—he is to do it **to all men.** Christ had taught His followers the true answer to the question 'Who is my neighbour?' (Luke x. 29 ff.), and had reminded them that the Father in Heaven gives His good gifts without discrimination (Matt. v. 45). When, therefore, the apostle adds '**and in particular to the household of the faith,**' he is not qualifying what he has just said, but enforcing a specific application. He is not in the least untrue here to the fundamental universalism of his gospel, and there is no need on that account to limit his reference to merely physical needs, on the principle that 'if a Christian were left in distress this would be even more to the discredit of the new religion than if a non-Christian went hungry' (Burton, *Commentary, ad loc.*). A man is not likely to do good to all men if he does not do it in the first place to those of his own household. And those who are sons of God by faith in Christ Jesus (iii. 26) will remember that they form a family; they are members of the household of God (Eph. ii. 19), or, as it is here called, *the household of ' the faith '* (cf. note on iii. 23). Paul's other Epistles show how distressed he was when there were factions or rivalries in a Christian congregation, and he was probably conscious that that danger was already a real one in Galatia (cf. note on v. 15).

V. CONCLUSION OF THE EPISTLE (vi. 11–18)

11 See what big letters I make, when I write you in my own hand !
12   These men who are keen upon you getting circumcised are just men who want to make a grand display in the flesh—it is simply to avoid being persecuted for the cross
13   of Christ. Why, even the circumcision party do not observe the Law themselves ! They merely want you to
14   get circumcised, so as to boast over your flesh ! But no boasting for me, none except in the cross of our Lord Jesus Christ, by which the world has been crucified to me
15   and I crucified to the world. For what counts is neither circumcision nor uncircumcision, it is the new creation.
16   On all who will be guided by this rule, may *peace* and mercy rest, even upon the Israel of God.
17 Let no one interfere with me after this, for I bear branded on my body the owner's stamp of Jesus.
18 The grace of our Lord Jesus Christ be with your spirit, brothers. Amen.

11   The Authorized Version translation (' Ye see how large a letter I have written unto you with mine own hand ') is clearly inconsistent with the Greek. Are we to picture the apostle taking the pen from the scribe to add a benediction and perhaps his signature (cf. 2 Thess. iii. 17, 1 Cor. xvi. 21)? Here, however, if he had meant now to bring the Epistle to a close, his surging thoughts and swelling emotions carry him away, and he adds verses 12–16 as a last appeal, a very personal one, in his own handwriting.

But what does he mean by the reference to **big letters ?** Is it merely that his handwriting is large and awkward as

compared with the neater script of the amanuensis ? Or is
it that he writes in big letters for the sake of emphasis—
another proof of the eagerness and intensity of his soul ?
If it be asked why Paul should call attention to his
indifferent penmanship, the answer is given by the emphatic
words ' in my own hand,' Paul's meaning being : ' Unlovely
writer though I am, I want you to have this in my own
handwriting and not merely in the writing of a scribe.'
From this we may go on to speculate whether Paul does
not write in his own hand more than these concluding
verses. May he have begun as far back as chap. v.,
verse 2, *or even have written the whole letter in his own
hand*? This last suggestion gives by far the best interpretation of the sentence. Style and contents alike proclaim
that, from first to last, Galatians was not dictated, but came
direct from the hand of the apostle.

In this concluding paragraph Paul asks the Galatians to 12
study the plain facts of the situation. ' What really is in the
mind of those *who are applying pressure* (it is more than **who
are keen**) *to get you circumcised ?* ' Some of the phrases used in
the following verses might suggest that Paul here seeks to
expose and denounce the motives of the Judaizers. But it is
not on so low and unworthy a note that he is to conclude his
great Epistle. Though for the sake of simplicity and directness
he makes his references concrete rather than abstract, what
he is primarily concerned to lay bare is not the motives of the
Judaizers but the implications of the movement for which
they stand, not their hypocrisy as men but the perversity of
their outlook, which has already misled themselves and is
now in danger of misleading others.

In the first place Paul says of them that they **want to make
a grand display in the flesh.** The emphasis is on the concluding
phrase. He is thinking primarily of the demand that the
flesh should be circumcised ; but at the very suggestion of
this he sees again the whole broad issue as one between flesh
and spirit. And these men are misguided enough to exalt
the flesh over the spirit, as if in God's sight a man who was
circumcised counted for more than a man who was not !

In explanation of this perversity of his opponents Paul introduces an unexpected reference to persecution : **they want to avoid being persecuted for the cross of Christ.** Here we may recall what was said in the commentary on v. 11 regarding *the stumbling-block of the cross,* viz. that the official policy of non-Christian Judaism was to tolerate Christianity so long as it operated within the sphere of Judaism—in other words, so long as it demanded of its Gentile converts that they should be incorporated through circumcision into Israel—but to persecute those who, like Paul, saw in the cross of Christ the inauguration on God's part of a new covenant which completely superseded the old, and which included in its scope all, Jews and Gentiles without distinction, who had faith in Christ.

13 The Judaizers would of course have claimed that this was an unfair presentation of the case—their attitude was dictated by zeal for the God of Israel and the Law which He had given to Israel. Was it to meet some such protestation that Paul asserted next that **the circumcision party do not observe the Law themselves ?** His thought here is not free from obscurity for us. The reference to *the circumcision party* (lit. *those who are being circumcised*) is perhaps not solely to the Judaizers who were urging circumcision or to the Galatians who were falling in with their demands, but includes in the most general way all those who accept circumcision. Paul's point would seem to be that circumcision, though it may make a man a member of God's people Israel, brings him next face to face with the impossible demands of the Law, and does not enable him to keep them. Why then should the Galatians seek to commit themselves to a way of salvation which experience has already shown to be ineffectual ? ' And when these people (there is here a slight change of subject) **want you** to become like them and **get circumcised,** they are not really bringing you to the living God, they are merely adding to the number of the circumcised, and finding cause therefore **to boast over your flesh.'** This *boasting* is of course in God's sight : they think God will be pleased that they have won so many adherents to Israel !

Such is the judaizing position, as Paul sees it according to **14** first principles. Over against it, by an emphatic contrast, he now sets his own. Using a phrase (*God forbid*, Authorized Version) which he frequently employs when he wishes to show that the standards of earth do not apply in the affairs of heaven, he declares that for himself there can be **no boasting except in the cross of our Lord Jesus Christ.** It is to the cross of Christ that Paul owes his redemption, and that new life which is only possible to those who have been redeemed ; he cannot therefore find anything to be proud of in the evil world out of which he has been delivered. And just as in ii. 21 he had said that he had been crucified with Christ, so now he declares that by the cross ' **the world has been crucified to me and I to the world.**' By ' the world ' Paul means the whole natural order of things so far as it is existent and operative without relation to the living and regenerating Spirit of God— we may compare it with his use of ' the flesh ' in the more limited sphere of human nature. All the things in life which to the natural man are imposing and attractive have lost significance for him—they have become *dead* things (' the veriest refuse ' he calls them in Phil. iii. 8). And he in turn has become dead to them—his ideals and outlook have now become so *spiritual* and *unworldly* that the world can ignore him just as if he had ceased to be.

In the new life to which redeemed men are introduced they **15** are confronted with entirely new standards. In the natural world *the Jew* may be proud of being a Jew, and *the Greek* of being a Greek ; but in the new world Jew and Greek are alike transformed, and there emerges a **new creation.** Paul operates with a similar thought in v. 6, but while there his argument was that these distinctions possess no validity as means of salvation, here he asserts that they now cease to exist (cf. p. 124), for the creative Spirit of God has brought into life something new. If they do not **count,** it is because they no longer have any *meaning.* The phrase *a new creation* occurs again in 2 Cor. v. 17 ; we may compare the Johannine teaching on *the new birth.*

The principle which he has just enunciated provides for **16**

the apostle a standard or rule for the Christian life. Hence
when he comes to pronounce a short benediction as a conclusion to this section, he includes in it all who will be guided
(or it may be, *who will march together*) by this rule, as opposed
to those who think that God attaches significance to such
externalities as circumcision. The word of benediction is
peace, as in Num. vi. 26, Ps. cxxv. 5. Thus the Epistle
closes, as it opened (i. 3), with a prayer for *peace*. As in i. 3
peace was combined with *grace*, so here it is combined with
mercy ; and *grace, mercy,* and *peace* occur together (and always
in that order) in the opening salutations of 1 Tim., 2 Tim.,
and 2 John, while Jude has *mercy, peace and love*.

When Paul adds : even upon the Israel of God, is he using
a phrase to cover the whole body of Christians, regarded as
the new Israel? This, which seems at first the most natural
explanation, is not without difficulty. The phrase *the Israel
of God* occurs nowhere else in the New Testament, and it is
perhaps preferable to refer it to *the faithful remnant in Israel*,
who looked to God for some other *rule* than that provided by
the bond of circumcision and obedience to the Law. On this
view, Paul's benediction is firstly to those who already 'belong
to Christ,' ordering their lives according to the principle of
the *new creation* stated in verse 15 ; but, just as he knows
that this excludes some (like the Judaizers) who, though they
call themselves Christ's, yet do not walk by this rule, so on
the other hand he recalls, with true sympathy for his brethren
after the flesh, that there are those in Israel who are waiting
for the Lord their God and are marked out by Him for salvation. If this is so, ought *mercy* to go with this second clause,
so as to give a translation as follows : *As many as shall be
guided by this rule, peace be on them, and mercy too upon the
Israel of God?* In this way we should be spared the collocation
peace and mercy—it is perhaps more natural from a religious
point of view, as it is more in accordance with Biblical usage,
that where these terms are joined together, *mercy* should
precede *peace*. And while the first part of the prayer is
naturally for *peace* on those who already are Christ's, the
second is for *mercy* on those in Israel to whom Christ has not

yet been revealed, though they are marked out for inclusion in the fellowship.

Is it permissible to see in this reference to the Israel of God, as in other allusions to the Church in this Epistle, an indication of an early date ? (see Introduction, p. xlv.).

So much of the Epistle has been occupied with a vindication 17 of his own personal position and outlook that Paul adds a brief closing word with regard to himself. He has said all he wants to say in self-defence. He is now prepared to go his own way with a conscience unruffled and serene. Using a phrase familiar in the Gospels (e.g. Luke xi. 7 ; Mark xiv. 6) to indicate *giving trouble*, he claims that **after this** he ought to be allowed the privilege of immunity. He bases his claim on the fact that **branded on** his **body** is **the owner's stamp of Jesus** (lit. marks : *stigmata*).

One cannot but ask what is the origin and precise meaning of this striking metaphor. (1) Slaves were sometimes branded with the name of their master, and Paul boasted that he was a slave of Jesus Christ. That explanation may almost certainly be accepted so far as it goes.[1] (2) What suggested the metaphor to Paul in the first place may have been a contrast with the stamp of circumcision. ' Some men lay stress on being stamped as belonging to Israel ; for me it is enough that I am stamped as belonging to Jesus.' (3) Are we then to say that in Paul's case *the owner's stamp* is entirely metaphorical? This may be so. But it is more probable that he is appealing to certain bodily scars or wounds received in the service of his Master ; and when we recall how in his later Epistles he interpreted his sufferings as linking him up with the Lord (e.g. Col. i. 24 ; cf. the thought in Gal. ii. 19 of being ' crucified with Christ ') we can understand how he would regard such

[1] The fact vouched for by Herodotus (ii. 113) that a runaway slave, taking refuge in a certain temple in Egypt, could have the mark of the God set upon him and so remain inviolate is not likely to have any bearing on the Pauline phrase. Neither need we find a parallel in the papyrus (3rd century A.D.), quoted by Deissmann, apparently a tiny scroll enclosed as a spell in an amulet, which says : ' I bear the tomb of Osiris. . . . If so-and-so gives me trouble, I shall throw it at him.' Though in that case we have the words *I bear* and *give trouble*, there is no reference to marks branded on the body.

wounds as marking him out as 'belonging to Jesus' (cf. iii. 29 ; v. 24). At Lystra Paul was stoned and almost killed (Acts xiv. 19) ; and if he meant his words to convey this reference to his readers, the Galatians would understand it. It is noteworthy that Paul uses here the personal name Jesus just as he does in an analogous passage in 2 Cor. iv. 10.

18 As a conclusion to the Epistle as a whole, just as verse 16 was to the section immediately preceding, there now comes the final benediction. **The grace of the Lord Jesus Christ is** the formula regularly employed in the Epistles—Ephesians, Colossians, and the Pastoral Epistles are exceptions. Here it is especially full of meaning in view of the emphasis throughout the letter on *grace* and *redemption*. Paul can speak of **your spirit** because the Galatians now recognize the living God in their lives and have received the Holy Spirit. With a sympathetic **brethren** and a reverential **Amen** the Epistle closes.

TEXTUAL NOTES ATTACHED TO DR. MOFFATT'S TRANSLATION

Dr. Moffatt has the following textual footnotes attached to his Translation :

On iv. 25 : 'Omitting Ἄγαρ as a gloss, with the Latin, Sahidic, and Ethiopic versions, ℵ C G, Origen, and many others.'

On v. 1 : 'Whether ᾗ is read after τῇ ἐλευθερίᾳ or instead of τῇ, the opening words of v. 1 must be connected with the closing words of iv. 31. I think on the whole that this interpretation of the text, which is advocated by modern editors like Lightfoot and Zahn, has the best claim to be regarded as authentic; it goes back to Marcion and has the powerful support of the Latin version, of G, of Origen, Ambrosiaster, Jerome, and others.'

On v. 24 : 'Omitting Ἰησοῦ with D G, the Latin, Gothic, and Armenian versions, Marcion, Chrysostom, and others.'

INDEX